Taste*of*Home.
BRUNCH
CLASSICS

TASTE OF HOME BOOKS • RDA ENTHUSIAST BRANDS, LLC • MILWAUKEE, WI

Taste of Home

ISBN: 978-1-61765-997-3
LOCC: 2020948508

Executive Editor: Mark Hagen
Senior Art Director: Raeann Thompson
Editor: Christine Rukavena
Art Director: Maggie Conners
Designer: Arielle Jardine
Deputy Editor, Copy Desk: Dulcie Shoener
Copy Editor: Ann Walter
Cover Photographer: Dan Roberts
Cover Set Stylist: Stacey Genaw
Cover Food Stylist: Shannon Norris

Pictured on front cover:
The Best Ever Pancakes, p. 206
Orange Dream Mimosas, p. 16
Everything Breakfast Sliders, p. 99

Pictured on spine:
Make-Ahead Eggs Benedict Toast Cups, p. 243

Pictured on title page:
Croque-Madame, p. 102

Pictured on back cover:
Overnight Yeast Waffle Sliders, p. 207
Denver Omelet Salad, p. 122
Cherry Danish, p. 174
Ham & Collards Quiche, p. 195

Printed in China
1 3 5 7 9 10 8 6 4 2

MORE WAYS TO
CONNECT WITH US:

TABLE OF CONTENTS

HOW TO THROW AN EPIC BRUNCH

TODAY'S HOSTS DON'T LOSE A WINK OF SLEEP WITH THESE PARTY TIPS. WHETHER PLANNING A CASUAL BUFFET OR FORMAL EVENT, TURN HERE FOR EASY EYE-OPENING SUCCESS.

1. CHOOSE A VARIETY OF DISHES

Include a mix of savory and sweet, hot and cold, simple and more-involved foods. Make it easy on yourself with our **Special Menus** (p. 190) or see this book's indexes (p. 252) for no-fuss planning.

Don't have time to make everything? You don't have to! It's perfectly fine to round out menus with items from the store or bakery. After all, from-scratch bagels may be a treat, but no one is coming to brunch expecting them. Create a menu that incorporates homemade entrees as well as store-bought bites, and you'll eliminate plenty of stress.

2. LOOK FOR MAKE AHEAD

Look for the Make Ahead icon throughout this book to get a jump on meal prep. Many appetizers, pastries and even quiches can be prepared and then frozen in advance. **Overnight Cinnamon Rolls** (p. 179) and hearty morning casseroles are delightful timesavers. Prep them the night before, then refrigerate until you're ready to bake. Not only are they delicious and aromatic, but they always beat the clock.

3. SET UP THE NIGHT BEFORE

It's never a good idea to rush things right before guests arrive. If your party begins early in the morning, it's especially important to set up your spread the night before.

Lay out place settings, polish glassware, decide which serving platters will be used, decorate if desired and make sure there are plenty of seats to go around.

Take time to jot down a game plan or create a to-do list for the morning of the brunch. Don't forget the little things such as brewing coffee, setting out the butter so it comes to room temperature, pouring pitchers of ice water, setting up the bar, creating garnishes for drinks and other tasks. These small jobs can eat up a lot of time if not well planned.

4. CREATE A LEISURELY TONE

Let guests settle in to chat and enjoy a drink before the meal starts. Have an easy snack or two such as cheese and crackers, small pastries or something from the **Brunch Bites** chapter (p. 24) to keep hunger at bay. This way, nothing is derailed in case someone (including the host!) is running behind.

5. KEEP HOT FOODS HOT

There's no need to cook your food at the last minute before guests arrive. Casseroles, breakfast meats and other hot foods are easily kept warm in a slow (200°) oven, slow cooker or chafing dish.

Late arrival? Make a plate, cover with foil and stash it in the warming drawer.

6. OFFER A SELF-SERVE BAR

A themed buffet station is not only easy on the host, but it's a blast for party guests. Make space for stations throughout the home, or on the kitchen island or countertop. These spreads allow guests to serve themselves and create their own specialty. Consider these ideas:

Pancake Bar (p.204). Fun for kids of all ages, this station gives guests the opportunity to customize their own flapjacks with berries, sprinkles and other tasty additions.

Bowl Bar (p. 234). Divvy out bowls of fresh fruit, granola, nuts and a few sweet toppings so guests can layer fixings into cups of plain yogurt, smoothie bowls or hot oatmeal.

Bloody Mary Bar (p. 19). Party-goers will love customizing their drinks with garnishes galore.

7. SERVE A SIGNATURE BEVERAGE

Are Bloody Marys not your thing? Then try classic **Mimosas** (p. 23), the Creamsicle®-inspired version on the cover (p. 16) or zesty **Mojito Slush** (p. 13). All of these drinks are easy to prep ahead and allow guests to help themselves. That's a win-win for busy brunch hosts.

BLOODY MARY BAR

1. FILL WITH ICE
2. SPLASH IN THE GOOD STUFF
3. SKEWER GARNISH
4. ENJOY!

You say tomato
I say...
Bloody Mary

8. KEEP IT TIDY

For a polished look, avoid setting foods on the table while still in their cartons, bottles or containers.

Pour syrups into small glass pitchers or servers, and scoop flavored cream cheese into tiny bowls. Make sure your butter dish is clean and presentable.

Brunch is a great time to break out items such as vintage or decorative gravy boats, which work well for hollandaise sauce and the like. Similarly, don't forget ceramic creamers and sugar bowls for coffee.

9. GET CREATIVE

Make your tablescape stand out by opting for unexpected serving dishes. Our Executive Culinary Director Sarah Farmer frequently relies on tartlet tins for her brunch-time bashes. "You can use them as holders for flatware bundles or even fill them with sliced fruit or pastries," she says.

The way you present the food can instantly set the mood. Make a kabob out of doughnut holes and fresh fruit, then set them inside a vase. Presto! You have a whimsical dessert bouquet.

10. ARRANGE A FUN CENTERPIECE

When it comes to decorations, this fantastic quote from the 1964 edition of *Joy of Cooking* still holds true today: "Don't make your effects so stagey that your guests' reactions will be 'she went to a lot of trouble.' Make them rather say, 'She had a lot of fun doing it.'"

We're all for having fun decor! Brighten up your brunch table by picking out a few small vases, jars or bowls. Fill them with simple flowers like baby's breath, daisies or baby tulips. Another easy trick is to incorporate fresh produce (such as a bowl of pretty lemons or baby radishes) on the table.

11. LIGHT IT UP

Candles always add festive elegance, even for a daytime event. Stick with unscented tea lights or votive candles to make the table sparkle. Taper candles add a more formal touch, but be sure to place them (and other table decor) carefully so they don't obstruct conversation or guests' view of one another.

12. SNEAK IN CONVERSATION STARTERS

If there are newcomers at the table, it might be a good idea to encourage inclusive conversation. Surprise your guests with a few open-ended questions written on cardboard coasters or DIY paper napkin rings. Here are a few of our favorites:

- What's the best meal you've ever eaten?
- Tell us about your favorite vacation.
- What was your highlight from the past week?

13. REMEMBER THE KIDS

If children are on the guest list, be sure to offer some colorful menu items as well as fruit and simple standbys such as cereal and milk.

Consider clever finger foods like a cute batch of **Pigs in a Pool** (p. 251). And no child will be able to resist **Birthday Cake Pancakes** (p. 49) or tasty **Rainbow Fruit Salad** (p. 76).

14. TOSS IN A TASTY TAKEAWAY

Who doesn't love a present? Surprise your guests with a tiny food gift as they leave the party. It could be a sweet take-home such as **Bird Nests** (p. 202) or a few **Strawberry Cheesecake Bites** (p. 231). You could also set jars of yummy **Berry Curd** (p. 149) or homemade jams or jellies into cute gift bags for great parting gifts.

15. RELAX & ENJOY

The whole point of throwing a party is to enjoy the company of friends and family, so don't panic if everything doesn't go according to plan. Guests will have a better time if they see that you are, too. Grab a drink and raise a toast to the best Sunday Funday ever!

BASIC TABLE SETTING

For most occasions, the dinner plate is positioned directly in the center of the place setting, and everything is simply oriented around it.

- Set the fork to the left.

- Place knife and spoon to the right, aligning flatware along the bottom edge of the place setting. The knife's sharp edge faces toward the plate.

- Beverages are placed above the knife, with the water glass in the prominent position. Down and to the right, you may set a wine glass, juice glass or coffee cup, in that order.

- If using, the bread and butter plate goes above the fork.

- Fold napkins under the fork or on the plate for an informal setting.

Drinks to Clink

Blend, brew, chill, ice and shake your way to the perfect morning bevvy. Get your sparkle on.

BELMONT BREEZE

BELMONT BREEZE

This sipper may be juicy, but it's not too sweet. This flavorful refresher is the perfect drink for whiskey lovers to sip on a hot day.
—*Taste of Home* Test Kitchen

- -

Takes: 5 min. • **Makes:** 1 serving

  ½ to ¾ **cup ice cubes**
1½ **oz. whiskey**
1½ **oz. orange juice**
1½ **oz. cranberry juice**
  1 **oz. sour mix**
  ¾ **oz. sherry**
  1 **oz. club soda**
  1 **oz. lemon-lime soda**
    Mint sprig and lemon wedge

1. Fill a shaker three-fourths full with ice. Place remaining ice in a cocktail glass; set aside.
2. Add the whiskey, juices, sour mix and sherry to shaker; cover and shake for 10-15 seconds or until condensation forms on outside of shaker. Strain into prepared glass. Top with sodas. Garnish with mint and lemon wedge.
1 serving: 223 cal., 0 fat (0 sat. fat), 0 chol., 13mg sod., 29g carb. (27g sugars, 0 fiber), 0 pro.

STRAWBERRY BANANA YOGURT SMOOTHIE

STRAWBERRY BANANA YOGURT SMOOTHIE

Frozen strawberries combine with banana to make these frosty smoothies extra thick. The recipe is a delightful way to get a substantial dose of nutrients early in the day.
—Christy Adkins, Martinez, GA

- -

Takes: 5 min. • **Makes:** 2 servings

  ½ **cup 2% milk**
  ⅓ **cup strawberry yogurt**
  ⅓ **cup frozen unsweetened strawberries**
  ½ **medium firm banana, chopped**
  4 **ice cubes**
  8 **tsp. sugar**

In a blender, combine all of the ingredients; cover and process for 30-45 seconds or until smooth. Stir if necessary. Pour into 2 chilled glasses; serve immediately.
1 cup: 171 cal., 2g fat (1g sat. fat), 7mg chol., 52mg sod., 36g carb. (32g sugars, 1g fiber), 4g pro.

PINEAPPLE-ORANGE SPICED TEA

PINEAPPLE-ORANGE SPICED TEA

The sweet aroma of this tea wafting from a slow cooker warms the dreariest day. My daughter served it for a holiday open house, and coffee drinkers were instantly converted. I bring it to the office to spice up our break room beverage selections.
—Carole J. Drennan, Abilene, TX

- -

Prep: 15 min. • **Cook:** 2 hours
Makes: 12 servings (3 qt.)

- 2 qt. boiling water
- 16 tea bags
- 2 cinnamon sticks (3 in.)
- 1 piece fresh gingerroot (½ in.), peeled and thinly sliced
- 4 whole cloves
- 1 cup sugar
- 1 can (12 oz.) frozen orange juice concentrate, thawed
- 1 can (12 oz.) frozen pineapple juice concentrate, thawed
- 1 cup pomegranate or cranberry juice
- ½ cup lemon juice
  Optional: Pomegranate seeds and lemon wedges

1. In a 5- or 6-qt. slow cooker, combine boiling water and tea bags. Cover and let stand 5 minutes.

2. Meanwhile, place cinnamon sticks, ginger and cloves on a double thickness of cheesecloth. Gather the corners of cloth to enclose seasonings; tie securely with string. Discard tea bags. Stir in remaining ingredients; add spice bag. Cook, covered, on low until heated through, 2-3 hours. Discard spice bag. Stir before serving. If desired, serve with pomegranate seeds and lemon slices.

1 cup: 173 cal., 0 fat (0 sat. fat), 0 chol., 10mg sod., 43g carb. (41g sugars, 1g fiber), 1g pro.

5i

LEMON-BASIL MOJITO MOCKTAILS

In this twist on the classic summer beverage, lemon and basil take the place of mint. For a grown-up version, just add your favorite rum or vodka.
—Cheryl Perry, Hertford, NC

- -

Prep: 15 min. + chilling
Makes: 12 servings

- 1½ cups sugar
- 4 cups water
- 6 cups fresh basil leaves, divided
- Crushed ice, divided
- 2 bottles (1 liter each) club soda

GARNISH
- Fresh lemon wedges

1. In a small saucepan, bring sugar and water to a boil. Cook and stir until sugar is dissolved. Place half of the basil in a small bowl. With a pestle or wooden spoon, crush basil until its aroma is released. Stir into sugar mixture. Remove from heat; cool completely. Strain; refrigerate until cold.

2. Place 2 cups crushed ice and remaining basil in a 4-qt. pitcher. Using a muddler or a wooden spoon, press basil leaves against ice until their aroma is released. Stir in basil syrup and soda. Serve over crushed ice in tall glasses; squeeze lemon wedges into drink.

1 serving: 101 cal., 0 fat (0 sat. fat), 0 chol., 36mg sod., 26g carb. (25g sugars, 0 fiber), 0 pro.

MAKE AHEAD

MOJITO SLUSH

Whether you're splashing poolside or watching the kids inside, this slushy beverage has just the right balance of minty crispness and limey tartness that's sure to tingle the taste buds.
—Jessica Ring, Chicago, IL

- -

Prep: 30 min. + freezing
Makes: 13 servings (about 2 qt. slush mix)

- 1 pkg. (3 oz.) lime gelatin
- 2 Tbsp. sugar
- 1 cup boiling water
- 1 cup fresh mint leaves
- 2 cans (12 oz. each) frozen limeade concentrate, thawed
- 2 cups cold water
- 1 cup grapefruit soda
- 1 cup rum or additional grapefruit soda

EACH SERVING
- ⅔ cup grapefruit soda

GARNISH
- Lime wedge and/or fresh mint leaves

1. In a small bowl, dissolve gelatin and sugar in boiling water; add mint leaves. Cover and steep 20 minutes. Press through a sieve; discard mint. Stir in the limeade concentrate, cold water, soda and rum. Pour into a 2½-qt. freezer container. Freeze overnight or until set.

2. For each serving, scoop ⅔ cup slush into a glass. Pour soda into the glass; garnish as desired.

1 serving: 278 cal., 0 fat (0 sat. fat), 0 chol., 28mg sod., 61g carb. (59g sugars, 0 fiber), 1g pro.

LEMON-BASIL
MOJITO MOCKTAILS

BLACK-EYED SUSAN

The Kentucky Derby has the mint julep; the Preakness has the Black-Eyed Susan. The drink is a sunny mix of vodka, rum, and pineapple and orange juices to toast your special events.
—*Taste of Home* Test Kitchen

- - - - - - - - - - - - - - - - - - - -

Takes: 5 min. • **Makes:** 1 serving

- ½ to ¾ cup crushed ice
- 1 oz. vodka
- 1 oz. light rum
- ½ oz. Triple Sec
- 2 oz. unsweetened pineapple juice
- 2 oz. orange juice
  Lime slice and pitted sweet dark cherry

Place desired amount of ice in a rocks glass. Pour vodka, rum, Triple Sec and juices into glass. Stir; serve with a lime slice and cherry.

1 serving: 242 cal., 0 fat (0 sat. fat), 0 chol., 3mg sod., 21g carb. (18g sugars, 0 fiber), 0 pro.

BLACK-EYED SUSAN

MINT JULEP

Here's a lovely brunchtime classic. The cool classic is beloved in the South.
—*Taste of Home* Test Kitchen

- - - - - - - - - - - - - - - - - - - -

Prep: 30 min. + chilling
Makes: 10 servings (2½ cups syrup)

MINT SYRUP
- 2 cups sugar
- 2 cups water
- 2 cups loosely packed chopped fresh mint

EACH SERVING
- ½ to ¾ cup crushed ice
- ½ to 1 oz. bourbon
  Mint sprig

1. For syrup, combine the sugar, water and chopped mint in a large saucepan. Bring to a boil over medium heat; cook until sugar is dissolved, stirring occasionally. Remove from the heat; cool to room temperature.

2. Line a mesh strainer with a double layer of cheesecloth or a coffee filter. Strain syrup; discard mint. Cover and refrigerate syrup for at least 2 hours or until chilled.

3. For each serving, place ice in a metal julep cup or rocks glass. Pour ¼ cup mint syrup and bourbon into the glass; stir until mixture is well chilled. Garnish with mint sprig.

⅓ cup: 197 cal., 0 fat (0 sat. fat), 0 chol., 6mg sod., 42g carb. (39g sugars, 1g fiber), 1g pro.

MINTY MOCHACCINOS

Cool off on a hot summer day with this yummy ice cream drink. It delightfully blends chocolate, coffee and mint for a frothy refresher you'll love.
—Edna Hoffman, Hebron, IN

- -

Takes: 5 min. • **Makes:** 4 servings

- 2 cups milk
- 1 tsp. vanilla extract
- ⅛ tsp. mint extract
- 1 envelope (.77 oz.) Irish cream instant cappuccino mix
- 2 cups chocolate ice cream, softened

In a blender, combine all ingredients; cover and process until blended. Stir if necessary. Pour into chilled glasses; serve immediately.

1 cup: 245 cal., 12g fat (7g sat. fat), 39mg chol., 127mg sod., 29g carb. (28g sugars, 1g fiber), 7g pro.

BRIGHT IDEA

For a pretty presentation, garnish each drink with whipped cream and chocolate shavings.

RAINBOW SPRITZER

RAINBOW SPRITZER

This drink gets its bubbly goodness from ginger ale and puckery lemonade.
—Olivia Thompson, Milwaukee, WI

- -

Takes: 20 min. • **Makes:** 4 servings

- ½ cup fresh blueberries
- ½ cup chopped peeled kiwifruit
- ½ cup chopped fresh pineapple
- ½ cup sliced fresh strawberries or fresh raspberries
- 1 cup chilled ginger ale
- ½ cup chilled unsweetened pineapple juice
- ½ cup chilled lemonade

In 4 tall glasses, layer blueberries, kiwi, pineapple and strawberries. In a 2-cup glass measure or small pitcher, mix remaining ingredients; pour over fruit. Serve immediately.

1 serving: 91 cal., 0 fat (0 sat. fat), 0 chol., 8mg sod., 23g carb. (18g sugars, 2g fiber), 1g pro.

ORANGE DREAM MIMOSAS

Toast the good times with this grown-up Creamsicle drink. For the kiddos, make a nonalcoholic version with sparkling cider, grape juice or ginger ale.
—Deirdre Cox, Kansas City, MO

- -

Prep: 15 min. + freezing
Makes: 16 servings (4 cups frozen mix)

  4 **tsp. grated orange zest**
2½ **cups orange juice**
  1 **cup half-and-half cream**
  ¾ **cup superfine sugar**
  2 **bottles (750 ml each) champagne or other sparkling wine**
     Fresh strawberries

1. Place the first 4 ingredients in a blender; cover and process until sugar is dissolved. Transfer to an 8-in. square dish; freeze, covered, 6 hours or overnight.
2. To serve, place ¼ cup orange mixture in each champagne glass. Top with champagne. Garnish with strawberries; serve immediately.
1 serving: 138 cal., 2g fat (1g sat. fat), 8mg chol., 8mg sod., 15g carb. (13g sugars, 0 fiber), 1g pro.
ORANGE DREAM MIMOSA MOCKTAILS: Substitute 2 bottles (750 ml each) sparkling apple cider for the champagne.

ORANGE DREAM MIMOSAS

Serve a Bottle of Champagne

1. Remove foil. Look for a tear-strip with a little tab on it, or cut the foil with a wine opener.

2. Carefully remove cage. Untwist the wire loop holding the cage in place on top of the cork. Careful— the cage is what's ensuring the cork stays in the bottle. Once it's removed or loosened, the cork could come out. Point bottle away from people, your face, and anything fragile.

3. Uncork. Place one hand on top of the bottle to help ease out the cork. Gently turn the bottle with your other hand. By controlling how quickly the cork comes out, the result will be a gentle hiss rather than a loud bang.

4. Enjoy! Bubbles last longer if you tilt the glass and gently pour wine against the side of it.

COCONUT
COLD-BREW
LATTE

5i

COCONUT COLD-BREW LATTE

Cold-brew lattes are all the rage at coffee shops, but they're easy to make at home. This coconut cold-brew latte is ridiculously refreshing and is even vegan!
—Natalie Larsen, Columbia, MD

- -

Prep: 20 min. + chilling
Makes: 4 servings

- ½ **cup coarsely ground medium-roast coffee**
- ½ **cup hot water (205°)**
- 3½ **cups cold water**

COCONUT SIMPLE SYRUP
- 1 **cup water**
- ½ **cup sugar**
- ½ **cup sweetened shredded coconut**

EACH SERVING
- **Ice cubes**
- 2 **Tbsp. coconut milk**

1. Place coffee grounds in a clean glass container. Pour hot water over grounds; let stand 10 minutes. Stir in cold water. Cover and refrigerate for 12-24 hours. (The longer the coffee sits, the stronger the flavor.)

2. Meanwhile, for coconut simple syrup, in a small saucepan, bring water, sugar and coconut to a boil. Reduce heat; simmer 10 minutes. Strain and discard the coconut. Cool completely.

3. Strain coffee through a fine mesh sieve; discard grounds. Strain coffee again through a coffee filter; discard the grounds. Store the coffee in the refrigerator for up to 2 weeks. For each serving, fill a large glass with ice. Add 1 cup cold brewed coffee and 4 Tbsp. coconut syrup; stir. Top with coconut milk.

1 cup: 145 cal., 5g fat (5g sat. fat), 0 chol., 12mg sod., 26g carb. (26g sugars, 0 fiber), 1g pro.

BLOODY MARY BAR

1. FILL WITH ICE
2. SPLASH IN THE GOOD STUFF
3. SKEWER GARNISH
4. ENJOY!

You say tomato I say... Bloody Mary

UNCLE MERLE'S BLOODY MARY

UNCLE MERLE'S BLOODY MARY

I had a very good friend who was not related to me, but everyone called him Uncle Merle. He gave me this recipe and made me promise not to give it to anyone until he passed away. Uncle Merle is gone now, but his recipe lives on.

—Ronald Roth, Three Rivers, MI

Takes: 10 min. • **Makes:** 5 servings

- 4 cups tomato juice
- 1 Tbsp. white vinegar
- 1½ tsp. sugar
- 1½ tsp. Worcestershire sauce
- 1 tsp. beef bouillon granules
- ½ tsp. salt
- ¼ tsp. onion powder
- ¼ tsp. celery salt
- ¼ tsp. pepper
- ⅛ tsp. garlic powder
- 1 drop hot pepper sauce
  Dash ground cinnamon, optional
  Ice cubes
- 7½ oz. vodka
  Optional garnishes: Celery ribs, cooked shrimp, cherry tomatoes, jalapeno peppers, string cheese, lemon wedges, cooked bacon, beef snack sticks, cucumber spears, olives, cubed cheese, old bay seasoning and celery salt

In a pitcher, mix the first 11 ingredients until blended. If desired, stir in cinnamon. For each serving, pour ¾ cup mixture over ice; stir in 1½ Tbsp. of vodka. Garnish as desired.

1 cup: 119 cal., 1g fat (0 sat. fat), 0 chol., 961mg sod., 9g carb. (7g sugars, 1g fiber), 2g pro.

BRIGHT IDEA

DIY Bloody Mary Bar

For decorative rims, wipe rim with a lemon wedge then dip in a mixture of coarse salt with smoked paprika, seafood seasoning and/or celery salt. Set out bowls of fixings so each person can create their own masterpiece. Add a beer chaser if desired.

PEACH CHAMPAGNE

I searched high and low for the perfect punch recipe and wound up creating this one. It's a big hit at parties, especially weddings. In summer, I freeze fresh peaches and strawberries.

—Linda Hall, Evington, VA

- -

Takes: 10 min.
Makes: 20 servings (3¾ qt.)

- 1 pkg. (16 oz.) frozen unsweetened sliced peaches
- 1 pkg. (14 oz.) frozen unsweetened sliced strawberries
- 2 cans (5½ oz. each) peach nectar, chilled
- 1 cup peach schnapps liqueur
- 2 liters lemon-lime soda, chilled
- 2 bottles (750 ml each) champagne or other sparkling wine, chilled

IN A PUNCH BOWL, COMBINE PEACHES, STRAWBERRIES, NECTAR AND LIQUEUR. STIR IN LEMON-LIME SODA AND CHAMPAGNE JUST BEFORE SERVING.
3/4 CUP: 135 CAL., 0 FAT (0 SAT. FAT), 0 CHOL., 11MG SOD., 18G CARB. (15G SUGARS, 1G FIBER), 0 PRO.

MAKE AHEAD 5ⁱ

COFFEE MILK

After one sip, you'll see why this is the official drink of Rhode Island... it's simply delectable!

—*Taste of Home* Test Kitchen

- -

Prep: 10 min.
Cook: 35 min. + chilling
Makes: 4 servings (1 cup syrup)

- ½ cup finely ground coffee
- 2 cups cold water
- 1 cup sugar

EACH SERVING

- 1 cup cold 2% milk

PLACE GROUND COFFEE IN FILTER BASKET OF A DRIP COFFEEMAKER. ADD 2 CUPS COLD WATER TO WATER RESERVOIR AND BREW COFFEE. IN A SMALL SAUCEPAN, COMBINE COFFEE AND SUGAR; BRING TO A BOIL. REDUCE HEAT; SIMMER UNTIL REDUCED BY HALF, ABOUT 30 MINUTES. REMOVE FROM HEAT; TRANSFER TO A SMALL BOWL OR COVERED CONTAINER. REFRIGERATE, COVERED, UNTIL COLD OR UP TO 2 WEEKS.
TO PREPARE COFFEE MILK: IN A TALL GLASS, MIX 1 CUP MILK AND 2-4 TBSP. COFFEE MILK SYRUP.
1 SERVING PREPARED WITH 1/4 CUP SYRUP: 324 CAL., 5G FAT (3G SAT. FAT), 20MG CHOL., 122MG SOD., 63G CARB. (62G SUGARS, 0 FIBER), 8G PRO.

BLUEBERRY PANCAKE SMOOTHIE

Have your blueberry pancakes and drink them, too! A smoothie loaded with fruit, oatmeal, maple syrup and cinnamon is great in the morning or at any time of day. If your berries are fresh instead of frozen, freeze the banana ahead of time.
—Kailey Thompson, Palm Bay, FL

- -

Takes: 5 min. • **Makes:** 2 servings

1 cup unsweetened almond milk
1 medium banana
½ cup frozen unsweetened blueberries
¼ cup instant plain oatmeal
1 tsp. maple syrup
½ tsp. ground cinnamon
Dash sea salt

Place the first 6 ingredients in a blender; cover and process until smooth. Pour the mixture into 2 chilled glasses; sprinkle with sea salt. Serve immediately.
1 cup: 153 cal., 3g fat (0 sat. fat), 0 chol., 191mg sod., 31g carb. (13g sugars, 5g fiber), 3g pro.
Diabetic exchanges: 2 starch.

BLUEBERRY PANCAKE SMOOTHIE

OLD-FASHIONED LEMONADE

This sweet-tart lemonade is a traditional part of my Memorial Day and Fourth of July menus. Folks can't get enough of the fresh-squeezed flavor.
—Tammi Simpson, Greensburg, KY

- -

Prep: 15 min. + chilling
Makes: 7 servings

1⅓ cups sugar
5 cups water, divided
1 Tbsp. grated lemon zest
1¾ cups lemon juice (about 10 large lemons)

In a large saucepan, combine sugar, 1 cup water and lemon zest. Cook and stir over medium heat until the sugar is dissolved, about 4 minutes. Remove from the heat. Stir in the lemon juice and remaining water; refrigerate until cold. Serve over ice.
1 cup: 142 cal., 0 fat (0 sat. fat), 0 chol., 1mg sod., 37g carb. (35g sugars, 0 fiber), 0 pro.
LIMEADE: Substitute lime zest for lemon zest and limes for lemons.
LAVENDER LEMONADE: Add 2 Tbsp. dried lavender to the sugar and lemon zest mixture before simmering. If desired, strain before serving.
GINGER-MINT LEMONADE: Add 1-2 Tbsp. grated fresh gingerroot and 1-2 mint sprigs to the sugar and lemon zest mixture before simmering. If desired, strain before serving.

GINGER-KALE SMOOTHIES

GINGER-KALE SMOOTHIES

Since I started drinking these spicy smoothies for breakfast every day, I honestly feel better! Substitute any fruit and juice you like to make this recipe your own healthy blend.
—Linda Green, Kilauea, Kauai, HI

- -

Takes: 15 min. • **Makes:** 2 servings

1¼ cups orange juice
1 tsp. lemon juice
2 cups torn fresh kale
1 medium apple, peeled and coarsely chopped
1 Tbsp. minced fresh gingerroot
4 ice cubes
⅛ tsp. ground cinnamon
⅛ tsp. ground turmeric or ¼-in. piece fresh turmeric, peeled and finely chopped
Dash cayenne pepper

Place all ingredients in a blender; cover and process until blended. Serve immediately.
1 cup: 121 cal., 0 fat (0 sat. fat), 0 chol., 22mg sod., 29g carb. (21g sugars, 2g fiber), 1g pro.
Diabetic exchanges: 1½ fruit, 1 vegetable.

MIMOSA

A standard offering at brunch, mimosas are as pretty to behold as they are tasty to sip. Make sure the wine you use is extra-dry or dry (not brut), so it doesn't overpower the orange juice.
—*Taste of Home* Test Kitchen

- -

Takes: 5 min. • **Makes:** 1 serving

2 oz. champagne or other sparkling wine, chilled
½ oz. Triple Sec
2 oz. orange juice
GARNISH
Orange slice

Pour champagne into a champagne flute or wine glass. Pour the Triple Sec and orange juice into the glass. Garnish as desired.
1 serving: 119 cal., 0 fat (0 sat. fat), 0 chol., 0 sod., 13g carb. (11g sugars, 0 fiber), 0 pro.

HOW-TO

Quick-Chill Champagne

The fastest way to chill a bottle of bubbly is to immerse it in ice water with a small handful of salt. Turn the bottle periodically. It'll be ready in about 20 minutes!

Brunch Bites

Go ahead and invite the gang. These mix-and-match dishes make for good morning grazing.

Bananas Foster
crunch mix

CHOCOLATE FRUIT DIP

I usually serve this popular dip with strawberries and pineapple, but it's good with other fruit, such as apples and melon. Your friends will think this one's really special.
—Sarah Maury Swan, Granite, MD

Takes: 10 min. • **Makes:** 2 cups

- 1 pkg. (8 oz.) cream cheese, softened
- ⅓ cup sugar
- ⅓ cup baking cocoa
- 1 tsp. vanilla extract
- 2 cups whipped topping
  Assorted fruit for dipping

In a large bowl, beat cream cheese and sugar until smooth. Beat in cocoa and vanilla. Beat in whipped topping until smooth. Serve with fresh fruit.

2 Tbsp.: 96 cal., 7g fat (5g sat. fat), 16mg chol., 42mg sod., 8g carb. (5g sugars, 0 fiber), 1g pro.

READER REVIEW
"Not only would I make this recipe again ... I've already made it over and over. I'm getting ready now to make three batches of it for a friend's recital reception. It's rich and delicious, yet light, like a mousse. I like it best with strawberries."
— RECIPEME579, TASTEOFHOME.COM

HAM & BRIE PASTRIES

HAM & BRIE PASTRIES

Growing up, I loved pocket pastries. Now with a busy family, I need quick bites. My spin on the classic ham and cheese delivers at snack, brunch or supper time.
—Jenn Tidwell, Fair Oaks, CA

- -

Takes: 30 min. • **Makes:** 16 pastries

- 1 **sheet frozen puff pastry, thawed**
- ⅓ **cup apricot preserves**
- 4 **slices deli ham, quartered**
- 8 **oz. Brie cheese, cut into 16 pieces**

1. Preheat oven to 400°. On a lightly floured surface, unfold puff pastry. Roll pastry to a 12-in. square; cut into sixteen 3-in. squares. Place 1 tsp. preserves in center of each square; top with ham, folding as necessary, and cheese. Overlap 2 opposite corners of each pastry over filling; pinch tightly to seal.

2. Place on a parchment-lined baking sheet. Bake 15-20 minutes or until golden brown. Cool on the pan for 5 minutes before serving.

Freeze option: Freeze cooled pastries in a freezer container, separating layers with waxed paper. To use, reheat pastries on a baking sheet in a preheated 400° oven until heated through.

1 appetizer: 144 cal., 8g fat (3g sat. fat), 17mg chol., 192mg sod., 13g carb. (3g sugars, 1g fiber), 5g pro.

BANANAS FOSTER CRUNCH MIX

Bananas Foster is one of my favorite desserts. So I thought that a crunchy, snackable version would be a hit. It is heated in the microwave and takes just a few minutes to make.
—David Dahlman, Chatsworth, CA

- -

Prep: 10 min.
Cook: 5 min. + cooling
Makes: 2½ qt.

  3 cups Honey Nut Chex
  3 cups Cinnamon Chex
2¼ cups pecan halves
1½ cups dried banana chips
 ⅓ cup butter, cubed
 ⅓ cup packed brown sugar
 ½ tsp. ground cinnamon
 ½ tsp. banana extract
 ½ tsp. rum extract

1. Place the first 4 ingredients in a large microwave-safe bowl. Place butter, brown sugar and cinnamon in a small microwave-safe bowl; microwave on high for 2 minutes, stirring once. Stir in extracts. Pour over cereal mixture; toss to coat.
2. Microwave cereal mixture on high for 3 minutes, stirring every minute. Spread onto baking sheets to cool. Store in an airtight container.
¾ cup: 358 cal., 24g fat (9g sat. fat), 14mg chol., 170mg sod., 36g carb. (18g sugars, 4g fiber), 4g pro.

**BANANAS FOSTER
CRUNCH MIX**

CHICKEN CAPRESE TOASTS

CHICKEN CAPRESE TOASTS

This unique, flavorful salad and bread combo will get rave reviews—guaranteed! It also makes a tasty side dish.
—Frances Pietsch, Flower Mound, TX

Prep: 40 min. • **Bake:** 5 min.
Makes: 8 cups salad
(6½ dozen crostini)

- 2 **cups shredded rotisserie chicken**
- 1 **lb. fresh mozzarella cheese, cubed**
- 2 **cups grape tomatoes, halved**
- 1 **can (14 oz.) water-packed artichoke hearts, rinsed, drained and coarsely chopped**
- ½ **cup pitted Greek olives, thinly sliced**
- ¼ **cup minced fresh basil**
- ¼ **cup olive oil**
- 2 **garlic cloves, minced**
- ½ **tsp. salt**
- ½ **tsp. coarsely ground pepper**

CROSTINI

- 2 **French bread baguettes (10½ oz. each)**
- 4 **garlic cloves**
- ¼ **cup olive oil**
- 1 **tsp. salt**

1. In a large bowl, combine the first 6 ingredients. In a small bowl, whisk the oil, garlic, salt and pepper; drizzle over the chicken mixture and toss to coat. Refrigerate until serving.

2. Cut the baguettes into ½-in. slices. Place on ungreased baking sheets. Bake at 425° for 2-4 minutes or until lightly browned. Cut the garlic in half lengthwise; rub over bread. Brush with oil and sprinkle with salt. Bake 2-3 minutes longer or until crisp. Serve crostini with salad.

1 piece: 179 cal., 10g fat (3g sat. fat), 19mg chol., 316mg sod., 16g carb. (1g sugars, 1g fiber), 7g pro.

5 Homemade Spreads in a Hurry

Whip up a couple of these toppings and pop them in the fridge the day before your brunch party. Then all you have to do is ask someone to pick up bagels. Done and done!

Beer Cheese
Combine 1 cup softened cream cheese, ½ cup shredded cheddar cheese, 3 Tbsp. beer and ½ envelope ranch dressing mix. Add salt and pepper to taste.

Pecan Pie
Combine 1 cup softened cream cheese, ½ cup toasted chopped pecans and ¼ cup caramel sauce.

Inside-Out "Everything"
Combine 1 cup cream cheese, 1 Tbsp. each poppy seeds and sesame seeds, 2 tsp. each dried minced garlic and dried minced onion, and 1 tsp. Worcestershire sauce. Season with salt and pepper to taste.

Mediterranean Goat Cheese
Combine 1 cup softened cream cheese, ⅓ cup goat cheese, ¼ cup chopped olives, ¼ cup chopped roasted red peppers and 2 tsp. grated lemon peel. Season with salt and pepper to taste.

Orange Marmalade
Combine 1 cup softened cream cheese with ⅓ cup orange marmalade.

BEER CHEESE

MEDITERRANEAN GOAT CHEESE

ORANGE MARMALADE

PECAN PIE

INSIDE-OUT "EVERYTHING"

BAGEL WITH A VEGGIE SCHMEAR

BAGEL WITH A VEGGIE SCHMEAR

I got this recipe from my favorite bagel shop in New York City. Now I make it every time I'm craving a quick and healthy meal. I like to add chopped pitted green olives to the schmear.

—Julie Merriman, Seattle, WA

Takes: 20 min. • **Makes:** 4 servings

- 4 oz. fat-free cream cheese
- 4 oz. fresh goat cheese
- ½ tsp. grated lime zest
- 1 Tbsp. lime juice
- ⅔ cup finely chopped cucumber
- ¼ cup finely chopped celery
- 3 Tbsp. finely chopped carrot
- 1 radish, finely chopped
- 2 Tbsp. finely chopped red onion
- 2 Tbsp. thinly sliced fresh basil
- 4 whole wheat bagels, split and toasted
- 8 slices tomato
  Coarsely ground pepper, optional

In a bowl, beat cheeses, lime zest and lime juice until blended. Fold in chopped vegetables and basil. Serve on bagels with tomato slices. If desired, sprinkle with pepper.

2 open-faced sandwiches: 341 cal., 6g fat (3g sat. fat), 22mg chol., 756mg sod., 56g carb. (15g sugars, 10g fiber), 20g pro.

HOW-TO

Cut Bagels for Low Commitment

Order bagels uncut so you can thinly slice them vertically at home. This makes for easy sampling.

DILL DIP

Be prepared—you'll likely need to make a double batch of this delightful dip. One is never enough when we have a get-together. It tastes fantastic with just about any vegetable, so you can use whatever you have on hand as a dipper.
—Kathy Beldorth, Three Oaks, MI

- - - - - - - - - - - - - - - - - - - -

Prep: 10 min. + chilling
Makes: 2 cups

- 1 cup mayonnaise
- 1 cup sour cream
- 2 Tbsp. dried parsley flakes
- 1 Tbsp. dried minced onion
- 2 tsp. dill weed
- 1½ tsp. seasoned salt
- 1 tsp. sugar
   Fresh vegetables or potato chips

In a small bowl, combine the first 7 ingredients. Chill for at least 1 hour. Serve with fresh vegetables or potato chips.
2 Tbsp.: 123 cal., 13g fat (3g sat. fat), 5mg chol., 219mg sod., 1g carb. (1g sugars, 0 fiber), 1g pro.

BRIGHT IDEA

To make the dip a bit lighter, swap in reduced-fat mayonnaise and sour cream.

SALMON MOUSSE CUPS

I make these tempting little tarts frequently for parties. They disappear at an astonishing speed, so I usually double or triple the recipe. They melt in your mouth!
—Fran Rowland, Phoenix, AZ

- - - - - - - - - - - - - - - - - - - -

Prep: 25 min. + chilling
Bake: 10 min. + cooling
Makes: 2 dozen

- 3 oz. cream cheese, softened
- ½ cup butter, softened
- 1 cup all-purpose flour
- FILLING
- 1 pkg. (8 oz.) cream cheese, softened
- 1 cup fully cooked salmon chunks, flaked or 1 can (7½ oz.) salmon, drained, bones and skin removed
- 2 Tbsp. chicken broth
- 2 Tbsp. sour cream
- 1 Tbsp. finely chopped onion
- 1 tsp. lemon juice
- ½ tsp. salt
- 2 Tbsp. minced fresh dill

1. In a small bowl, beat the cream cheese and butter until smooth. Add flour and mix well. Shape into 24 balls; press onto the bottom and up the sides of greased miniature muffin cups.
2. Bake at 350° for 10-15 minutes or until golden brown. Cool 5 minutes before removing from pans to wire racks to cool completely.
3. For filling, in a large bowl, beat cream cheese until smooth. Add the salmon, broth, sour cream, onion, lemon juice and salt until blended. Spoon into the shells. Refrigerate for at least 2 hours. Sprinkle with dill.
2 appetizers: 228 cal., 18g fat (11g sat. fat), 58mg chol., 359mg sod., 9g carb. (1g sugars, 0 fiber), 7g pro.

SALMON MOUSSE CUPS

BACON-WRAPPED APRICOT BITES

These sweet and slightly smoky snacks are easy to prepare and fun to eat. For a change, sprinkle them with a bit of blue cheese or toasted chopped almonds.
—Tammie Floyd, Plano, TX

Prep: 20 min. • **Bake:** 20 min.
Makes: about 2 dozen (⅔ cup sauce)

8   **maple-flavored bacon strips**
1   **pkg. (6 oz.) dried apricots**
½   **cup honey barbecue sauce**
1   **Tbsp. honey**
1½ **tsp. prepared mustard**

1. Cut bacon strips widthwise into thirds. In a large skillet, cook bacon over medium heat until partially cooked but not crisp. Remove to paper towels to drain.
2. Wrap a bacon piece around each apricot; secure with a toothpick. Place in an ungreased 15x10x1-in. baking pan.

3. Bake at 350° until bacon is crisp, 18-22 minutes. Meanwhile, in a small bowl, combine the barbecue sauce, honey and mustard. Serve with warm apricot bites.

1 appetizer: 47 cal., 1g fat (0 sat. fat), 3mg chol., 105mg sod., 8g carb. (6g sugars, 1g fiber), 1g pro.

PULLED PORK
DOUGHNUT HOLE
SLIDERS

PULLED PORK DOUGHNUT HOLE SLIDERS

This slider recipe was created by accident when we had a surplus of root beer pulled pork from a party. Now we can't have barbecue any other way!
—Eden Dranger, Los Angeles, CA

Prep: 55 min. • **Cook:** 8 hours
Makes: 5 dozen

1	**bottle (2 liters) root beer**
1½	**cups barbecue sauce**
1½	**tsp. salt**
1	**tsp. minced fresh gingerroot**
1	**bone-in pork shoulder roast (about 3 lbs.)**

SLAW
½	**cup mayonnaise or Miracle Whip**
2	**Tbsp. white vinegar**
1	**Tbsp. maple syrup**
1	**pkg. (14 oz.) coleslaw mix**

ASSEMBLY
60	**plain doughnut holes**
60	**appetizer skewers**
	Additional barbecue sauce, optional

1. In a large saucepan, bring the root beer to a boil. Reduce heat to medium-high; cook, uncovered, until the liquid is reduced by half, 30-45 minutes. Transfer to a 5- or 6-qt. slow cooker. Stir in barbecue sauce, salt and ginger. Add roast, turning to coat.

2. Cook, covered, on low until pork is tender, 8-10 hours. For slaw, in a large bowl, mix mayonnaise, vinegar and syrup. Stir in the coleslaw mix. Refrigerate, covered, until flavors are blended, at least 1 hour.

3. Remove the pork from the slow cooker; skim fat from cooking juices. Remove meat from bones; shred with 2 forks. Return juices and pork to slow cooker; heat through.

4. To serve, cut the doughnut holes in half; cut a thin slice off bottoms to level. Serve pork and slaw in doughnut holes; secure with skewers. If desired, serve with additional barbecue sauce.

Freeze option: Freeze cooled pork mixture in freezer containers. To use, partially thaw in refrigerator overnight. Heat through in a covered saucepan, stirring gently.

1 slider: 138 cal., 7g fat (2g sat. fat), 13mg chol., 218mg sod., 14g carb. (10g sugars, 0 fiber), 5g pro.

HERBED LEEK TARTS

This savory tart is a favorite among our family and friends! It's delicious and different—and surprisingly simple to make.
—Jean Ecos, Hartland, WI

- -

Prep: 25 min.
Bake: 20 min. + cooling
Makes: 2 tarts (8 servings each)

 3 **cups thinly sliced leeks (about 4 medium)**
 ½ **cup chopped sweet red pepper**
 4 **garlic cloves, minced**
 2 **Tbsp. olive oil**
 1½ **cups shredded Swiss cheese**
 2 **Tbsp. Dijon mustard**
 1 **tsp. herbes de Provence**
 2 **sheets refrigerated pie crust**
 1 **tsp. 2% milk**
 2 **Tbsp. chopped almonds or walnuts, optional**

1. In a large skillet, saute the leeks, red pepper and garlic in oil until tender. Remove from heat; cool for 5 minutes. Stir in the cheese, mustard and herbs; set aside.
2. On a lightly floured surface, roll each sheet of crust into a 12-in. circle. Transfer to parchment-lined baking sheets. Spoon leek mixture over crusts to within 2 in. of edges. Fold edges of crust over filling, leaving center uncovered. Brush folded crust with milk; sprinkle with nuts if desired.
3. Bake at 375° for 20-25 minutes or until crust is golden and filling is bubbly. Using parchment, slide tarts onto wire racks. Cool for 10 minutes before cutting. Serve warm. Refrigerate leftovers.

1 slice: 194 cal., 12g fat (5g sat. fat), 14mg chol., 177mg sod., 17g carb. (2g sugars, 1g fiber), 5g pro.

CHICKEN WING DINGS

Your guests will have a ball sampling this appetizer that has all the flavor and saucy goodness of traditional Buffalo chicken wings, just without the bones.
—Suzanne Clark, Phoenix, AZ

- -

Prep: 30 min. • **Cook:** 10 min./batch
Makes: 2½ dozen meatballs (1½ cups dip)

 ¼ **cup finely chopped celery**
 ¼ **cup finely chopped onion**
 ¼ **cup finely chopped carrot**
 1 **envelope ranch salad dressing mix**
 1 **large egg, lightly beaten**
 1 **lb. ground chicken**
 2 **cups crushed potato chips**
 2 **Tbsp. canola oil**
 1 **container (8 oz.) spreadable cream cheese**
 ¾ **cup crumbled blue cheese**
 2 **Tbsp. 2% milk**
 2 **garlic cloves, minced**
 ½ **cup Buffalo wing sauce**

1. Combine the first 5 ingredients. Crumble chicken over mixture and mix well. Shape into 1-in. balls; roll in potato chips. In a large skillet, heat oil over medium heat. Cook meatballs in batches until no longer pink; drain.
2. For dip, combine cream cheese, blue cheese, milk and garlic. Drizzle meatballs with wing sauce; serve with dip.

1 appetizer with 2 tsp. dip: 87 cal., 6g fat (3g sat. fat), 24mg chol., 300mg sod., 4g carb. (1g sugars, 0 fiber), 4g pro.

HERBED LEEK TARTS

LAYERED HUMMUS DIP

2 Tbsp. brown sugar
¾ tsp. Dijon mustard
½ tsp. maple syrup
⅛ tsp. salt
2 tsp. bourbon, optional
4 thick-sliced bacon strips
EGGS
12 hard-boiled large eggs
¾ cup mayonnaise
1 Tbsp. maple syrup
1 Tbsp. Dijon mustard
¼ tsp. pepper
¼ tsp. ground chipotle pepper
   Minced fresh chives

1. Preheat oven to 350°. In a small bowl, mix the brown sugar, ¾ tsp. mustard, ½ tsp. syrup and salt. If desired, stir in bourbon. Coat bacon with brown sugar mixture. Place on a rack in a foil-lined 15x10x1-in. baking pan. Bake 25-30 minutes or until crisp. Cool completely.
2. Cut the eggs in half lengthwise. Remove yolks, reserving whites. In a small bowl, mash yolks. Add mayonnaise, 1 Tbsp. syrup, 1 Tbsp. mustard and both types of pepper; stir until smooth. Chop the bacon finely; fold half into the egg yolk mixture. Spoon or pipe into egg whites. Sprinkle with remaining bacon and chives. Refrigerate, covered, until serving.
1 stuffed egg half: 107 cal., 9g fat (2g sat. fat), 97mg chol., 142mg sod., 2g carb. (2g sugars, 0 fiber), 4g pro.

LAYERED HUMMUS DIP

My love for Greece inspired this fast-to-fix Mediterranean dip. It is fabulous for parties and is a perfect way to include garden-fresh veggies on your menu.
—Cheryl Snavely, Hagerstown, MD

- -

Takes: 15 min. • **Makes:** 12 servings

1 carton (10 oz.) hummus
¼ cup finely chopped red onion
½ cup Greek olives, chopped
2 medium tomatoes, seeded and chopped
1 large English cucumber, chopped
1 cup crumbled feta cheese
   Baked pita chips

Spread hummus into a shallow 10-in. round dish. Layer with onion, olives, tomatoes, cucumber and cheese. Refrigerate until serving. Serve with pita chips.
1 serving: 88 cal., 5g fat (2g sat. fat), 5mg chol., 275mg sod., 6g carb. (1g sugars, 2g fiber), 4g pro.
Diabetic Exchanges: 1 fat, ½ starch.

BOURBON CANDIED BACON DEVILED EGGS

At our house, it doesn't get any better than deviled eggs with bacon—bourbon candied bacon, that is. See if you can resist them. We can't.
—Colleen Delawder, Herndon, VA

- -

Prep: 20 min. • **Bake:** 25 min.
Makes: 2 dozen

BOURBON CANDIED BACON
DEVILED EGGS

SHRIMP COCKTAIL

During the '60s, shrimp cocktail was one of the most popular party foods around. And it is still a crowd favorite. It's the one appetizer that I serve for every special occasion.

—Peggy Allen, Pasadena, CA

Prep: 30 min. + chilling
Makes: about 6 dozen
(1¼ cups sauce)

- 3   qt. water
- 1   small onion, sliced
- ½   medium lemon, sliced
- 2   sprigs fresh parsley
- 1   Tbsp. salt
- 5   whole peppercorns
- 1   bay leaf
- ¼   tsp. dried thyme
- 3   lbs. uncooked large shrimp, peeled and deveined (tails on)

SAUCE
- 1   cup chili sauce
- 2   Tbsp. lemon juice
- 2   Tbsp. prepared horseradish
- 4   tsp. Worcestershire sauce
- ½   tsp. salt
  Dash cayenne pepper

1. In a Dutch oven, combine the first 8 ingredients; bring to a boil. Add the shrimp. Reduce heat; simmer, uncovered, for 4-5 minutes or until shrimp turn pink.

2. Drain the shrimp and immediately rinse in cold water. Refrigerate for 2-3 hours or until cold. In a small bowl, combine sauce ingredients. Refrigerate until serving.

3. Arrange the shrimp on a serving platter; serve with sauce.

3 shrimp with 2 tsp. sauce: 59 cal., 1g fat (0 sat. fat), 66mg chol., 555mg sod., 4g carb. (2g sugars, 0 fiber), 9g pro.

HOW-TO

Keep Shrimp Cold on a Buffet

You can serve shrimp attractively and keep it at a safe temperature with a lettuce-lined bowl. Fill a large shallow bowl (plastic works well because it's a natural insulator) two-thirds full with crushed ice placed in a zippered plastic bag. Disguise the ice with lettuce leaves, then place shrimp on top. If serving a shrimp sauce, nestle the bowl down into the center.

CAPRESE SALAD KABOBS

CAPRESE SALAD KABOBS

Trade in the usual veggie party platter for these fun kabobs. I often make these for my family to snack on, and it's a wonderful recipe for the kids to help with.
—Christine Mitchell, Glendora, CA

- -

Takes: 10 min. • **Makes:** 12 kabobs

24 **grape tomatoes**
12 **cherry-size fresh mozzarella cheese balls**
24 **fresh basil leaves**
2 **Tbsp. olive oil**
2 **tsp. balsamic vinegar**

On each of 12 appetizer skewers, alternately thread 2 tomatoes, 1 cheese ball and 2 basil leaves. Whisk the olive oil and vinegar; drizzle over kabobs.

1 kabob: 44 cal., 4g fat (1g sat. fat), 5mg chol., 10mg sod., 2g carb. (1g sugars, 0 fiber), 1g pro.
Diabetic exchanges: 1 fat.

READER REVIEW
"I made this for a wedding I catered, and everyone loved it. I couldn't find fresh basil leaves in the quantity I needed at a price the bride could afford, so I used chopped fresh basil. I mixed it with the oil and vinegar and marinated the cheese. Then I brushed additional mixture over the kabobs before serving."
—FAITHANDCHOCOLATE, TASTEOFHOME.COM

CHILAQUILAS APPETIZER

I learned how to make this recipe when I was attending high school in California. It's been a family favorite for years.
—Joy Frost, Wood River, IL

Prep: 10 min. • **Cook:** 30 min.
Makes: 10 servings

- 1 lb. ground beef
- 1 can (16 oz.) chili beans, undrained
- 1 can (14½ oz.) diced tomatoes, undrained
- 1 can (6 oz.) pitted ripe olives, drained and sliced
- 6 green onions, sliced
- 1 to 2 Tbsp. chili powder
    Salt and pepper to taste
- 1 pkg. (20 oz.) tortilla or corn chips
- 1 to 2 cups shredded cheddar cheese

1. In a large skillet, cook beef over medium heat until no longer pink, breaking into crumbles; drain. Add the beans, tomatoes, olives, onions, chili powder, salt and pepper.
2. Bring to a boil. Reduce the heat; simmer, uncovered, for 20 minutes or until thickened. Arrange chips on a platter; top with meat mixture and sprinkle with cheese.
1 serving: 465 cal., 22g fat (7g sat. fat), 34mg chol., 688mg sod., 51g carb. (2g sugars, 6g fiber), 18g pro.

TOMATO-GOAT CHEESE SPREAD

A good friend shared this recipe with me. It is super easy and so delicious. Guests will love it! It's best served with crackers that aren't strongly seasoned.
—Linda Alexander, Madison, WI

Takes: 10 minutes
Makes: 12 servings

- 1 jar (8½ oz.) julienned oil-packed sun-dried tomatoes
- 2 garlic cloves, minced
- 1 log (11 oz.) fresh goat cheese
    Minced fresh parsley, optional
    Assorted crackers

1. Drain the tomatoes, reserving 3 Tbsp. of oil.
2. In a small skillet, heat the reserved oil, tomatoes and garlic over medium-high heat. Cook and stir 5 minutes or until the garlic is golden and the tomatoes are heated through. To serve, place the cheese on a serving plate. Pour the tomato mixture over cheese. If desired, sprinkle with parsley. Serve with crackers.
1 serving: 117 cal., 9g fat (3g sat. fat), 17mg chol., 158mg sod., 6g carb. (0 sugars, 1g fiber), 4g pro.

TOMATO-GOAT CHEESE SPREAD

COASTAL CAROLINA
MUFFIN-TIN FRITTATAS

COASTAL CAROLINA MUFFIN-TIN FRITTATAS

Incorporating the flavors of a South Carolina low country crab boil, these tasty frittatas are simple and delightful. If you have leftover cooked potatoes (roasted or boiled), try dicing them and substituting them for the refrigerated shredded potatoes in this recipe!
—Shannon Kohn, Summerville, SC

Prep: 30 min. • **Bake:** 30 min.
Makes: 1 dozen

- ½ cup mayonnaise
- 1 Tbsp. lemon juice
- 2 tsp. sugar
- 1 tsp. seafood seasoning
- 2 cups refrigerated shredded hash brown potatoes
- 1½ cups chopped smoked sausage
- 1 can (8 oz.) jumbo lump crabmeat, drained
- ¼ cup chopped roasted sweet red peppers
- 7 large eggs
- ¾ cup heavy whipping cream
- 1 Tbsp. Louisiana-style hot sauce
- ½ tsp. salt
- 12 bacon strips, cooked and crumbled
- ¼ cup thinly sliced green onions

1. Preheat oven to 350°. In a small bowl, combine mayonnaise, lemon juice, sugar and seafood seasoning. Refrigerate until serving.

2. Meanwhile, in a large bowl, combine potatoes, sausage, crab and red peppers. Divide among 12 greased jumbo muffin cups. In another large bowl, whisk the eggs, cream, hot sauce and salt. Pour over the potato mixture. Top with bacon.

3. Bake 30-35 minutes or until a knife inserted in center comes out clean. Serve with sauce and green onions.

1 frittata: 292 cal., 23g fat (8g sat. fat), 164mg chol., 768mg sod., 7g carb. (2g sugars, 1g fiber), 13g pro.

Pancakes & Waffles

Got a sweet spot for crepes, French toast and more lazy-day favorites? Brunch is the time to break them out.

BAKED PEACH PANCAKE

This dish makes for a dramatic presentation. I usually take it right from oven to table, fill it with peaches and sour cream, and serve it with bacon or ham. Whenever I go home, my mom asks me to make it.

—Nancy Wilkinson, Princeton, NJ

Prep: 10 min. • **Bake:** 25 min.
Makes: 6 servings

- 2   cups fresh or frozen sliced peeled peaches
- 4   tsp. sugar
- 1   tsp. lemon juice
- 3   large eggs, room temperature
- ½   cup all-purpose flour
- ½   cup 2% milk
- ½   tsp. salt
- 2   Tbsp. butter
      Ground nutmeg
      Sour cream, optional

1. In a small bowl, combine peaches, sugar and lemon juice; set aside. In a large bowl, beat eggs until fluffy. Add the flour, milk and salt; beat until smooth.

2. Place butter in a 10-in. ovenproof skillet in a 400° oven for 3-5 minutes or until melted. Immediately pour batter into hot skillet. Bake until the pancake has risen and puffed all over, 20-25 minutes.

3. Fill with peach slices and sprinkle with nutmeg. Serve immediately, with sour cream if desired.

1 piece: 149 cal., 7g fat (4g sat. fat), 105mg chol., 272mg sod., 17g carb. (8g sugars, 1g fiber), 5g pro.
Diabetic exchanges: 1 medium-fat meat, 1 fat, ½ starch, ½ fruit.

BAKED PEACH PANCAKE

RASPBERRY-BANANA
BREAKFAST TACOS

RASPBERRY-BANANA BREAKFAST TACOS

My sweet take on breakfast tacos uses in pancakes in place of tortillas! They're so easy and absolutely delicious. Vary the fruits and berries depending on what's in season.
—Joan Hallford,
North Richland Hills, TX

- -

Prep: 25 min. • **Cook:** 5 min./batch
Makes: 4 servings

- ¾ **cup all-purpose flour**
- ¾ **cup whole wheat flour**
- 3 **Tbsp. sugar**
- 2 **tsp. baking powder**
- ¾ **tsp. ground cinnamon**
- ½ **tsp. salt**
- 1 **large egg, room temperature**
- 1 **cup 2% milk**
- 2 **Tbsp. canola oil**
- 1 **tsp. vanilla extract**
- ⅓ **cup cream cheese, softened**
- 3 **Tbsp. vanilla yogurt**
- 1 **small banana, sliced**
- 1 **cup fresh raspberries**

1. Whisk together flours, sugar, baking powder, cinnamon and salt. Combine egg, milk, canola oil and vanilla; stir into dry ingredients just until moistened.

2. Preheat a griddle over medium heat. Lightly grease griddle. Pour batter by ½ cupfuls onto griddle; cook until bubbles on top begin to pop and bottoms are golden brown. Turn; cook until second side is golden brown.

3. Meanwhile, beat together cream cheese and yogurt. Spread over pancakes; top with banana and raspberries. Fold up.

1 taco: 429 cal., 17g fat (6g sat. fat), 71mg chol., 651mg sod., 59g carb. (19g sugars, 6g fiber), 11g pro.

AUNT BETTY'S JELLY CREPES

My Aunt Betty made these for me when I was a boy. They're so easy and taste so good I've been eating them ever since.
—Richard Ward, Three Rivers, MI

Takes: 20 min. • **Makes:** 3 crepes

- 2 large eggs, room temperature
- ¾ cup 2% milk
- ⅛ tsp. salt
- ½ cup all-purpose flour
  Butter, softened
  Strawberry or grape jelly
  Confectioners' sugar

In a small bowl, whisk eggs, milk and salt. Add flour; beat until smooth. Melt 1 tsp. butter in a 10-in. nonstick skillet. Pour ¼ cup batter into center of skillet; lift and turn pan to cover bottom. Cook until lightly browned; turn and brown the other side. Remove and keep warm. Repeat with the remaining batter, adding butter to skillet as needed. Spread the crepes with butter and jelly; roll up. Dust with confectioners' sugar. Serve immediately.

1 crepe: 161 cal., 5g fat (2g sat. fat), 130mg chol., 172mg sod., 19g carb. (3g sugars, 1g fiber), 8g pro.

APPLE PIE RICOTTA WAFFLES

I had apples and ricotta cheese to use up, and the result was these fluffy, tender waffles with just a hint of sweetness.
—Teri Rasey, Cadillac, MI

Prep: 25 min. • **Cook:** 10 min./batch
Makes: 6 servings

- ¼ cup butter
- 6 medium apples, peeled and chopped
- 2 Tbsp. sugar
- 1 Tbsp. honey
- 1 tsp. ground cinnamon
- 1 tsp. vanilla extract

WAFFLES
- 2 cups all-purpose flour
- 2 Tbsp. quick-cooking grits
- 1 Tbsp. cornstarch
- 1 tsp. baking soda
- ½ tsp. salt
- 2 large eggs, room temperature
- 2 cups buttermilk
- 1 cup reduced-fat ricotta cheese
- ½ cup canola oil
- 2 tsp. vanilla extract
- 1½ cups fat-free vanilla Greek yogurt
  Fresh blueberries, optional

1. In a large skillet, melt butter over medium-high heat. Add the apples, sugar, honey, cinnamon and vanilla; cook and stir until the apples are crisp-tender, 10-12 minutes. Remove from heat and keep warm.

2. Preheat waffle iron. In a large bowl, whisk flour, grits, cornstarch, baking soda and salt. Whisk eggs, buttermilk, ricotta, oil and vanilla; add stir into dry ingredients just until moistened.

3. Bake waffles according to manufacturer's directions until golden brown. Serve with topping, yogurt and, if desired, blueberries.

1 waffle: 633 cal., 31g fat (8g sat. fat), 96mg chol., 709mg sod., 70g carb. (31g sugars, 4g fiber), 18g pro.

APPLE PIE RICOTTA WAFFLES

STRAWBERRY CHEESECAKE PANCAKES

More of a dessert than breakfast food, these luscious pancakes really showcase the darlings of summertime—strawberries! The pancakes, sauce and sweet cream cheese filling all feature them. This is a wonderful recipe for Mother's Day.
—Shirley Warren, Thiensville, WI

- -

Prep: 40 min. • **Cook:** 5 min./batch
Makes: 20 pancakes (¾ cup spread and 3 cups sauce)

6	oz. cream cheese, softened
1	Tbsp. sugar
½	cup crushed strawberries

PANCAKES

2	cups all-purpose flour
¼	cup sugar
4	tsp. baking powder
½	tsp. salt
2	large eggs, room temperature
1½	cups 2% milk
1	cup sour cream
⅓	cup butter, melted
1	cup chopped fresh strawberries

SAUCE

3	cups crushed strawberries
¼	cup seedless strawberry jam
¼	cup water

1. In a small bowl, beat cream cheese and sugar until smooth; stir in the strawberries. Chill until serving.

2. In a large bowl, combine the flour, sugar, baking powder and salt. Combine the eggs, milk, sour cream and butter. Stir into dry ingredients just until moistened. Fold in fresh chopped strawberries.

3. Pour batter by ¼ cupfuls onto a greased hot griddle; turn when bubbles form on top. Cook until the second side is golden brown.

4. For sauce, in a small saucepan, combine the strawberries, jam and water; heat through. Spread cream cheese mixture over pancakes; top with sauce. (Refrigerate remaining sauce for another use.)

2 pancakes with 1 Tbsp. spread and 2 Tbsp. sauce: 335 cal., 18g fat (11g sat. fat), 96mg chol., 413mg sod., 35g carb. (14g sugars, 2g fiber), 8g pro.

RABANADAS (PORTUGUESE FRENCH TOAST)

I find this dish a comforting reminder of my childhood. The creamy custard center contrasts deliciously with the cinnamon sugar crust.
—Ana Paula Cioffi, Hayward, CA

- -

Prep: 15 min. • **Cook:** 5 min./batch
Makes: 6 servings

- 1   **cup sugar**
- 2   **Tbsp. ground cinnamon**
- 4   **large eggs**
- 2   **cups 2% milk**
      Oil for frying
- 1   **loaf (8 oz.) French bread, cut into 1-in. slices**

1. In a small bowl, mix sugar and cinnamon until blended. In a large shallow dish, whisk eggs and milk. Dip both sides of bread in egg mixture, soaking lightly.

2. In an electric skillet, heat 1 in. of oil to 350°. Working with a few slices at a time, remove bread from egg mixture, allowing excess to drain, and fry 2-3 minutes on each side or until golden brown. Drain on paper towels.

3. Dip warm rabanadas in cinnamon-sugar to coat all sides. Serve warm or at room temperature.

2 slices: 391 cal., 21g fat (3g sat. fat), 131mg chol., 313mg sod., 42g carb. (23g sugars, 2g fiber), 11g pro.

BIRTHDAY CAKE PANCAKES

BIRTHDAY CAKE PANCAKES

To make plain old pancake mix extra special for my kids, I add cake mix and sprinkles. Frosting closes the deal.

—Dina Crowell, Fredericksburg, VA

- -

Prep: 15 min. + standing
Cook: 5 min./batch
Makes: 6 servings

- 1 **cup pancake mix**
- 1 **cup yellow or white cake mix**
- 2 **large eggs, room temperature**
- 1½ **cups plus 1 Tbsp. 2% milk, divided**
- 1 **tsp. vanilla extract**
- ¼ **cup sprinkles**
- ¾ **cup vanilla frosting**
  Additional sprinkles

1. Whisk pancake mix and cake mix. In a separate bowl, whisk eggs, 1½ cups milk and vanilla until blended. Add to dry ingredients, stirring just until moistened. Let stand for 10 minutes. Fold in ¼ cup sprinkles.

2. On a lightly greased griddle over medium heat, pour the batter by ¼ cupfuls to create 6 large pancakes. Cook until bubbles on top begin to pop; turn. Cook until golden brown. Repeat, using smaller amounts of batter to create pancakes of different sizes.

3. Microwave frosting and remaining milk, covered, on high until melted, 10-15 seconds. On each of the large pancakes, layer smaller pancakes in order of decreasing size with the smallest on top; drizzle with frosting. Top with additional sprinkles.

Freeze option: Freeze cooled pancakes between layers of waxed paper in a freezer container. To use, place pancakes on an ungreased baking sheet, cover with foil and reheat in a preheated 375° oven 5-10 minutes. Or, place a stack of pancakes on a microwave-safe plate and microwave on high until heated through, 30-90 seconds.

1 serving: 396 cal., 12g fat (3g sat. fat), 67mg chol., 558mg sod., 65g carb. (38g sugars, 1g fiber), 7g pro.

Make Fanciful Flapjacks

Use a squeeze bottle to make pancakes in fun shapes such as snowmen, hearts, caterpillars—or your loved one's name.

BANANA CREPES

BANANA CREPES

I like to serve this impressive treat at parties. The pleasant banana-orange flavor makes it wonderful for after dinner or for brunch.
—Freda Becker, Garrettsville, OH

- -

Prep: 20 min. + standing
Cook: 10 min. • **Makes:** 12 crepes

- 2 **large eggs, room temperature**
- ¾ **cup 2% milk**
- ½ **cup all-purpose flour**
- 1 **Tbsp. butter, melted**
- 1 **Tbsp. sugar**
- ⅛ **tsp. salt**

FILLING
- ½ **cup butter, cubed**
- ⅔ **cup sugar**
- 4 **tsp. grated orange zest**
- ⅔ **cup orange juice**

- 6 **medium firm bananas, peeled and sliced**
  Fresh raspberries, optional

1. In a bowl, whisk together first 6 ingredients; let stand 20 minutes.
2. Heat a lightly greased 8-in. nonstick skillet over medium heat. Fill a ¼-cup measure halfway with batter; pour into center of pan. Quickly lift, tilt and rotate pan to coat bottom evenly. Cook crepe until top appears dry; turn over and cook until bottom is cooked, 15-20 seconds longer. Remove to a wire rack. Repeat with remaining batter, greasing pan as needed.
3. For filling, place butter, sugar, orange zest and orange juice in a large skillet; bring to a boil, stirring to dissolve sugar. Reduce heat to medium; add bananas to warm.

4. To serve, spoon bananas onto crepes; fold into quarters. Top with remaining filling and, if desired, raspberries.
2 filled crepes: 443 cal., 20g fat (12g sat. fat), 110mg chol., 226mg sod., 64g carb. (43g sugars, 3g fiber), 6g pro.

BRIGHT IDEA

Try these crepes with a more wholesome filling of sliced bananas, strawberries, Greek yogurt and a sprinkle of granola for crunch.

SWEET POTATO DUTCH BABY WITH PRALINE SYRUP

This recipe reminds me of my favorite Dutch baby breakfast from when I was a child. It's a perfect comfort dish morning or evening.
—Angela Spengler, Niceville, FL

- -

Prep: 10 min. • **Cook:** 30 min.
Makes: 6 servings

- 4 **Tbsp. butter, divided**
- 3 **large eggs, room temperature**
- ½ **cup 2% milk**
- ¼ **cup mashed canned sweet potatoes in syrup**
- ½ **cup all-purpose flour**
- ¼ **tsp. salt**
- ½ **cup maple syrup**
- ¼ **cup chopped pecans**

1. Preheat the oven to 400°. Place 2 Tbsp. butter in a 10-in. cast-iron or other ovenproof skillet. Place in oven until butter is melted, 4-5 minutes; carefully swirl to coat evenly.
2. Meanwhile, in a large bowl, whisk eggs, milk and sweet potatoes until blended. Whisk in flour and salt. Pour into hot skillet. Bake until puffed and sides are golden brown and crisp, 20-25 minutes.
3. In a small saucepan, combine syrup, pecans and remaining 2 Tbsp. butter. Cook and stir over medium heat until butter is melted. Remove the pancake from oven; serve immediately with syrup.
1 serving: 261 cal., 14g fat (6g sat. fat), 115mg chol., 210mg sod., 30g carb. (19g sugars, 1g fiber), 5g pro.

SWEET POTATO
DUTCH BABY WITH
PRALINE SYRUP

BLINTZ PANCAKES

Blending sour cream and cottage cheese—ingredients traditionally associated with blintzes—into the batter of these pancakes gives them their old-fashioned flavor. Top these family favorites with berry syrup to turn an ordinary morning into an extraordinary day.
—Dianna Digoy, San Diego, CA

- -

Takes: 30 min. • **Makes:** 12 pancakes

- 1 **cup all-purpose flour**
- 1 **Tbsp. sugar**
- ½ **tsp. salt**
- 1 **cup sour cream**
- 1 **cup 4% cottage cheese**
- 4 **large eggs, room temperature, lightly beaten**
  Strawberry or blueberry syrup
  Sliced fresh strawberries, optional

1. In a large bowl, combine the flour, sugar and salt. Stir in the sour cream, cottage cheese and eggs until blended.
2. Pour batter by ¼ cupfuls onto a greased hot griddle in batches; turn when bubbles form on top. Cook until the second side is golden brown. Serve with syrup and, if desired, strawberries.
2 pancakes: 248 cal., 13g fat (7g sat. fat), 136mg chol., 371mg sod., 21g carb. (5g sugars, 1g fiber), 11g pro.

CHOCOLATE CHIP DUTCH BABY

I modified a traditional Dutch baby recipe given to me by a friend to come up with this version, which my family thinks is terrific. You'll be surprised at how easy it is to make.
—Mary Thompson, La Crosse, WI

Takes: 30 min. • **Makes:** 4 servings

¼   cup miniature semisweet
       chocolate chips
¼   cup packed brown sugar

DUTCH BABY

½   cup all-purpose flour
2   large eggs, room
       temperature
½   cup half-and-half cream
⅛   tsp. ground nutmeg
       Dash ground cinnamon
3   Tbsp. butter
       Optional: Maple syrup and
       additional butter

1. In a small bowl, combine the miniature chocolate chips and brown sugar; set aside. In a small bowl, beat the flour, eggs, cream, nutmeg and cinnamon until smooth.

2. Place butter in a 9-in. pie plate or an 8-in. cast-iron skillet. Heat in a 425° oven until melted, about 4 minutes. Pour batter into hot pie plate or skillet. Sprinkle with the chocolate chip mixture. Bake for 13-15 minutes or until top edges are golden brown. Serve immediately, with syrup and butter if desired.

1 piece: 313 cal., 17g fat (10g sat. fat), 144mg chol., 140mg sod., 33g carb. (21g sugars, 1g fiber), 6g pro.

CHOCOLATE CHIP
DUTCH BABY

BAKED BANANAS FOSTER FRENCH TOAST

MAKE AHEAD

BAKED BANANAS FOSTER FRENCH TOAST

This yummy baked French toast serves up all the taste of the spectacular dessert in fine fashion. It's sure to delight.
—Laurence Nasson, Hingham, MA

- -

Prep: 20 min. + chilling
Bake: 35 min. • **Makes:** 6 servings

½ cup butter, cubed
⅔ cup packed brown sugar
½ cup heavy whipping cream
½ tsp. ground cinnamon
½ tsp. ground allspice
¼ cup chopped pecans, optional
3 large bananas, sliced
12 slices egg bread or challah (about ¾ lb.)
1½ cups 2% milk
3 large eggs
1 Tbsp. sugar
1 tsp. vanilla extract

1. Place butter in a microwave-safe bowl; microwave, covered, until melted, 30-45 seconds. Stir in brown sugar, cream, cinnamon, allspice and, if desired, pecans. Add bananas; toss gently to coat.

2. Transfer to a greased 13x9-in. baking dish. Arrange bread over top, trimming to fit as necessary.

3. Place remaining ingredients in a blender; process just until blended. Pour over the bread. Refrigerate, covered, 8 hours or overnight.

4. Preheat oven to 375°. Remove the French toast from refrigerator while oven heats. Bake, uncovered, until a knife inserted in the center comes out clean, 35-40 minutes. Let stand 5-10 minutes. Invert to serve.

1 piece: 658 cal., 31g fat (17g sat. fat), 218mg chol., 584mg sod., 84g carb. (39g sugars, 4g fiber), 14g pro.

OVERNIGHT PANCAKES

Our kids love waking up to these golden, fluffy pancakes. The buttermilk batter is refrigerated overnight, making them perfect for busy mornings and special occasion breakfasts alike.
—Lisa Sammons, Cut Bank, MT

Prep: 10 min. + chilling
Cook: 10 min. • **Makes:** 30 pancakes

1 pkg. (¼ oz.) active dry yeast
¼ cup warm water (110° to 115°)
4 cups all-purpose flour
1 Tbsp. baking powder
2 tsp. baking soda
2 tsp. sugar
1 tsp. salt
6 large eggs, room temperature
4 cups buttermilk
¼ cup canola oil

1. Dissolve yeast in warm water; let stand for 5 minutes. Meanwhile, in another bowl, combine the next 5 ingredients. Whisk the eggs, buttermilk and oil; stir into flour mixture just until moistened. Stir in yeast mixture. Refrigerate, covered, for 8 hours or overnight.
2. To make pancakes, lightly grease griddle and preheat over medium heat. Pour batter by ¼ cupfuls onto griddle; cook until bubbles on top begin to pop and bottoms are golden brown. Turn; cook until second side is golden brown.
3 pancakes: 319 cal., 10g fat (2g sat. fat), 116mg chol., 862mg sod., 44g carb. (6g sugars, 2g fiber), 12g pro.

BUTTERMILK PECAN WAFFLES

I like cooking with buttermilk. These nutty, golden waffles are my husband's favorite breakfast, so we enjoy them often. They're as easy to prepare as regular waffles, but their unique taste makes them exceptional.
—Edna Hoffman, Hebron, IN

Prep: 10 min. **Cook:** 5 min./batch
Makes: 7 waffles

2 cups all-purpose flour
1 Tbsp. baking powder
1 tsp. baking soda
½ tsp. salt
4 large eggs, room temperature
2 cups buttermilk
½ cup butter, melted
3 Tbsp. chopped pecans

1. In a large bowl, whisk flour, baking powder, baking soda and salt. In another bowl, whisk the eggs and buttermilk until blended. Add to dry ingredients; stir just until moistened. Stir in butter.
2. Pour about ¾ cup batter onto a lightly greased preheated waffle maker. Sprinkle with a few pecans. Bake according to manufacturer's directions until golden brown. Repeat with the remaining batter and chopped pecans.
1 waffle: 337 cal., 19g fat (10g sat. fat), 159mg chol., 762mg sod., 31g carb. (4g sugars, 1g fiber), 10g pro.

BUTTERMILK PECAN WAFFLES

BANANA
BLUEBERRY
PANCAKES

BANANA BLUEBERRY PANCAKES

This recipe is a favorite in our home. My kids don't even realize how healthy it is!
—Kelly Reinicke, Wisconsin Rapids, WI

- -

Prep: 15 min. • **Cook:** 5 min./batch
Makes: 14 pancakes

- 1 **cup whole wheat flour**
- ½ **cup all-purpose flour**
- 2 **Tbsp. sugar**
- 2 **tsp. baking powder**
- ½ **tsp. salt**
- 1 **large egg, room temperature, lightly beaten**
- 1¼ **cups fat-free milk**
- 3 **medium ripe bananas, mashed**
- 1 **tsp. vanilla extract**
- 1½ **cups fresh or frozen blueberries**
  Optional: Maple syrup and sliced bananas

1. In a large bowl, combine the flours, sugar, baking powder and salt. Combine the egg, milk, bananas and vanilla; stir into dry ingredients just until moistened.

2. Pour batter by ¼ cupfuls onto a hot griddle coated with cooking spray; sprinkle with blueberries. Turn when bubbles form on top; cook until second side is golden brown. If desired, serve pancakes with syrup and sliced bananas.

Freeze option: Freeze cooled pancakes between layers of waxed paper in a resealable freezer container. To use, place pancakes on an ungreased baking sheet, cover with foil, and reheat in a preheated 375° oven 6-10 minutes. Or, place a stack of pancakes on a microwave-safe plate and microwave on high for 1¼-1½ minutes or until heated through.
Note: If using frozen blueberries, do not thaw.
2 pancakes: 195 cal., 2g fat (0 sat. fat), 31mg chol., 317mg sod., 41g carb. (19g sugars, 4g fiber), 6g pro.
Diabetic exchanges: 1½ starch, 1 fruit.

Incredible Eggs

Humble, healthy eggs are the very symbol of life.
Here are 15 wonderful ways to celebrate them.

CLASSIC EGGS BENEDICT

MUFFIN CUP EGGS

My children loved these even when they were toddlers.
—Lisa Walder, Urbana, IL

Takes: 30 min.
Makes: 6 servings

- 12 **thin slices deli roast beef**
- 6 **slices American cheese, quartered**
- 12 **large eggs**

1. Press 1 slice of beef onto the bottom and up the sides of each greased muffin cup, forming a shell. Arrange 2 cheese pieces in each shell. Break 1 egg into each cup.
2. Bake, uncovered, at 350° for 20-25 minutes or until eggs are completely set.

2 muffin cups: 238 cal., 15g fat (7g sat. fat), 452mg chol., 551mg sod., 3g carb. (2g sugars, 0 fiber), 22g pro.

HOW-TO

Test Doneness of Hollandaise

Dip a spoon in the sauce and run your finger across the back. A fully cooked sauce will hold a firm line and not run down.

CLASSIC EGGS BENEDICT

Legend has it that poached eggs on an English muffin started at Delmonico's in New York.
—Barbara Pletzke, Herndon, VA

Takes: 30 min. • **Makes:** 8 servings

- 4 **large egg yolks**
- 2 **Tbsp. water**
- 2 **Tbsp. lemon juice**
- ¾ **cup butter, melted**
  Dash white pepper

ASSEMBLY
- 8 **large eggs**
- 4 **English muffins**
- 8 **slices warm Canadian bacon**
  Paprika

1. For hollandaise sauce, in top of a double boiler or a metal bowl over simmering water, whisk egg yolks, water and lemon juice until blended; cook until the mixture is just thick enough to coat a metal spoon and temperature reaches 160°, whisking constantly. Remove from heat. Very slowly drizzle in warm melted butter, whisking constantly. Whisk in white pepper. Transfer to a small bowl if necessary. Place bowl in a larger bowl of warm water. Keep warm, stirring occasionally, until ready to serve, up to 30 minutes.
2. Place 2-3 in. of water in a large saucepan or skillet with high sides. Bring to a boil; adjust the heat to maintain a gentle simmer. Break 1 egg into a small bowl; holding bowl close to surface of water, slip egg into water. Repeat with 3 more eggs.
3. Cook, uncovered, 2-4 minutes or until whites are completely set and yolks begin to thicken but are not hard. With a slotted spoon, lift eggs out of water. Repeat with remaining 4 eggs.
4. Split and toast English muffins; top each half with Canadian bacon, a poached egg and 2 Tbsp. sauce. Sprinkle with paprika.

1 serving: 345 cal., 26g fat (14g sat. fat), 331mg chol., 522mg sod., 15g carb. (1g sugars, 1g fiber), 13g pro.

HAM & SWISS EGG CASSEROLE

The buttery crunch of croissants goes perfectly with smooth Swiss and tender eggs. Breakfast for a crew doesn't get much easier than this!

—Kathy Harding, Richmond, MO

- -

Prep: 20 min. • **Bake:** 35 min.
Makes: 12 servings

- 16 **large eggs**
- 2 **cups 2% milk**
- ½ **tsp. salt**
- ¼ **tsp. ground nutmeg**
- 4 **cups shredded Swiss cheese**
- 8 **oz. sliced deli ham, chopped**
- 4 **croissants, torn into 1½-in. pieces**
- 1 **Tbsp. minced chives**

1. Preheat oven to 350°. Whisk together eggs, milk, salt and nutmeg. Sprinkle the cheese and ham into a greased 13x9-in. baking dish or pan; pour in egg mixture. Sprinkle the croissant pieces over top.

2. Bake, uncovered, until puffed and golden brown, 35-40 minutes. Sprinkle with chives. Let stand for 5-10 minutes before serving.

To Make Ahead: Refrigerate the unbaked casserole, covered, several hours or overnight. To use, preheat oven to 350°. Remove casserole from refrigerator while oven heats. Bake as directed.

1 piece: 354 cal., 23g fat (11g sat. fat), 306mg chol., 545mg sod., 12g carb. (5g sugars, 1g fiber), 24g pro.

HAM & SWISS
EGG CASSEROLE

LOADED TATER TOT BAKE

I keep frozen Tater Tots on hand for meals like this delicious casserole. It's a super brunch, breakfast or side dish that kids of all ages love.

—Nancy Heishman, Las Vegas, NV

Prep: 15 min. • **Bake:** 35 min.
Makes: 6 servings

- 1 Tbsp. canola oil
- 1 medium onion, finely chopped
- 6 oz. Canadian bacon, cut into ½-in. strips
- 4 cups frozen Tater Tots, thawed
- 6 large eggs, lightly beaten
- ½ cup reduced-fat sour cream
- ½ cup half-and-half cream
- 1 Tbsp. dried parsley flakes
- ¾ tsp. garlic powder
- ½ tsp. pepper
- 1½ cups shredded cheddar cheese

1. Preheat oven to 350°. In a large skillet, heat oil over medium heat. Add onion; cook and stir until tender, 2-3 minutes. Add Canadian bacon; cook until lightly browned, 1-2 minutes, stirring occasionally. Remove from heat.
2. Line bottom of a greased 11x7-in. baking dish with Tater Tots; top with Canadian bacon mixture. In a large bowl, whisk eggs, sour cream, cream and seasonings until blended. Stir in the cheese; pour over top. Bake, uncovered, until golden brown, 35-40 minutes.

1 piece: 443 cal., 29g fat (12g sat. fat), 243mg chol., 917mg sod., 23g carb. (4g sugars, 2g fiber), 22g pro.

EGG BURRITOS

EGG BURRITOS

Zap one of these frozen burritos in the microwave and you'll stave off hunger all morning. Bacon with cheese is my family's favorite combo, but I sometimes use breakfast sausage instead.
—Audra Niederman, Aberdeen, SD

Takes: 25 min. • **Makes:** 10 burritos

- 12 bacon strips, chopped
- 12 large eggs
- ½ tsp. salt
- ¼ tsp. pepper
- 10 flour tortillas (8 in.), warmed
- 1½ cups shredded cheddar cheese
- 4 green onions, thinly sliced

1. In a large cast-iron or other heavy skillet, cook bacon until crisp; drain on paper towels. Remove all but 1-2 Tbsp. drippings from pan.

2. Whisk eggs, salt and pepper. Heat skillet over medium heat; pour in egg mixture. Cook and stir until eggs are thickened and no liquid egg remains; remove from heat.

3. Spoon about ¼ cup egg mixture onto center of each tortilla; sprinkle with cheese, bacon and green onions. Roll into burritos.

Freeze option: Cool eggs before making burritos. Individually wrap burritos in paper towels and foil; freeze in an airtight container. To use, remove foil; place paper towel-wrapped burrito on a microwave-safe plate. Microwave on high until heated through, turning once. Let stand 15 seconds.

1 burrito: 376 cal., 20g fat (8g sat. fat), 251mg chol., 726mg sod., 29g carb. (0 sugars, 2g fiber), 19g pro.

MANCHEGO MUSHROOM SCRAMBLE

MIGAS BREAKFAST TACOS

Unless you grew up in the Southwest or visit there often, you might be hearing of migas for the first time. Think of them as the best scrambled eggs ever. The secret ingredient: corn tortillas. They really make my migas tacos special!

—Stephen Exel, Des Moines, IA

- -

Takes: 30 min. • **Makes:** 3 servings

- ¼ cup finely chopped onion
- 1 jalapeno pepper, seeded and chopped
- 1 Tbsp. canola oil
- 2 corn tortillas (6 in.), cut into thin strips
- 4 large eggs
- ¼ tsp. salt
- ⅛ tsp. pepper
- ½ cup crumbled queso fresco or shredded Monterey Jack cheese
- ¼ cup chopped seeded tomato
- 6 flour tortillas (6 in.), warmed
  Optional toppings: Refried beans, sliced avocado, sour cream and minced fresh cilantro

1. In a large skillet, saute onion and jalapeno in oil until tender. Add the tortilla strips; cook 3 minutes longer. In a small bowl, whisk the eggs, salt and pepper. Add to skillet; cook and stir until almost set. Stir in cheese and tomato.

2. Serve in flour tortillas with toppings of your choice.

2 tacos: 424 cal., 21g fat (5g sat. fat), 295mg chol., 821mg sod., 39g carb. (2g sugars, 1g fiber), 21g pro.

MANCHEGO MUSHROOM SCRAMBLE

This savory breakfast dish takes everyday scrambled eggs up a few notches. The rich flavor is so satisfying.

—Thomas Faglon, Somerset, NJ

- -

Takes: 25 min. • **Makes:** 8 servings

- 2 Tbsp. extra virgin olive oil, divided
- ½ cup diced onion
- ½ cup diced sweet red pepper
- 2 cups thinly sliced fresh shiitake mushrooms (about 4 oz.)
- 1 tsp. prepared horseradish
- 8 large eggs, beaten
- 1 cup heavy whipping cream
- 1 cup shredded Manchego cheese
- 1 tsp. kosher salt
- 1 tsp. coarsely ground pepper

1. In a large nonstick skillet, heat 1 Tbsp. olive oil over medium heat. Add onion and red pepper; cook and stir until crisp-tender, 2-3 minutes. Add the mushrooms; cook and stir until tender, 3-4 minutes. Stir in the horseradish; cook 2 minutes more.

2. In a small bowl, whisk together remaining ingredients and remaining olive oil. Pour into skillet; cook and stir until eggs are thickened and no liquid egg remains.

1 serving: 274 cal., 24g fat (12g sat. fat), 234mg chol., 405mg sod., 4g carb. (2g sugars, 1g fiber), 11g pro.

MIGAS BREAKFAST
TACOS

CURRY SCRAMBLE

I have eggs every morning, and this is a great change from the classic scrambled egg meal. I like to add sliced peppers on top if I have them on hand.
—Valerie Belley, St. Louis, MO

- -

Takes: 15 min. • **Makes:** 4 servings

- 8 **large eggs**
- ¼ **cup fat-free milk**
- ½ **tsp. curry powder**
- ¼ **tsp. salt**
- ⅛ **tsp. pepper**
- ⅛ **tsp. ground cardamom, optional**
- 2 **medium tomatoes, sliced or chopped**

1. In a large bowl, whisk eggs, milk, curry powder, salt, pepper and, if desired, cardamom until blended.
2. Place a lightly greased large nonstick skillet over medium heat. Pour in egg mixture; cook and stir until eggs are thickened and no liquid egg remains. Serve with tomatoes.
1 serving: 160 cal., 10g fat (3g sat. fat), 372mg chol., 299mg sod., 4g carb. (3g sugars, 1g fiber), 14g pro.
Diabetic exchanges: 2 medium-fat meat.

SPINACH-EGG BREAKFAST PIZZAS

I like my food pretty, and this breakfast pizza is eye-popping. Bring it to the table with a bowl of berries or grapes and hot cafe au lait.
—Lily Julow, Lawrenceville, GA

- -

Prep: 20 min. • **Bake:** 15 min.
Makes: 4 pizzas

Cornmeal
- 1 **loaf (1 lb.) frozen pizza dough, thawed**
- 1 **Tbsp. plus additional extra virgin olive oil, divided**
- 5 **to 6 oz. fresh baby spinach**
- ⅓ **cup plus additional grated Parmesan cheese, divided**
- 3 **Tbsp. sour cream**
- 1 **small garlic clove, minced**
- ¼ **tsp. sea salt**
- ⅛ **tsp. plus additional coarsely ground pepper, divided**
- 4 **large eggs**

1. Preheat oven to 500°. Line two 15x10x1-in. baking pans with parchment; sprinkle lightly with cornmeal. Cut dough into 4 pieces; stretch and shape into 6- to 7-in. circles and place in pans.
2. Meanwhile, in a large skillet, heat 1 Tbsp. olive oil over medium-high heat. Add spinach; cook and stir until just starting to wilt, 1-2 minutes. Combine spinach with the next 5 ingredients; spread the spinach mixture over each pizza. Leave a slight border of raised dough along edge. Bake on a lower oven rack about 5 minutes.
3. Remove from oven; break an egg into center of each pizza. Return to lower oven rack, baking until egg whites are set but yolks are still runny, 6-10 minutes. Drizzle olive oil over pizzas; top with additional Parmesan cheese and pepper. Serve immediately.
1 pizza: 433 cal., 14g fat (4g sat. fat), 199mg chol., 865mg sod., 55g carb. (3g sugars, 1g fiber), 16g pro.

SPINACH-EGG
BREAKFAST
PIZZAS

ITALIAN EGGS BENEDICT
WITH PESTO
HOLLANDAISE

ITALIAN EGGS BENEDICT WITH PESTO HOLLANDAISE

My husband and I have a standing breakfast date on Saturday mornings. When we want something fancy, we make Italian-inspired eggs Benedict with pesto and prosciutto.
—Jackie Dodd, Los Angeles, CA

Takes: 30 min. • **Makes:** 4 servings

½ cup butter, cubed
1 Tbsp. prepared pesto
4 large egg yolks
2 Tbsp. water
1 Tbsp. lemon juice
2 tsp. white vinegar
4 large eggs
8 thin slices prosciutto or deli ham
4 fresh basil leaves
4 slices tomato
4 slices Italian bread (1 in. thick), toasted

1. In a small saucepan, melt butter; stir in pesto. In top of a double boiler or a metal bowl over simmering water, whisk egg yolks, water and lemon juice until blended; cook until mixture is just thick enough to coat a metal spoon and temperature reaches 160°, whisking constantly. Reduce heat to very low. Very slowly drizzle in warm melted butter mixture, whisking constantly.
2. Transfer to a small bowl if necessary. Place bowl in a larger bowl of warm water. Keep warm, stirring occasionally, until ready to serve. Place 2-3 in. of water in a large saucepan or skillet with high sides; add vinegar. Bring to a boil; adjust heat to maintain a gentle simmer. Break cold eggs, 1 at a time, into a small bowl; holding the bowl close to the surface of the water, slip each egg into water.
3. Cook, uncovered, 3-5 minutes or until whites are completely set and yolks begin to thicken but are not hard. Using a slotted spoon, lift eggs out of water.
4. To serve, layer prosciutto or ham, basil leaves, tomato and eggs over toast. Top with hollandaise sauce. Serve immediately.

1 serving: 525 cal., 39g fat (19g sat. fat), 457mg chol., 1092mg sod., 24g carb. (2g sugars, 2g fiber), 21g pro.

MEDITERRANEAN OMELET

This fluffy omelet gives us reason to rush to the breakfast table. For extra flair, add chopped fresh herbs such as basil, oregano or tarragon.
—Milynne Charlton, Scarborough, ON

Takes: 10 min. • **Makes:** 2 servings

- 4   large eggs
- ¼   cup water
- ⅛   tsp. salt
  Dash pepper
- 1   Tbsp. butter
- ¼   cup crumbled feta or goat cheese
- ¼   cup chopped tomato
- 1   green onion, chopped

1. In a small bowl, whisk eggs, water, salt and pepper until blended. In a large nonstick skillet, heat butter over medium-high heat. Pour in egg mixture. Mixture should set immediately at edge. As eggs set, push cooked portions toward the center, letting the uncooked eggs flow underneath.

2. When eggs are thickened and no liquid egg remains, add cheese, tomato and green onion to 1 side. Fold omelet in half and cut into 2 portions; slide onto plates.

½ omelet: 236 cal., 18g fat (8g sat. fat), 395mg chol., 472mg sod., 3g carb. (1g sugars, 1g fiber), 15g pro.

MEDITERRANEAN OMELET

SAUSAGE PIZZA FRITTATA

I love this frittata because the combination of fresh flavors makes it special. It's the perfect sunny South Florida breakfast.
—Wolfgang Hanau,
West Palm Beach, FL

- -

Takes: 30 min. • **Makes:** 4 servings

    4 oz. bulk Italian sausage
    2 cups sliced fresh mushrooms
    2 Tbsp. diced red onion
    2 Tbsp. diced green pepper
    ¼ cup diced fresh pineapple
    6 large eggs, beaten
    6 Tbsp. marinara sauce
    2 Tbsp. shredded part-skim
       mozzarella cheese
    2 Tbsp. grated Parmigiano-
       Reggiano cheese
    2 Tbsp. minced fresh parsley

1. Preheat broiler. In a 10-in. ovenproof skillet, cook sausage, mushrooms, onion and pepper over medium heat until sausage is no longer pink and vegetables are tender, 6-8 minutes, breaking sausage into crumbles; drain.
2. Return sausage mixture to skillet; stir in pineapple. Pour in beaten eggs. Cook, covered, until nearly set, 4-6 minutes. Spread marinara over top; sprinkle with cheeses.
3. Broil 3-4 in. from heat until eggs are completely set and cheese is melted, 2-3 minutes. Let stand 5 minutes. Sprinkle with parsley; cut into wedges.
1 wedge: 226 cal., 15g fat (5g sat. fat), 299mg chol., 459mg sod., 7g carb. (4g sugars, 1g fiber), 16g pro.

SOUTHERN HASH BROWNS & HAM SHEET-PAN BAKE

CALICO SCRAMBLED EGGS

When you're short on time, this recipe is eggs-actly what you need. With green pepper and tomato, it's colorful and good for you, too.
—*Taste of Home* Test Kitchen

Takes: 15 min. • **Makes:** 4 servings

8	large eggs
¼	cup 2% milk
⅛	to ¼ tsp. dill weed
⅛	to ¼ tsp. salt
⅛	to ¼ tsp. pepper
1	Tbsp. butter
½	cup chopped green pepper
¼	cup chopped onion
½	cup chopped fresh tomato

1. In a bowl, whisk first 5 ingredients until blended. In a 12-in. nonstick skillet, heat butter over medium-high heat. Add green pepper and onion; cook and stir until tender. Remove from pan.

2. In same pan, pour in egg mixture; cook and stir over medium heat until eggs begin to thicken. Add tomato and pepper mixture; cook until heated through and no liquid egg remains, stirring gently.

1 cup: 188 cal., 13g fat (5g sat. fat), 381mg chol., 248mg sod., 4g carb. (3g sugars, 1g fiber), 14g pro.
Diabetic exchanges: 2 medium-fat meat, ½ fat.

SOUTHERN HASH BROWNS & HAM SHEET-PAN BAKE

Why not apply the convenience of sheet-pan cooking to breakfast? I love how easily it comes together.
—Colleen Delawder, Herndon, VA

Prep: 15 min. • **Bake:** 35 min. •
Makes: 4 servings

1	pkg. (20 oz.) refrigerated shredded hash brown potatoes
3	Tbsp. olive oil
½	tsp. salt
½	tsp. pepper
¼	cup apple jelly
¼	cup apricot preserves
1	Tbsp. horseradish sauce
1	tsp. Dijon mustard
¼	tsp. garlic powder
¼	tsp. onion powder
2	cups cubed fully cooked ham
4	large eggs
2	green onions, finely chopped

1. Preheat oven to 400°. Place potatoes in a greased 15x10x1-in. baking pan. Drizzle with oil; sprinkle with salt and pepper. Toss to coat. Bake until edges are golden brown, 25-30 minutes.

2. In a small bowl, combine jelly, preserves, horseradish sauce, Dijon, garlic powder and onion powder. Pour over potatoes; add ham. Toss to coat.

3. With the back of a spoon, make 4 wells in potato mixture. Break an egg into each well. Bake until egg whites are completely set and yolks begin to thicken but are not hard, 10-12 minutes. Sprinkle with green onions and additional pepper.

1 serving: 483 cal., 19g fat (4g sat. fat), 228mg chol., 1340mg sod., 55g carb. (23g sugars, 3g fiber), 24g pro.

SHIITAKE EGGS IN PUFF PASTRY

These easy pastry shells present beautifully at the table.

—Jamie Brown-Miller, Napa, CA

Takes: 30 min. • **Makes:** 4 servings

- 1   sheet thawed puff pastry
- 2   Tbsp. butter, divided
- 1½ cups sliced fresh shiitake mushrooms
- 1   cup fresh baby spinach
- 6   large eggs, lightly beaten
- ½ cup crumbled goat cheese
- 1   Tbsp. Sriracha chili sauce
- 4   thin slices prosciutto
- 1   Tbsp. minced fresh tarragon

1. Preheat oven to 425°. Place four 6-oz. ramekins upside-down on a baking sheet. Grease outsides of ramekins well. Cut pastry into quarters; shape each around a ramekin. Bake 14-16 minutes or until golden brown.

2. In a large skillet, melt 1 Tbsp. butter over medium-high heat. Add mushrooms; saute 2-3 minutes or until lightly browned. Stir in spinach until wilted. Remove from pan.

3. In same pan, heat remaining butter over medium heat. Pour in eggs; cook and stir until thickened and no liquid egg remains. Gently stir in goat cheese, chili sauce and mushroom mixture.

4. Carefully remove pastries from ramekins and place right-side up on plates. Line bottoms and sides of pastries with prosciutto. Fill with egg mixture; sprinkle with tarragon.

1 serving: 545 cal., 35g fat (13g sat. fat), 324mg chol., 826mg sod., 39g carb. (2g sugars, 6g fiber), 21g pro.

SHIITAKE EGGS
IN PUFF PASTRY

Sunny Salads

From garden-fresh greats to pasta favorites, the perfect cold course is here.

STRAWBERRY ARUGULA SALAD WITH FETA

The combination of peppery arugula, sweet strawberries and robust feta cheese may sound unusual, but one bite wins over the taste buds.
—Carla Horne, Meridian, MS

- -

Takes: 15 min. • **Makes:** 12 servings

6	cups fresh arugula or baby spinach
1½	cups sliced fresh strawberries
½	cup slivered almonds or pine nuts
½	cup crumbled garlic and herb feta cheese
4	green onions, chopped

VINAIGRETTE

⅓	cup olive oil
1	Tbsp. Dijon mustard
1	Tbsp. red wine vinegar
2	tsp. lemon juice
1½	tsp. balsamic vinegar
1	tsp. minced fresh rosemary or ¼ tsp. dried rosemary, crushed
1	tsp. fresh sage or ¼ tsp. dried sage leaves
½	tsp. celery seed
⅛	tsp. pepper

In a salad bowl, combine the first 5 ingredients. In a small bowl, whisk the vinaigrette ingredients. Drizzle over salad; toss to coat.

¾ cup: 106 cal., 9g fat (2g sat. fat), 3mg chol., 88mg sod., 4g carb. (2g sugars, 1g fiber), 2g pro.

STRAWBERRY ARUGULA SALAD WITH FETA

HONEY POPPY SEED
FRUIT SALAD

HONEY POPPY SEED FRUIT SALAD

Though fresh fruit steals the show in this morning medley, the honey sauce makes it an especially sweet treat. It takes just 10 minutes to assemble this easy salad, which tastes so good with brunch.
—Dorothy Dinnean, Harrison, AR

- -

Takes: 10 min. • **Makes:** 8 servings

- 2 **medium firm bananas, chopped**
- 2 **cups fresh blueberries**
- 2 **cups fresh raspberries**
- 2 **cups sliced fresh strawberries**
- 5 **Tbsp. honey**
- 1 **tsp. lemon juice**
- ¾ **tsp. poppy seeds**

In a large bowl, combine the bananas and berries. In a small bowl, combine the honey, lemon juice and poppy seeds. Pour over fruit; toss to coat.
¾ cup: 117 cal., 1g fat (0 sat. fat), 0 chol., 2mg sod., 30g carb. (23g sugars, 5g fiber), 1g pro.

Quickly Hull a Strawberry

Insert a drinking straw into the tip of the berry and push it through the other end.

BANANA SPLIT FLUFF

This pretty pink mixture, rich with yummy fruit and nuts, is sure to disappear in a hurry. It's a sweet and speedy treat that can be served as a dessert or salad.
—Anne Powers, Munford, AL

Takes: 10 min. • **Makes:** 10 servings

- 1   **can (14 oz.) sweetened condensed milk**
- 1   **carton (12 oz.) frozen whipped topping, thawed**
- 1   **can (21 oz.) cherry pie filling**
- 3   **medium firm bananas, cut into chunks**
- 1   **can (8 oz.) crushed pineapple, drained**
- ½   **cup chopped nuts**

In a large bowl, combine the milk and whipped topping until well blended. Fold in pie filling, bananas, pineapple and nuts.

¾ cup: 374 cal., 13g fat (8g sat. fat), 13mg chol., 62mg sod., 58g carb. (49g sugars, 2g fiber), 5g pro.

READER REVIEW

"Just made this about an hour ago. Husband said this was the best salad I have ever made. Good with miniature marshmallows sprinkled on top just before serving. Yum!"
—MISS LYNN, TASTEOFHOME.COM

BANANA SPLIT FLUFF

KALE & BACON
SALAD WITH
HONEY-HORSERADISH
VINAIGRETTE

KALE & BACON SALAD WITH HONEY-HORSERADISH VINAIGRETTE

Totally scrumptious and packed with nutrition, this salad was my response to friends who asked how they could incorporate kale into their diets without sacrificing taste. It is also wonderful made with collard or mustard greens.
—Elizabeth Warren,
Oklahoma City, OK

- -

Prep: 35 min. • **Makes:** 8 servings

- 10 kale leaves, stems removed, thinly sliced
- ¼ cup loosely packed basil leaves, thinly sliced
- ½ cup alfalfa sprouts
- 4 bacon strips, cooked and crumbled
- ½ cup crumbled feta cheese
- ½ medium ripe avocado, peeled and thinly sliced
- 1 hard-boiled large egg, chopped
- 1 cup grape tomatoes, chopped

VINAIGRETTE

- ⅓ cup olive oil
- 3 Tbsp. lemon juice
- 2 Tbsp. prepared horseradish
- 2 Tbsp. honey
- 1½ tsp. garlic powder
- 1½ tsp. spicy brown mustard
- ¼ tsp. crushed red pepper flakes
- ⅛ tsp. pepper
  Dash salt

1. Divide kale and basil among 8 salad plates. Top with sprouts, bacon, feta cheese, avocado, egg and tomatoes.

2. In a small bowl, whisk all the vinaigrette ingredients. Drizzle over salads; serve immediately.

1 serving: 236 cal., 15g fat (3g sat. fat), 34mg chol., 248mg sod., 21g carb. (6g sugars, 4g fiber), 8g pro.

CRUNCHY APPLE SIDE SALAD

CRUNCHY APPLE SIDE SALAD

With fiber-rich fruit, light dressing and crunchy walnuts, this makes a great side salad or snack. Try it with low-fat granola.
—Kathy Armstrong, Post Falls, ID

Takes: 15 min. • **Makes:** 5 servings

- ⅓ cup fat-free sugar-free vanilla yogurt
- ⅓ cup reduced-fat whipped topping
- ¼ tsp. plus ⅛ tsp. ground cinnamon, divided
- 2 medium red apples, chopped
- 1 large Granny Smith apple, chopped
- ¼ cup dried cranberries
- 2 Tbsp. chopped walnuts

In a large bowl, combine yogurt, the whipped topping and ¼ tsp. cinnamon. Add chopped apples and cranberries; toss to coat. Refrigerate until serving. Sprinkle with chopped walnuts and remaining cinnamon before serving.

¾ cup: 109 cal., 3g fat (1g sat. fat), 0 chol., 12mg sod., 22g carb. (16g sugars, 3g fiber), 2g pro.

Diabetic exchanges: 1 fruit, ½ starch, ½ fat.

RAINBOW FRUIT SALAD

When my children were young, I would often dress up fresh fruit in this easy salad. Decades later, my grandchildren and even my great-grandchildren love digging into the fruity layers. This salad goes well with barbecued meats or cold sandwiches.
—Jonnie Adams Sisler, Stevensville, MT

Prep: 20 min. + chilling
Makes: 20 servings

- 2 large firm bananas, sliced
- 2 Tbsp. lemon juice
- 2 cups seeded cubed watermelon
- 2 cups fresh or canned pineapple chunks
- 1 pint fresh blueberries
- 3 kiwifruit, peeled and sliced
- 1 pint fresh strawberries, halved
- 6 oz. cream cheese, softened
- ⅓ cup confectioners' sugar
- 2 Tbsp. fresh lime juice
- ½ tsp. grated lime zest
- 1 cup heavy whipping cream, whipped

1. Toss bananas and lemon juice; place in a 4-qt. glass serving bowl. Add remaining fruit in layers.
2. In a bowl, beat cream cheese until smooth. Gradually add sugar, lime juice and zest. Stir in a small amount of whipped cream; mix well. Fold in remaining whipped cream. Spread over fruit. Chill until serving.

¾ cup: 123 cal., 7g fat (5g sat. fat), 22mg chol., 31mg sod., 14g carb. (10g sugars, 2g fiber), 1g pro.

CUCUMBER CRUNCH COLESLAW

CUCUMBER CRUNCH COLESLAW

This recipe came about as a way to use a julienne peeler that I had received as a gift. Leftover sparkling wine was my other inspiration, and I combined it with cucumbers to create a refreshing slaw. It's a nice way to round out a brunch or picnic.
—Merry Graham, Newhall, CA

Takes: 30 min. • **Makes:** 8 servings

⅓ cup olive oil
¼ cup sparkling or dry white wine
1 Tbsp. minced fresh basil
1 Tbsp. Key lime juice
1 serrano pepper, seeded and minced
1½ tsp. minced fresh mint
1½ tsp. molasses
1 tsp. sugar
1 garlic clove, minced
¾ tsp. salt
¾ tsp. grated lime zest
½ tsp. pepper

COLESLAW
3 English cucumbers, julienned
2 cups fresh arugula or baby spinach, coarsely chopped
1 cup fresh snow peas, cut into ½-in. pieces
½ cup sliced almonds, toasted
1 cup dried cranberries

1. Combine first 12 ingredients; set aside. In a large bowl, combine the remaining ingredients.
2. Just before serving, pour dressing over salad; toss to coat.

¾ cup: 178 cal., 12g fat (2g sat. fat), 0 chol., 227mg sod., 16g carb. (11g sugars, 2g fiber), 2g pro.
Diabetic exchanges: 2 fat, 1 vegetable, ½ starch.

CALIFORNIA AVOCADO SALAD

Spread a little sunshine with this easy salad. Just four ingredients drizzled with dressing and you have a light lunch or a pretty side to serve with dinner.

—James Schend,
Pleasant Prairie, WI

Takes: 20 min. • **Makes:** 8 servings

- 3 medium oranges, peeled and sectioned
- 2 medium ripe avocados, peeled and sliced
- ¼ cup toasted pine nuts
- 2 tsp. minced fresh rosemary
  Orange Yogurt Dressing (recipe at right) or dressing of your choice

Arrange oranges and avocados on a platter; sprinkle with pine nuts and rosemary. Drizzle dressing over salad. Serve immediately.

½ cup with 2 Tbsp. Orange Yogurt Dressing: 135 cal., 11g fat (1g sat. fat), 3mg chol., 129mg sod., 10g carb. (5g sugars, 3g fiber), 2g pro. **Diabetic exchanges:** 2 fat, ½ fruit.

Orange Yogurt Dressing: Whisk ¼ cup reduced-fat mayonnaise, ¼ cup fat-free palin yogurt, 2 Tbsp. orange juice, 2 tsp. honey, 1 tsp. grated orange zest, ¼ tsp. salt and a dash of white pepper. Refrigerate until serving.

FAVORITE CRAB PASTA SALAD

Wanda, a friend at work, made this for a party and boy, did it catch on fast! It's especially wonderful for summer picnics and barbecues.

—Cheryl Seweryn, Lemont, IL

Takes: 20 min. • **Makes:** 7 servings

- 3 cups uncooked medium pasta shells
- 1 lb. creamy coleslaw
- ½ cup mayonnaise
- 1 Tbsp. chopped onion
- 1 tsp. dill weed
  Dash salt
- 2 cups chopped imitation crabmeat

1. Cook pasta according to package directions. Meanwhile, in a large serving bowl, combine the coleslaw, mayonnaise, onion, dill and salt. Stir in crab.

2. Drain the pasta and rinse in cold water. Add to coleslaw mixture; toss to coat. Chill until serving.

¾ cup: 376 cal., 20g fat (3g sat. fat), 17mg chol., 508mg sod., 39g carb. (9g sugars, 2g fiber), 10g pro.

CALIFORNIA AVOCADO SALAD

LIME-HONEY FRUIT SALAD

Nothing is more refreshing to me than a seasonal fruit salad enhanced with this simple lime-honey dressing.
—Victoria Shevlin, Cape Coral, FL

- -

Prep: 20 min. + chilling
Makes: 12 servings

1	tsp. cornstarch
¼	cup lime juice
¼	cup honey
½	tsp. poppy seeds
3	medium Gala or Red Delicious apples, cubed
2	medium pears, cubed
2	cups seedless red grapes
2	cups green grapes

1. In a small microwave-safe bowl, combine cornstarch and lime juice until smooth. Microwave, uncovered, on high for 20 seconds; stir. Cook 15 seconds longer; stir. Stir in honey and poppy seeds.

2. In a large bowl, combine the apples, pears and grapes. Pour dressing over fruit; toss to coat. Cover and refrigerate overnight.

¾ cup: 96 cal., 0 fat (0 sat. fat), 0 chol., 2mg sod., 25g carb. (21g sugars, 2g fiber), 1g pro.
Diabetic exchanges: 1½ fruit.

LIME-HONEY FRUIT SALAD

GRANDMA'S SPINACH SALAD

With all its fresh ingredients, this pretty salad was my grandma's favorite. Even little ones like it. But you don't have to tell yours that spinach is good for them!
—Shelley Riebel, Armada, MI

Takes: 20 min. • **Makes:** 8 servings

- ½ **cup sugar**
- ½ **cup canola oil**
- ¼ **cup white vinegar**
- ½ **tsp. celery seed**
- 10 **oz. fresh baby spinach (about 13 cups)**
- 1 **small red onion, thinly sliced**
- ½ **lb. sliced fresh mushrooms**
- 5 **hard-boiled large eggs, sliced**
- 8 **bacon strips, cooked and crumbled**

1. Whisk first 4 ingredients until sugar is dissolved.

2. In a 13x9-in. dish, layer half of each of the following: spinach, onion, mushrooms and sliced eggs. Repeat layers. Drizzle with dressing; top with crumbled bacon.

1¼ cups: 280 cal., 21g fat (3g sat. fat), 125mg chol., 214mg sod., 16g carb. (14g sugars, 1g fiber), 9g pro.

GRANDMA'S
SPINACH SALAD

HOW-TO

Hard-Cook Eggs in a Pressure Cooker

- Place trivet insert and 1 cup water in a 6-qt. electric pressure cooker. Set up to 12 eggs on trivet.
- Lock lid; close pressure-release valve. Adjust to pressure-cook on high for 5 minutes (for large eggs). Meanwhile, prepare an ice bath.
- Let pressure release naturally for 5 minutes; quick-release any remaining pressure. Immediately place eggs in ice water to cool. Peel when ready to use.

Hot Breakfast Sides

Round out an abundant a.m. spread with meat, potatoes and hot veggie sides.

BAKED FRUIT COMPOTE

A splash of Madeira wine makes canned fruit fancy and festive . This dish brightens any winter brunch. Mix and match canned fruits to suit your family's tastes.
—Myrt Pfannkuche, Pell City, AL

Takes: 30 min. • **Makes:** 11 servings

- 1 can (29 oz.) sliced peaches, drained
- 1 can (20 oz.) pineapple chunks, drained
- 2 cans (8 oz. each) grapefruit sections, drained
- 1 can (15¼ oz.) sliced pears, drained
- 1 can (11 oz.) mandarin oranges, drained
- 1 cup pitted dried plums
- ½ cup butter, cubed
- ½ cup packed brown sugar
- ¼ cup Madeira wine, optional
  Fresh mint leaves, optional

1. Preheat oven to 350°. In a 13x9-in. baking dish, combine the first 6 ingredients.
2. In a small saucepan, combine butter and brown sugar. Bring to a boil over medium heat; cook and stir until sugar is dissolved, 2-3 minutes. Remove from heat; stir in Madeira wine if desired. Pour over fruit and toss to coat.
3. Bake, uncovered, until heated through, 20-25 minutes. Garnish with mint if desired.
¾ cup: 257 cal., 8g fat (5g sat. fat), 22mg chol., 75mg sod., 46g carb. (39g sugars, 2g fiber), 1g pro.

PUMPKIN & CHICKEN SAUSAGE HASH

This lovely hash can be served as a side or as the main dish for breakfast, lunch or dinner. I like to serve it topped with poached or fried eggs in the morning.
—Valerie Donn, Williamsburg, MI

Prep: 15 min. • **Cook:** 25 min.
Makes: 4 servings

- 2 Tbsp. olive oil
- 2 cups cubed fresh pumpkin or butternut squash
- ¼ tsp. salt
- ¼ tsp. pepper
- ½ cup chopped onion
- 1 pkg. (12 oz.) fully cooked apple chicken sausage links or flavor of your choice, cut into ½-in. slices
- 1 cup sliced fresh mushrooms
- ½ cup chopped sweet red pepper
- ½ cup chopped green pepper
- 1 tsp. garlic powder
- ¼ cup minced fresh parsley

In a large skillet, heat olive oil over medium heat. Add pumpkin; sprinkle with salt and pepper. Cook and stir until crisp-tender, 8-10 minutes. Add onion; cook 3 minutes longer. Add sausage, mushrooms, red and green peppers and garlic powder. Cook and stir until pumpkin is tender, 10-12 minutes. Top with parsley before serving.
1 serving: 260 cal., 14g fat (3g sat. fat), 60mg chol., 634mg sod., 19g carb. (13g sugars, 2g fiber), 16g pro.
Diabetic exchanges: 2 lean meat, 1½ fat, 1 starch.

PUMPKIN & CHICKEN SAUSAGE HASH

MUSHROOM-GRUYERE SCALLOPED POTATOES

MUSHROOM-GRUYERE SCALLOPED POTATOES

When I started cooking, the only mushrooms I used were the button variety. Now I love to experiment with different types. This is wonderful as a side dish to accompany a hearty breakfast, at dinnertime with grilled steak or roasted ham, or anytime as a main dish with a green salad.
—Nadine Mesch, Mount Healthy, OH

Prep: 30 min.
Bake: 1 hour + standing
Makes: 10 servings

6   Tbsp. butter, divided
½   lb. each sliced fresh shiitake, baby portobello and button mushrooms
1   Tbsp. sherry, optional
5   Tbsp. all-purpose flour
3   cups half-and-half cream
3   Tbsp. minced fresh rosemary
1½   tsp. salt
1   tsp. pepper
2   cups shredded Gruyere cheese
2   lbs. red potatoes, thinly sliced
½   tsp. paprika

1. Preheat oven to 350°. In a large skillet, heat 1 Tbsp. butter over medium-high heat. Add mushrooms; cook and stir until tender. If desired, stir in the sherry and cook until evaporated, 1-2 minutes longer. Remove from pan.

2. In same pan, melt remaining butter over medium heat. Stir in flour until smooth; gradually whisk in cream. Bring to a boil, stirring constantly; cook and stir until thickened, about 2 minutes. Reduce heat to medium-low. Stir in minced rosemary, salt and pepper. Gradually add cheese, stirring until melted. Remove from heat.

3. Arrange potatoes in an even layer in a greased 13x9-in. baking dish. Top with mushrooms and sauce mixture; sprinkle with paprika.

4. Bake, covered, 40 minutes. Bake, uncovered, until golden brown and bubbly, 20-25 minutes longer. Let stand 15 minutes before serving.
¾ cup: 442 cal., 29g fat (18g sat. fat), 104mg chol., 599mg sod., 23g carb. (4g sugars, 3g fiber), 20g pro.

LATKES WITH LOX

Lox, a salty smoked salmon, is a year-round delicacy. This recipe, inspired by one from the Jewish Journal, *uses lox as a topping.*
—*Taste of Home* Test Kitchen

LATKES
WITH LOX

Prep: 20 min. • **Cook:** 5 min./batch
Makes: 3 dozen

- 2 **cups finely chopped onion**
- ¼ **cup all-purpose flour**
- 6 **garlic cloves, minced**
- 2 **tsp. salt**
- 1 **tsp. coarsely ground pepper**
- 4 **large eggs, lightly beaten**
- 4 **lbs. russet potatoes, peeled and shredded**
- ¾ **cup canola oil**

TOPPINGS

- 4 **oz. lox**
  Optional: Sour cream and minced fresh chives

1. In a large bowl, combine the first 5 ingredients. Stir in the eggs until blended. Add potatoes; toss to coat.
2. Heat 2 Tbsp. canola oil in a large nonstick skillet over medium heat. Drop batter by ¼ cupfuls into oil; press lightly to flatten. Fry in batches until golden brown on both sides, using remaining oil as needed. Drain on paper towels. Serve with lox; top with sour cream and chives if desired.

3 latkes with ⅓ oz. lox: 270 cal., 16g fat (2g sat. fat), 73mg chol., 610mg sod., 26g carb. (3g sugars, 2g fiber), 6g pro.

**BAVARIAN HARVEST
APPLE HASH**

BAVARIAN HARVEST
APPLE HASH

*This awesome recipe reflects
my German roots. In the cooler
months, nothing is as comforting
as a hearty hash. You can serve
this versatile dish as a side, or as
an entree with cheddar grits or
topped with a fried egg.*
—Crystal Schlueter,
Northglenn, CO

- -

Takes: 30 min. • **Makes:** 4 servings

- 2 Tbsp. canola oil
- ½ cup chopped onion
- 4 fully cooked apple chicken
  sausages or flavor of your
  choice, sliced
- 1½ cups thinly sliced Brussels
  sprouts
- 1 large tart apple, peeled
  and chopped

- 1 tsp. caraway seeds
- ¼ tsp. salt
- ⅛ tsp. pepper
- 2 Tbsp. finely chopped walnuts
- 1 Tbsp. brown sugar
- 1 Tbsp. whole grain mustard
- 1 Tbsp. cider vinegar

1. In a large skillet, heat oil over
medium-high heat; saute onion
until tender, 1-2 minutes. Add
sausages, Brussels sprouts, apple
and seasonings; saute until lightly
browned, 6-8 minutes.
2. Stir in walnuts, brown sugar,
mustard and vinegar; cook and stir
2 minutes.

1 cup: 310 cal., 17g fat (3g sat. fat),
60mg chol., 715mg sod., 25g carb.
(19g sugars, 3g fiber), 16g pro.

CHEESY SAUSAGE POTATOES

CHEESY SAUSAGE POTATOES

For a satisfying brunch, try these tender potato slices with lots of sausage and cheese. Everyone loves them and the pan always ends up empty.
—Linda Hill, Marseilles, IL

Takes: 25 min. • **Makes:** 10 servings

- 3 lbs. potatoes, peeled and cut into ¼-in. slices
- 1 lb. bulk pork sausage
- 1 medium onion, chopped
- ¼ cup butter, melted
- 2 cups shredded cheddar cheese

1. Place potatoes in a large saucepan and cover with water. Bring to a boil. Reduce heat; simmer, uncovered, until tender, 8-10 minutes

2. Meanwhile, crumble sausage into a large skillet; add onion. Cook over medium heat until meat is no longer pink; drain if necessary.

3. Drain potatoes; arrange in an ungreased 13x9-in. baking dish. Drizzle with butter. Add sausage mixture and stir gently. Sprinkle with cheese.

4. Bake, uncovered, at 350° until cheese is melted, 5-7 minutes.

¾ cup: 252 cal., 13g fat (8g sat. fat), 37mg chol., 220mg sod., 26g carb. (2g sugars, 3g fiber), 9g pro.

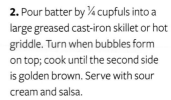

SALSA CORN CAKES

Spice things up with these tasty Tex-Mex cakes! The salsa is subtle but adds flavor. For lunch or dinner, serve these alongside tacos or nachos. You can use fresh corn when it is in season.
—Lisa Boettcher, Rosebush, MI

- -

Takes: 20 min. • **Makes:** 8 servings

- 6 oz. cream cheese, softened
- ¼ cup butter, melted
- 6 large eggs
- 1 cup 2% milk
- 1½ cups all-purpose flour
- ½ cup cornmeal
- 1 tsp. baking powder
- 1 tsp. salt
- 1 can (15¼ oz.) whole kernel corn, drained
- ½ cup salsa, drained
- ¼ cup minced green onions
  Sour cream and additional salsa

1. In a large bowl, beat cream cheese and butter until smooth; add the eggs and mix well. Beat in the milk until smooth. Combine the flour, cornmeal, baking powder and salt; stir into cream cheese mixture just until moistened. Fold in the corn, salsa and onions.

2. Pour batter by ¼ cupfuls into a large greased cast-iron skillet or hot griddle. Turn when bubbles form on top; cook until the second side is golden brown. Serve with sour cream and salsa.

1 serving: 324 cal., 15g fat (8g sat. fat), 191mg chol., 715mg sod., 34g carb. (5g sugars, 3g fiber), 11g pro.

ORANGE-GLAZED BACON

Just when you thought bacon couldn't get any tastier, here's a delightful version that's worth the extra effort.
—*Taste of Home* Test Kitchen

- -

Prep: 20 min. • **Bake:** 25 min.
Makes: 8 servings

- ¾ cup orange juice
- ¼ cup honey
- 1 Tbsp. Dijon mustard
- ¼ tsp. ground ginger
- ⅛ tsp. pepper
- 1 lb. bacon strips

1. In a small saucepan, combine the first 5 ingredients. Bring to a boil; cook until liquid is reduced to ⅓ cup.
2. Place bacon on a rack in an ungreased 15x10x1-in. baking pan. Bake at 350° for 10 minutes; drain.
3. Drizzle half of glaze over bacon. Bake for 10 minutes. Turn bacon and drizzle with remaining glaze. Bake 5-10 minutes longer or until golden brown. Place bacon on waxed paper until set. Serve warm.
3 glazed bacon strips: 146 cal., 8g fat (3g sat. fat), 21mg chol., 407mg sod., 12g carb. (11g sugars, 0 fiber), 7g pro.

SALSA CORN CAKES

BOHEMIAN COLLARDS

MUFFIN-TIN TAMALE CAKES

Here is some wonderful snacking inspiration. These muffin tamales have all the flavor without the fuss. Pair them with fruit skewers.
—Suzanne Clark, Phoenix, AZ

Prep: 25 min. • **Bake:** 20 min.
Makes: 2 dozen

- 2   pkg. (8½ oz. each) cornbread/muffin mix
- 1   can (14¾ oz.) cream-style corn
- 2   large eggs, room temperature, lightly beaten
- 1½ cups shredded reduced-fat Mexican cheese blend, divided
- 1½ cups chopped cooked chicken breast
- ¾ cup red enchilada sauce

1. Preheat oven to 400°. In a large bowl, combine muffin mix, corn and eggs; stir just until moistened. Stir in 1 cup cheese. In another bowl, toss chicken with enchilada sauce.
2. Fill each of 24 foil-lined muffin cups with 2 Tbsp. batter. Place 1 Tbsp. chicken mixture into center of each; cover with about 1 Tbsp. of batter.
3. Bake until muffins are golden brown, 13-15 minutes. Sprinkle tops with remaining cheese. Bake until cheese is melted, 3-5 minutes longer. Cool 5 minutes before removing from pan to wire racks. Serve warm. Refrigerate leftovers.
1 muffin: 137 cal., 5g fat (2g sat. fat), 28mg chol., 313mg sod., 18g carb. (5g sugars, 2g fiber), 7g pro.
Diabetic exchanges: 1 starch, 1 lean meat.

BOHEMIAN COLLARDS

I've added some unconventional ingredients to these collards that make them unique and exquisite on the palate and on the plate.
—Ally Phillips, Murrells Inlet, SC

Prep: 20 min. • **Cook:** 35 min.
Makes: 8 servings

- 1   large bunch collard greens (about 2 lbs.)
- 6   bacon strips, chopped
- 1   Tbsp. olive oil
- ½ cup chicken broth
- 1½ cups fresh or frozen corn (about 7½ oz.)
- 1   cup chopped sweet red pepper
- ½ tsp. salt
- ¼ tsp. crushed red pepper flakes
- ¼ tsp. pepper

1. Trim thick stems from collard greens; coarsely chop leaves. In a Dutch oven, cook bacon over medium heat until crisp, stirring occasionally. Remove with a slotted spoon; drain on paper towels. Cook and stir collard greens in bacon drippings and oil just until coated. Add broth; bring to a boil. Reduce heat; simmer, covered, until greens are very tender, 25-30 minutes.
2. Add corn, red pepper, salt, pepper flakes and pepper. Cook and stir until heated through. Sprinkle with bacon.
½ cup: 168 cal., 11g fat (3g sat. fat), 14mg chol., 369mg sod., 13g carb. (2g sugars, 5g fiber), 7g pro.
Diabetic exchanges: 2 fat, 1 starch.

**MUFFIN-TIN
TAMALE CAKES**

LEMON MINT BEANS

This side is a delightful addition to warm-weather meals.
—Dorothy Pritchett, Wills Point, TX

- -

Takes: 10 min. • **Makes:** 4 servings

- 1 lb. fresh or frozen cut green beans or wax beans
- 1 Tbsp. lemon juice
- 1 Tbsp. snipped fresh mint
- ¼ tsp. grated lemon zest
- ½ tsp. salt

In a saucepan, cook beans in a small amount of water until tender; drain. Add the remaining ingredients; toss to coat.

1 cup: 39 cal., 0 fat (0 sat. fat), 0 chol., 297mg sod., 9g carb. (0 sugars, 3g fiber), 2g pro.
Diabetic exchanges: 2 vegetable.

HOW-TO

Get the Most Juice

Warm a lemon in the microwave 7-10 seconds. Then roll it back and forth under your palm, giving it firm pressure. You'll get more juice and the lemon will be easier to squeeze. Works for limes, too.

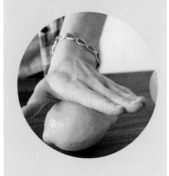

SWEET POTATO PANCAKES WITH CINNAMON CREAM

Topped with a rich cinnamon cream, these pancakes are an ideal dish for celebrating the tastes and aromas of fall.
—Tammy Rex, New Tripoli, PA

- -

Prep: 25 min. • **Cook:** 5 min./batch
Makes: 24 pancakes (1½ cups topping)

- 1 pkg. (8 oz.) cream cheese, softened
- ¼ cup packed brown sugar
- ½ tsp. ground cinnamon
- ½ cup sour cream

PANCAKES
- 6 large eggs, room temperature
- ¾ cup all-purpose flour
- ½ tsp. ground nutmeg
- ½ tsp. salt
- ¼ tsp. pepper
- 6 cups shredded peeled sweet potatoes (about 3 large)
- 3 cups shredded peeled apples (about 3 large)
- ⅓ cup grated onion
- ½ cup canola oil

1. In a small bowl, beat the cream cheese, brown sugar and cinnamon until blended; beat in sour cream. Set mixture aside.

2. In a large bowl, whisk the eggs, flour, nutmeg, salt and pepper. Add the sweet potatoes, apples and onion; toss to coat.

3. In a large nonstick skillet, heat 2 Tbsp. canola oil over medium heat. Working in batches, drop sweet potato mixture by ⅓ cupfuls into oil; press slightly to flatten. Fry until golden brown, 2-3 minutes on each side, using remaining oil as needed. Drain on paper towels. Serve with cinnamon topping.

2 pancakes with 2 Tbsp. topping: 325 cal., 21g fat (7g sat. fat), 114mg chol., 203mg sod., 30g carb. (15g sugars, 3g fiber), 6g pro.

SWEET POTATO PANCAKES WITH CINNAMON CREAM

**PEPPER JACK
HASH BROWN
CASSEROLE**

PEPPER JACK HASH BROWN CASSEROLE

I needed an impromptu potato dish, but had no potatoes. Frozen hash browns and the plethora of cheeses I'd stashed in the freezer offered the tasty solution to my side-dish dilemma.
—Cyndy Gerken, Naples, FL

- -

Prep: 25 min. • **Bake:** 30 min.
Makes: 12 servings

1 pkg. (30 oz.) frozen shredded hash brown potatoes, thawed
1 can (10½ oz.) condensed cream of chicken soup, undiluted
2 cups shredded pepper jack cheese
1½ cups heavy whipping cream
½ cup butter, melted
½ cup sour cream
¼ cup shredded Parmesan cheese
½ tsp. salt
½ tsp. onion powder
¼ tsp. garlic powder
¼ tsp. pepper

TOPPING

1 cup crushed potato chips
5 bacon strips, cooked and crumbled
¾ cup shredded Parmesan cheese
1 tsp. paprika

1. Preheat oven to 350°. In a large bowl, combine first 11 ingredients. Transfer to a greased 13x9-in. baking dish. For topping, combine potato chips, bacon and Parmesan; sprinkle over casserole. Top with paprika.
2. Bake, uncovered, until edges are bubbly and topping is golden brown, 25-30 minutes.

⅔ cup: 416 cal., 33g fat (19g sat. fat), 87mg chol., 682mg sod., 20g carb. (2g sugars, 2g fiber), 12g pro.

BRIGHT IDEA

If you're making this dish for kiddos, or an adult who doesn't like spicy food, use Monterey Jack cheese instead of pepper jack.

MAKE AHEAD

SLOW-COOKER GOETTA

My husband's grandfather, a German, introduced goetta to me when we first got married. I found a slow-cooker recipe and changed some of the ingredients to make it the best goetta around. Now, many people request the recipe. It makes a lot of sausage, but it also freezes well.

—Sharon Geers, Wilmington, OH

- -

Prep: 45 min. + chilling
Cook: 4 hours
Makes: 2 loaves (16 slices each)

6	cups water
2½	cups steel-cut oats
6	bay leaves
3	Tbsp. beef bouillon granules
¾	tsp. salt
1	tsp. each garlic powder, rubbed sage and pepper
½	tsp. ground allspice
½	tsp. crushed red pepper flakes
2	lbs. bulk pork sausage
2	medium onions, chopped

1. In a 5-qt. slow cooker, combine water, oats and seasonings. Cook, covered, on high 2 hours. Remove bay leaves.

2. In a large skillet, cook sausage and onions over medium heat until meat is no longer pink, 8-10 minutes, breaking up sausage into crumbles. Drain, reserving 2 Tbsp. drippings. Stir sausage mixture and reserved drippings into oats. Cook, covered, on low 2 hours.

3. Transfer mixture to 2 waxed paper-lined 9x5-in. loaf pans. Refrigerate, covered, overnight.

4. To serve, cut each loaf into 16 slices. In a large skillet, cook in batches over medium heat until lightly browned and heated through, 3-4 minutes on each side.

Freeze option: After shaping the goetta in loaf pans, cool and freeze, covered, until firm. Transfer goetta to freezer containers or wrap securely in foil; return to freezer. Partially thaw in the refrigerator overnight; slice and cook as directed.

1 slice: 121 cal., 7g fat (2g sat. fat), 15mg chol., 450mg sod., 10g carb. (1g sugars, 1g fiber), 5g pro.

BACON CHEESE MUFFINS

Flavored with bacon, cheese and veggies, these little bites are just the thing for your next brunch spread. They're fun to eat, and kids love them.

—Kendra Schertz, Nappanee, IN

- -

Prep: 15 min. • **Bake:** 20 min.
Makes: 8 servings

- 6 **oz. cream cheese, softened**
- 5 **tsp. 2% milk**
- 2 **large eggs, room temperature**
- ½ **cup shredded Colby cheese**
- 2 **Tbsp. chopped green pepper**
- 1 **Tbsp. finely chopped onion**
- 1 **tube (8 oz.) refrigerated crescent rolls**
- 5 **bacon strips, cooked and crumbled**
  Sliced green onions, optional

1. In a small bowl, beat cream cheese and milk until smooth. Add the eggs, cheese, green pepper and onion.
2. Separate crescent dough into 8 triangles; press onto the bottom and up the sides of greased muffin cups. Sprinkle half of the bacon into cups. Pour egg mixture over bacon; top with remaining bacon.
3. Bake at 375° for 18-22 minutes or until a knife inserted in center comes out clean. Serve warm. If desired, top with chopped green onion.
Freeze option: Freeze cooled muffins in a freezer container. To use, heat on a baking sheet in a preheated 375° oven until heated through.
1 muffin: 258 cal., 19g fat (9g sat. fat), 87mg chol., 409mg sod., 12g carb. (3g sugars, 0 fiber), 8g pro.

BACON
CHEESE
MUFFINS

Brunch-Worthy Sandwiches

Meet the delicious handhelds that make for glorious mornings.

RANCH CHICKEN SLIDERS

RANCH CHICKEN SLIDERS

When my grandson was younger, we always joked that nothing could make ranch chicken taste better. Then one day Avery's eyes lit up and he suggested we fry it! Our fried chicken burger was born. You won't believe how good these little sliders are.

—Tamara Hire, Decatur, IL

Prep: 2¾ hours + chilling
Cook: 10 min./batch
Makes: 6 servings

- 1 **lb. boneless skinless chicken breast halves**
- 1 **envelope ranch salad dressing mix**
- 1 **pkg. (8 oz.) cream cheese, cubed**
- 2 **cups crushed pretzels**
- 2 **cups crushed regular or barbecue potato chips**
- ¼ **cup grated Parmesan cheese**
- 2 **large eggs**
- 1 **Tbsp. 2% milk**
- 1 **cup all-purpose flour**
- 1 **tsp. garlic salt**
- ½ **tsp. pepper**
- ¼ **tsp. paprika**
  Oil for frying
- 12 **mini buns**
  Optional toppings: Lettuce, tomato, bacon and cheddar cheese

1. Place chicken in a 3- or 4-qt. slow cooker. Sprinkle with dressing mix; top with cubed cream cheese. Cook, covered, on low until a thermometer inserted in chicken reads 165°, 2½-3½ hours (mixture may appear curdled). Meanwhile, place pretzels, potato chips and Parmesan cheese in a food processor; pulse until combined. Reserve 1 cup for sliders. Transfer remaining pretzel mixture to a shallow bowl.

2. Remove the chicken from slow cooker; shred with 2 forks. Return the chicken to slow cooker; stir to combine. Add reserved 1 cup pretzel mixture; cool completely. Refrigerate at least 30 minutes.

3. In a shallow bowl, whisk the eggs and milk. Combine flour, garlic salt, pepper and paprika in another shallow bowl.

4. Shape chicken mixture into twelve ½-in.-thick patties. Dip patties in flour mixture to coat both sides; shake off excess. Dip in egg mixture, then in remaining pretzel mixture, patting to help coating adhere.

5. In a cast-iron or other heavy skillet, heat ¼ in. of oil to 375°. Fry sliders, a few at a time, until golden brown, 3-4 minutes on each side. Drain on paper towels. Serve on buns with toppings as desired.

2 sliders: 705 cal., 40g fat (12g sat. fat), 138mg chol., 1299mg sod., 59g carb. (5g sugars, 2g fiber), 29g pro.

EVERYTHING BREAKFAST SLIDERS

These breakfast sliders combine all of your favorite morning foods—like eggs, bacon and bagels—into one tasty package.
—Rashanda Cobbins, Milwaukee, WI

Prep: 30 min. • **Bake:** 15 min.
Makes: 8 servings

- 8 large eggs
- ¼ cup 2% milk
- 2 green onions, thinly sliced
- ¼ tsp. pepper
- 8 Tbsp. spreadable chive and onion cream cheese
- 8 miniature bagels, split
- 8 slices cheddar cheese, halved
- 8 slices Canadian bacon
- 8 cooked bacon strips, halved

GLAZE
- 2 Tbsp. butter, melted
- 1½ tsp. maple syrup
- ⅛ tsp. garlic powder
- 2 Tbsp. everything seasoning blend

1. Preheat oven to 375°. Heat a large nonstick skillet over medium heat. In a large bowl, whisk eggs, milk, green onions and pepper until blended; pour into skillet. Cook and stir until eggs are thickened and no liquid egg remains; remove from heat.

2. Spread cream cheese over bagel bottoms; place in a greased 13x9-in. baking dish. Layer each with half a slice of cheese and Canadian bacon. Spoon scrambled eggs over top. Layer with remaining halved cheese slices, bacon and bagel tops. Stir together butter, maple syrup and garlic powder; brush over tops of bagels. Sprinkle with everything seasoning blend.

3. Bake until tops are golden brown and cheese is melted, 12-15 minutes.

1 slider: 415 cal., 26g fat (13g sat. fat), 253mg chol., 1070mg sod., 18g carb. (4g sugars, 1g fiber), 24g pro.

EGG SALAD & BACON SANDWICH

On days I don't have much time to cook, egg salad on croissants hits the spot. It's also nice made with toasted bread or English muffins. Our family loves egg dishes of any kind. Luckily, my mom owns 30 chickens and she keeps me supplied with plenty of farm-fresh ingredients.
—Jane Ozment, Purcell, OK

Prep: 25 min. + chilling
Makes: 8 servings

- 4 bacon strips, cooked and crumbled
- ½ cup shredded cheddar cheese
- ½ cup sour cream
- ⅓ cup mayonnaise
- 2 Tbsp. minced chives
- ¼ tsp. salt
- ¼ tsp. pepper
- 10 hard-boiled large eggs, chopped
- 8 lettuce leaves
- 8 croissants, split

In a large bowl, combine the first 7 ingredients. Add eggs and mix well. Cover and chill at least 2 hours. Serve on lettuce-lined croissants.

1 serving: 470 cal., 32g fat (13g sat. fat), 327mg chol., 727mg sod., 28g carb. (3g sugars, 2g fiber), 16g pro.

EVERYTHING BREAKFAST SLIDERS

PESTO EGG WRAPS

PESTO EGG WRAPS

I wanted to create an easy recipe to use some remaining pesto that I had. I put a few ingredients together, and came up with a breakfast that really satisfies.
—Lisa Waterman, Lewistown, MT

- -

Takes: 15 min. • **Makes:** 2 servings

- ¼ cup oil-packed sun-dried tomatoes, chopped
- 4 large eggs, lightly beaten
- 2 Tbsp. crumbled feta cheese
- 2 Tbsp. prepared pesto
- 2 whole wheat tortillas (8 in.)

1. Heat a large skillet over medium heat. Add tomatoes; cook and stir until heated through. Pour in eggs; cook and stir until eggs are thickened and no liquid egg remains. Remove from heat; sprinkle with cheese.
2. Spread 1 Tbsp. pesto across center of each tortilla; top with egg mixture. Fold bottom and sides of tortilla over filling and roll up.

1 wrap: 407 cal., 23g fat (6g sat. fat), 432mg chol., 533mg sod., 27g carb. (2g sugars, 3g fiber), 21g pro.

HOW-TO

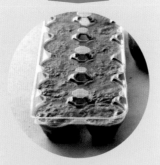

Upcycle Egg Cartons

Washed plastic egg cartons are a great stand-in if you don't have ice cube trays on hand. Portion homemade sauces, leftover wine or other foods into the egg cartons and freeze. Leave cubes in the carton, or pop them out to store in a freezer container.

**MINI CHICKEN
& BISCUIT
SANDWICHES**

MINI CHICKEN & BISCUIT SANDWICHES

My 11-year-old son, Jake, invented these sliders at dinner one night when he plunked his chicken on a biscuit. The rest of us tried it his way, and now we have them a lot.
—Jodie Kolsan, Palm Coast, FL

- -

Takes: 30 min. • **Makes:** 5 servings

- 1 tube (12 oz.) refrigerated buttermilk biscuits
- 5 boneless skinless chicken breasts (4 oz. each)
- ½ tsp. salt
- ½ tsp. dried thyme
- ¼ tsp. pepper
- 1 Tbsp. canola oil
- 1 Tbsp. butter
  Optional toppings: Cranberry chutney, lettuce leaves, sliced tomato and red onion

1. Bake biscuits according to package directions. Meanwhile, cut chicken crosswise in half. Pound with a meat mallet to ¼-in. thickness. Sprinkle with salt, thyme and pepper.
2. In a large skillet, heat oil and butter over medium-high heat. Add chicken in batches; cook until no longer pink, 2-3 minutes on each side. Split the biscuits in half; top with chicken and toppings as desired. Replace tops.
2 mini sandwiches: 367 cal., 16g fat (4g sat. fat), 69mg chol., 1029mg sod., 28g carb. (4g sugars, 0 fiber), 27g pro.

TRIPLE-DECKER SALMON CLUBS

You're in for a tasty treat with these deliciously different clubs. Guests love them.

—Jane Bone, Cape Coral, FL

- -

Takes: 15 min. • **Makes:** 2 servings

- ¾ cup 4% cottage cheese
- ¼ cup dill pickle relish
- 1 can (6 oz.) salmon, drained, bones and skin removed
- 1 celery rib, chopped
- 6 slices bread, toasted
- 2 lettuce leaves, optional

1. In a small bowl, combine the cottage cheese and pickle relish. In another bowl, combine salmon and celery.

2. For each sandwich, top 1 piece of toast with lettuce if desired and half of the cottage cheese mixture. Top with a second piece of toast; spread with half of the salmon mixture. Top with a third piece of toast.

1 sandwich: 455 cal., 13g fat (4g sat. fat), 57mg chol., 1494mg sod., 51g carb. (15g sugars, 3g fiber), 33g pro.

BRIGHT IDEA

Wild salmon is 20% leaner than farm-raised fish, while being higher in heart-healthy omega-3 fatty acids. Some people prefer its flavor over farm-raised fish, too.

CROQUE-MADAME

My son and I prefer a fried egg atop our grilled ham and cheese, but you can make the sandwich without it (and that makes it a croque-monsieur).

—Carolyn Turner, Reno, NV

- -

Takes: 30 min. • **Makes:** 8 servings

- 1 lb. thinly sliced Gruyere cheese, divided
- 16 slices sourdough bread
- 1½ lbs. thinly sliced deli ham
- ½ cup butter, softened
- 4 to 6 Tbsp. mayonnaise

EGGS

- 2 Tbsp. butter
- 8 large eggs
- ½ tsp. salt
- ½ tsp. pepper

1. Preheat oven to 400°. Place half of the cheese on 8 bread slices; top with sliced ham and remaining bread. Spread outsides of sandwiches with softened butter.

2. On a griddle, toast sandwiches over medium heat 2-3 minutes on each side or until golden brown. Spread tops with mayonnaise; top with remaining cheese. Transfer to an ungreased baking sheet; bake 4-5 minutes or until cheese is melted.

3. Meanwhile, for eggs, heat 1 Tbsp. butter on griddle over medium-high heat. Break 4 eggs, 1 at a time, onto griddle. Reduce heat to low. Cook to desired doneness, turning after whites are set if desired. Sprinkle with salt and pepper. Place eggs over sandwiches. Repeat with remaining ingredients.

1 sandwich: 758 cal., 47g fat (24g sat. fat), 344mg chol., 1691mg sod., 40g carb. (2g sugars, 2g fiber), 46g pro.

CROQUE-MADAME

GRILLED CHEESE BURGERS WITH SAUTEED ONIONS

My husband loves both my grilled cheese and my iron skillet burgers, so I decided to combine the two. He said it was the best burger he ever ate. It's just the thing to satsify anyone with a hearty appetite.

—Lisa Allen, Joppa, AL

Prep: 35 min. • **Cook:** 25 min.
Makes: 4 servings

- 1 **lb. lean ground beef (90% lean)**
- 2 **Tbsp. Worcestershire sauce**
- 1 **tsp. garlic powder**
- ½ **tsp. salt**
- ¼ **tsp. pepper**
- 1 **Tbsp. liquid smoke, optional**
- 1 **Tbsp. olive oil**
- 5 **Tbsp. butter, softened, divided**
- 1 **large onion, thinly sliced**
- 16 **slices American cheese**
- 16 **slices sandwich bread**

1. In a large bowl, combine beef, Worcestershire sauce, garlic powder, salt, pepper and liquid smoke if desired, mixing lightly but thoroughly. Shape into four 4-in. square patties.

2. In a large nonstick skillet, cook burgers in oil over medium heat until a thermometer reads 160°, 4-5 minutes on each side. Remove and keep warm.

3. In the same skillet, heat 1 Tbsp. butter over medium-high heat. Add onion; cook and stir until tender, 6-8 minutes. Remove and keep warm. Place cheese on 8 bread slices; top with remaining bread. Spread outsides of sandwiches with remaining 4 Tbsp. butter.

4. In the same skillet, toast sandwiches over medium heat until golden brown and cheese is melted, 1-2 minutes on each side. Top 4 sandwiches with burgers and onions. Top with the remaining sandwiches.

1 sandwich: 900 cal., 50g fat (27g sat. fat), 129mg chol., 1954mg sod., 56g carb. (12g sugars, 3g fiber), 47g pro.

CLASSIC AVOCADO TOAST

Here's an easy way to add some healthy avocados to your diet every morning. Use fiber-rich multigrain bread and top with sliced radishes and cracked pepper or lime zest, or chipotle peppers and cilantro.
—*Taste of Home* Test Kitchen

- -

Takes: 5 min. • **Makes:** 1 serving

- 1   **slice hearty bread, toasted**
- 1   **to 2 tsp. extra virgin olive oil or coconut oil**
- ¼   **medium ripe avocado, sliced**
- ⅛   **tsp. sea salt**

Spread toast with olive oil; top with avocado slices. If desired, mash avocado slightly and drizzle with additional oil. Sprinkle with salt.
1 slice: 160 cal., 11g fat (2g sat. fat), 0 chol., 361mg sod., 15g carb. (1g sugars, 3g fiber), 3g pro.
Diabetic exchanges: 2 fat, 1 starch.

STRAWBERRY MONTE CRISTOS

A gooey Monte Cristo sandwich never fails to please. This recipe comes together quickly with deli meats, sliced cheese and bottled dressing.
—Debbie Brunssen, Randolph, NE

- -

Takes: 25 min. • **Makes:** 4 servings

- ¼   **cup mayonnaise**
- 2   **tsp. Thousand Island salad dressing**
- 1   **tsp. Dijon mustard**
- 8   **slices white bread**
- ¼   **lb. thinly sliced deli turkey**
- ¼   **lb. thinly sliced deli ham**
- 4   **slices Swiss cheese**
- 2   **large eggs, beaten**
- 1   **cup half-and-half cream**
- ¼   **tsp. ground mustard**
- 2   **Tbsp. butter**
- ¼   **cup strawberry preserves**

1. In a small bowl, combine the mayonnaise, salad dressing and Dijon mustard; spread over 1 side of each slice of bread. On 4 slices, layer the turkey, ham and Swiss cheese; top with remaining bread. In a shallow bowl, combine the eggs, cream and ground mustard. Dip sandwiches in egg mixture.
2. On a griddle or in a large skillet, melt butter. Toast sandwiches over medium heat for 2-3 minutes on each side or until bread is golden brown. Serve sandwiches with strawberry preserves.
1 sandwich: 630 cal., 36g fat (15g sat. fat), 185mg chol., 1208mg sod., 46g carb. (18g sugars, 2g fiber), 27g pro.

Easily Pit an Avocado

• Cut ripe avocado top to bottom until you hit the seed. Turn avocado and cut again to make quarters.

• Gently twist the halves to separate.

• Pull out the seed.

• Pull the skin back like a banana peel. Slice as you like.

STRAWBERRY MONTE CRISTOS

ENGLISH MUFFIN EGG SANDWICHES

You can't beat the delicious combination of mushrooms, onions, peppers and cream cheese! Leave out the pepper flakes for a less spicy taste.
—Amy Lloyd, Madison, WI

- -

Takes: 25 min. • **Makes:** 8 servings

- ½ **lb. sliced fresh mushrooms**
- 1 **small sweet red pepper, chopped**
- 1 **small sweet onion, chopped**
- ½ **tsp. garlic salt**
- ¼ **tsp. pepper**
- ¼ **tsp. crushed red pepper flakes, optional**
- 7 **large eggs, lightly beaten**
- 8 **whole wheat English muffins, split and toasted**
- 4 **oz. reduced-fat cream cheese**

1. Place a large nonstick skillet over medium-high heat. Add mushrooms, red pepper, onion, garlic salt, pepper and red pepper flakes; cook and stir 5-7 minutes or until mushrooms are tender. Remove from pan.

2. Wipe skillet clean and coat with cooking spray; place skillet over medium heat. Add eggs; cook and stir just until the eggs are thickened and no liquid egg remains. Add vegetable mixture; heat through, stirring gently.

3. Spread muffin bottoms with cream cheese; top with egg mixture. Replace tops.

1 sandwich: 244 cal., 9g fat (4g sat. fat), 173mg chol., 425mg sod., 30g carb. (7g sugars, 5g fiber), 14g pro. **Diabetic exchanges:** 2 starch, 1 medium-fat meat, ½ fat.

CHICKEN FLORENTINE PANINI

This grilled sandwich combines chicken with provolone cheese, spinach and red onion.

—Lee Bremson, Kansas City, MO

Takes: 25 min. • **Makes:** 4 servings

- 1 **pkg. (5 oz.) fresh baby spinach**
- 2 **tsp. olive oil**
- ¼ **cup butter, softened**
- 8 **slices sourdough bread**
- ¼ **cup creamy Italian salad dressing**
- 8 **slices provolone cheese**
- ½ **lb. shaved deli chicken**
- 2 **slices red onion, separated into rings**

1. In a large cast-iron or other heavy skillet, saute spinach in oil until wilted, 2 minutes. Drain; wipe the skillet clean.

2. Spread 4 bread slices with the salad dressing. Layer with a cheese slice, chicken, spinach, onion and another cheese slice. Top with remaining bread. Butter outsides of sandwiches.

3. Cook in same skillet or panini maker until bread is golden brown and cheese is melted.

1 sandwich: 582 cal., 26g fat (10g sat. fat), 62mg chol., 1688mg sod., 63g carb. (4g sugars, 5g fiber), 23g pro.

CAPRESE TURKEY BAGEL CLUBS

I went to a friend's party and had bruschetta with Caprese salad on top. I loved the taste and started serving it at my parties. One day I had no bread, only bagels, and added turkey and a few other items. My young daughter said it was great. I started making the sandwiches for parties and everyone loved them!

—Maria Higginson, Bountiful, UT

Takes: 30 min.
Makes: 12 sandwiches

- 6 **garlic cloves, peeled and halved**
- 12 **Asiago cheese bagels, split and toasted**
- ¼ **cup mayonnaise**
- 2 **lbs. sliced deli turkey**
- 24 **slices fresh mozzarella cheese**
- 4 **plum tomatoes, thinly sliced**
- 1 **large red onion, thinly sliced**
- 12 **fresh basil leaves, thinly sliced**
- 2 **Tbsp. olive oil**

1. Rub the garlic cloves over cut sides of bagels.

2. For each sandwich, spread 1 tsp. mayonnaise over bagel bottom. Layer with turkey, cheese, tomatoes, onion and basil. Drizzle with olive oil. Replace tops. Cut sandwiches in half if desired.

1 sandwich: 709 cal., 29g fat (15g sat. fat), 96mg chol., 1444mg sod., 66g carb. (8g sugars, 3g fiber), 45g pro.

CHICKEN FLORENTINE PANINI

SALMON CROQUETTE BREAKFAST SANDWICH

I'm obsessed with smoked salmon on bagels! I could seriously eat it every day for breakfast. But smoked salmon can get pricey, so I found a cheaper alternative without losing the flavor.

—Jessi Hampton, Richmond Hill, GA

- -

Prep: 25 min. • **Cook:** 10 min.
Makes: 2 servings

- 1   large egg, lightly beaten
- ¼   cup dry bread crumbs
- 1   tsp. garlic powder
- 1   tsp. smoked paprika
- 1   pouch (6 oz.) boneless skinless pink salmon
- 1   Tbsp. olive oil
- 2   everything bagels, split and toasted
- 4   Tbsp. cream cheese, softened
- 1   Tbsp. capers, drained
- 1   medium tomato, sliced
- ½   medium red onion, thinly sliced into rings
  -   Snipped fresh dill, optional

1. In a small bowl, combine egg, bread crumbs, garlic powder and smoked paprika. Add salmon and mix well. Shape into 2 patties.

2. In a large skillet, cook patties in oil over medium heat until browned, 5-6 minutes on each side. Spread bagels with cream cheese; top with capers. Serve patties on bagels with tomato, red onion and, if desired, dill.

1 sandwich: 656 cal., 25g fat (10g sat. fat), 152mg chol., 1205mg sod., 75g carb. (14g sugars, 4g fiber), 34g pro.

SALMON CROQUETTE BREAKFAST SANDWICH

THE BEST EVER GRILLED CHEESE SANDWICH

THE BEST EVER GRILLED CHEESE SANDWICH

Spreading a mixture of mayo and butter on the bread creates a delightfully crispy crust with the well-loved, wonderful flavor of butter one expects in a grilled cheese sandwich.

—Josh Rink, Milwaukee, WI

Takes: 25 min. • **Makes:** 4 servings

- 6 **Tbsp. butter, softened, divided**
- 8 **slices sourdough bread**
- 3 **Tbsp. mayonnaise**
  3 **Tbsp. finely shredded Manchego or Parmesan cheese**
- ⅛ **tsp. onion powder**
- ½ **cup shredded sharp white cheddar cheese**
- ½ **cup shredded Monterey Jack cheese**
- ½ **cup shredded Gruyere cheese**
- 4 **oz. Brie cheese, rind removed, sliced**

1. Spread 3 Tbsp. butter on 1 side of bread slices. Toast bread, butter side down, in a large skillet or electric griddle over medium-low heat until golden brown, 2-3 minutes; remove. In a small bowl, mix together the mayonnaise, Manchego cheese, onion powder and remaining 3 Tbsp. butter. In another bowl, combine cheddar, Monterey Jack and Gruyere.

2. To assemble sandwiches, top toasted side of 4 bread slices with sliced Brie. Sprinkle cheddar cheese mixture evenly over Brie. Top with remaining bread slices, toasted side facing inward. Spread mayonnaise mixture on the outsides of each sandwich. Place in same skillet and cook until bread is golden brown and cheese is melted, 5-6 minutes on each side. Serve immediately.

1 sandwich: 659 cal., 49g fat (27g sat. fat), 122mg chol., 1017mg sod., 30g carb. (3g sugars, 1g fiber), 24g pro.

PESTO TURKEY SANDWICHES WITH STRAWBERRY MUSTARD

This is a popular choice when we're looking for something warm, quick and easy. The strawberry mustard is adjustable to suit your tastes. I've never been a big fan of mustard and neither have my kids, but we all love this sauce!
—Shannon Humphrey, Hampton, VA

- -

Takes: 15 min. • **Makes:** 4 sandwiches

- 4 Asiago cheese bagels, split
- 2 Tbsp. prepared pesto
- 3 Tbsp. seedless strawberry jam
- 2 tsp. Dijon mustard
- 8 oz. sliced oven roasted turkey breast

1. Preheat oven to 350°. Place bagels on an ungreased baking sheet, cut side up; spread with pesto. Bake until lightly toasted, 5-8 minutes.
2. In a small microwave-safe bowl, combine jam and Dijon mustard. Microwave, uncovered, on high until jam is melted, 15-30 seconds; stir to blend. Spread over bagel bottoms. Top with turkey; replace bagel tops.
1 sandwich: 489 cal., 11g fat (4g sat. fat), 32mg chol., 1260mg sod., 72g carb. (14g sugars, 2g fiber), 28g pro.

HUMMUS & VEGGIE WRAP-UP

I had a sandwich similar to this once when I stopped at a diner while on a long and arduous walk. I enjoyed it so much that I modified it to my own taste and now have it for lunch on a regular basis. Everyone at work wants to know how to make it.
—Michael Steffens, Indianapolis, IN

- -

Takes: 15 min. • **Makes:** 1 serving

- 2 Tbsp. hummus
- 1 whole wheat tortilla (8 in.)
- ¼ cup torn mixed salad greens
- 2 Tbsp. finely chopped sweet onion
- 2 Tbsp. thinly sliced cucumber
- 2 Tbsp. alfalfa sprouts
- 2 Tbsp. shredded carrot
- 1 Tbsp. balsamic vinaigrette

Spread hummus over tortilla. Layer with salad greens, onion, cucumber, sprouts and carrot. Drizzle with vinaigrette. Roll up tightly.
1 wrap: 235 cal., 8g fat (1g sat. fat), 0 chol., 415mg sod., 32g carb. (4g sugars, 5g fiber), 7g pro.
Diabetic exchanges: 2 starch, 1 fat.

READER REVIEW
"A bit different from the everyday. Inventive flavor (combo of balsamic and hummus), without much effort. A perfect little snack that's easy to make. I made this for people coming over, and everyone loved it. It tastes gourmet but is so quick and casual. Absolutely a little gem of a recipe."
— MARINA, TASTEOFHOME.COM

HUMMUS & VEGGIE WRAP-UP

TOAD IN THE HOLE BACON SANDWICH

Switch up the cheese—pepper jack gives a nice kick—or use sliced kielbasa, ham or sausage in place of the bacon in this versatile grilled cheese sandwich.
—Kallee Krong-McCreery, Escondido, CA

- -

Takes: 15 min. • **Makes:** 1 serving

- 2 **slices sourdough bread**
- 1 **Tbsp. mayonnaise**
- 1 **large egg**
- 1 **slice cheddar cheese**
- 2 **cooked bacon strips**

1. Using a biscuit cutter or round cookie cutter, cut out center of 1 slice of bread (discard center or save for another use). Spread the mayonnaise on 1 side of bread slices. In a large skillet coated with cooking spray, lightly toast cutout slice, mayonnaise side down, over medium-low heat. Flip slice; crack an egg into center. Add remaining bread slice, mayonnaise side down, to skillet; layer with cheddar cheese and bacon.

2. Cook, covered, until egg white is set, yolk is soft-set and cheese begins to melt. If needed, flip slice with the egg to finish cooking. To assemble sandwich, use solid bread slice as the bottom and cutout slice as the top.

1 sandwich: 610 cal., 34g fat (11g sat. fat), 240mg chol., 1220mg sod., 46g carb. (4g sugars, 2g fiber), 30g pro.

TOAD IN THE HOLE BACON SANDWICH

ATHENIAN CHICKEN
GRILLED CHEESE
SANDWICHES

ATHENIAN CHICKEN GRILLED CHEESE SANDWICHES

Mozzarella and feta cheese make one delicious duo in this upscale grilled cheese that also features tender chicken and the flavor of fresh herbs.

—Michael Cohen, Los Angeles, CA

- -

Takes: 30 min. • **Makes:** 4 servings

- 1 **lb. boneless skinless chicken breasts, cubed**
- ¼ **tsp. kosher salt**
- ¼ **tsp. pepper**
- 3 **garlic cloves, minced**

- 1 **Tbsp. plus ¼ cup olive oil, divided**
- 6 **oz. fresh mozzarella cheese, shredded**
- ½ **cup crumbled feta cheese**
- ½ **cup grated Parmesan cheese**
- ½ **cup fresh mint leaves, chopped**
- 2 **Tbsp. minced fresh oregano**
- 2 **Tbsp. capers, drained**
- 8 **slices olive or Italian bread (½ in. thick)**

1. Sprinkle chicken with salt and pepper. In a large skillet, cook chicken and garlic in 1 Tbsp. oil over medium heat until meat is no longer pink. Set aside and keep warm.

2. In a small bowl, combine the cheeses, mint, oregano and capers. Distribute half the cheese mixture evenly among 4 bread slices. Layer with chicken and remaining cheese mixture. Top with remaining bread. Brush outsides of sandwiches with remaining oil.

3. On a griddle, toast sandwiches for 2-3 minutes on each side or until cheese is melted.

1 sandwich: 605 cal., 36g fat (13g sat. fat), 112mg chol., 918mg sod., 27g carb. (1g sugars, 3g fiber), 41g pro.

BREAKFAST BURGER

My husband is big on eggs and bacon, so I wanted to merge his breakfast favorites with a grilled burger for an over-the-top treat. Topping it with my homemade blackberry jam sealed the deal.
—Tina Janssen, Walworth, WI

Prep: 25 min. • **Grill:** 30 min.
Makes: 4 servings

- 1 lb. ground beef
- 1 Tbsp. Worcestershire sauce
- 1 tsp. Montreal steak seasoning
- ½ tsp. salt, divided
- ½ tsp. pepper, divided
- 3 Tbsp. butter, softened and divided
- 8 slices Texas toast
- 2 Tbsp. canola oil
- 2½ cups frozen shredded hash brown potatoes, thawed
- 4 large eggs
- ¼ cup seedless blackberry spreadable fruit
- 4 slices American cheese
- 8 cooked bacon strips

1. Combine the ground beef, Worcestershire sauce, steak seasoning, ¼ tsp. salt and ¼ tsp. pepper; mixi lightly but thoroughly. Shape into four ½-in.-thick patties. Grill hamburgers, covered, on a greased grill rack over medium heat until a thermometer reads 160°, 4-5 minutes on each side.
2. Meanwhile, spread 2 Tbsp. butter over 1 side of Texas toast slices; grill with burgers until golden brown. Remove burgers and toast from heat; keep warm.
3. Increase heat to high. In a large skillet on grill rack, heat oil. Drop hash browns by ½ cupfuls into oil; press to flatten. Sprinkle with the remaining salt and pepper. Fry, covered, until golden brown and crisp, 12-15 minutes on each side, adding oil as needed. Remove and keep warm.

4. Reduce heat to medium. In same skillet, heat remaining butter. Add eggs; fry over easy.
5. To assemble, spread blackberry preserves over 4 slices of Texas toast. Layer each slice with 1 hash brown patty, 1 burger, 1 fried egg, 1 cheese slice and 2 bacon strips. Top with remaining toast slices.
1 burger: 859 cal., 49g fat (19g sat. fat), 307mg chol., 1703mg sod., 55g carb. (13g sugars, 2g fiber), 45g pro.

SMOKED SALMON EGG SALAD

Smoked salmon and croissants elevate egg salad sandwiches to a delicious and decidedly grown-up level.
—Cathy Tang, Redmond, WA

Takes: 10 min. • **Makes:** 6 servings

- ¾ cup mayonnaise
- 1 tsp. dill weed
- ½ tsp. lemon juice
- ¼ tsp. salt
- ⅛ tsp. pepper
- 6 hard-boiled large eggs, chopped
- 4 oz. smoked salmon, chopped
- 6 croissants, split
- 1½ cups fresh baby spinach

1. In a large bowl, combine the first 5 ingredients. Stir in eggs and salmon.
2. Place ⅓ cup on the bottom of each croissant; top with spinach leaves and replace croissant tops.
1 sandwich: 533 cal., 40g fat (11g sat. fat), 265mg chol., 889mg sod., 27g carb. (7g sugars, 2g fiber), 15g pro.

BREAKFAST BURGER

Midday Mains

Find the ideal dish for that magical time when morning, noon and beyond all blend together.

MUSHROOM & BROWN RICE HASH WITH POACHED EGGS

I made my mother's famous roast beef hash healthier by using cremini mushrooms instead of beef and brown rice instead of potatoes. This hearty favorite makes a light vegetarian main dish.

—Lily Julow, Lawrenceville, GA

- -

Takes: 30 min. • **Makes:** 4 servings

- 2   Tbsp. olive oil
- 1   lb. sliced baby portobello mushrooms
- ½   cup chopped sweet onion
- 1   pkg. (8.8 oz.) ready-to-serve brown rice
- 1   large carrot, grated
- 2   green onions, thinly sliced
- ½   tsp. salt
- ¼   tsp. pepper
- ¼   tsp. caraway seeds
- 4   large eggs, cold

1. In a large skillet, heat olive oil over medium-high heat; saute mushrooms until lightly browned, 5-7 minutes. Add sweet onion; cook 1 minute. Add rice and carrot; cook and stir until vegetables are tender, 4-5 minutes. Stir in sliced green onions, salt, pepper and caraway seeds; heat through.

2. Meanwhile, place 2-3 in. of water in a large saucepan or skillet with high sides. Bring to a boil; adjust heat to maintain a gentle simmer. Break cold eggs, 1 at a time, into a small bowl; holding bowl close to surface of water, slip egg into water.

3. Cook, uncovered, until the whites are completely set and the yolks begin to thicken but are not hard, 3-5 minutes. Using a slotted spoon, lift eggs out of water. Serve over rice mixture.

1 serving: 282 cal., 13g fat (3g sat. fat), 186mg chol., 393mg sod., 26g carb. (4g sugars, 3g fiber), 13g pro. **Diabetic exchanges:** 1½ starch, 1½ fat, 1 medium-fat meat.

HOW-TO

Poach Eggs

Place 2-3 in. water in a large skillet with high sides; add 1 Tbsp. vinegar. Bring to a boil; reduce heat and simmer gently. Break cold eggs, 1 at a time, into a custard cup or saucer; holding cup close to the surface of the water, slip each egg into water. Acidic poaching liquid makes it easier to get good results.

MUSHROOM & BROWN RICE HASH WITH POACHED EGGS

IRISH OATMEAL BRULEE

With its mild maple flavor and crispy broiled topping, this special oatmeal is an ultimate comfort food. I often use dried cherries instead of the raisins and add star anise to spice it up a bit.
—Rose Ann Wilson, Germantown, WI

- -

Prep: 15 min. + simmering
Broil: 5 min. • **Makes:** 8 servings

8 **cups 2% milk**
2 **cups steel-cut oats**
1 **cinnamon stick (3 in.)**
1 **orange peel strip (1 to 3 in.)**
   Dash salt
¾ **cup dried cranberries**
½ **cup golden raisins**
½ **cup maple syrup**
   Buttermilk, optional
½ **cup packed brown sugar**

1. In a large heavy saucepan, bring milk to a boil over medium heat. Add the oats, cinnamon, orange peel and salt. Reduce heat; simmer until thick and creamy, about 30 minutes, stirring occasionally.
2. Remove from the heat; discard cinnamon and orange peel. Stir in the cranberries, raisins, syrup and a small amount of buttermilk if desired. Cover and let stand for 2 minutes.
3. Transfer to 8 ungreased 6-oz. ramekins. Place on a baking sheet. Sprinkle with brown sugar. Broil 8 in. from the heat until sugar is caramelized, 4-7 minutes. Serve immediately.
1 serving: 437 cal., 8g fat (3g sat. fat), 18mg chol., 154mg sod., 83g carb. (51g sugars, 5g fiber), 14g pro.

ITALIAN SAUSAGE EGG BAKE

ITALIAN SAUSAGE EGG BAKE

This hearty entree warms up any breakfast or brunch menu with |its herb-seasoned flavor.
—Darlene Markham, Rochester, NY

Prep: 20 min. + chilling
Bake: 50 min. • **Makes:** 12 servings

- 8 **slices white bread, cubed**
- 1 **lb. Italian sausage links, casings removed, sliced**
- 2 **cups shredded sharp cheddar cheese**
- 2 **cups shredded part-skim mozzarella cheese**
- 9 **large eggs, lightly beaten**
- 3 **cups 2% milk**
- 1 **tsp. dried basil**
- 1 **tsp. dried oregano**
- 1 **tsp. fennel seed, crushed**

1. Place bread cubes in a greased 13x9-in. baking dish; set aside. In a large skillet, cook sausage over medium heat until no longer pink; drain. Spoon sausage over bread; sprinkle with the cheddar and mozzarella cheese.

2. In a large bowl, whisk the eggs, milk and seasonings; pour over casserole. Cover and refrigerate overnight.

3. Remove from the refrigerator 30 minutes before baking. Bake, uncovered, at 350° until a knife inserted in the center comes out clean, 50-55 minutes. Let stand for 5 minutes before cutting.

1 piece: 316 cal., 20g fat (10g sat. fat), 214mg chol., 546mg sod., 13g carb. (5g sugars, 1g fiber), 21g pro.

SAUSAGE-SWEET POTATO HASH & EGGS

When I first began making this dish for breakfast I served it with fried eggs on top. Now I sometimes make it for supper and serve it without eggs.
—Nancy Murphy, Mount Dora, FL

- -

Takes: 25 min. • **Makes:** 4 servings

- ½ **lb. Italian turkey sausage links, casings removed**
- 2 **medium sweet potatoes, peeled and diced**
- 2 **medium Granny Smith apples, chopped**
- ¼ **cup dried cranberries**
- ¼ **cup chopped pecans**
- ¼ **tsp. salt**
- 4 **green onions, sliced**
- 4 **large eggs**

1. In a large nonstick skillet coated with cooking spray, cook sausage and sweet potatoes over medium-high heat 8-10 minutes or until sausage is no longer pink, breaking up sausage into crumbles.

2. Add apples, cranberries, pecans and salt; cook and stir 4-6 minutes longer or until potatoes are tender. Remove from pan; sprinkle with green onions. Keep warm.

3. Wipe skillet clean and coat with cooking spray; place skillet over medium-high heat. Break 1 egg at a time into pan. Reduce heat to low. Cook as desired. Serve with hash.

1 serving: 338 cal., 14g fat (3g sat. fat), 207mg chol., 465mg sod., 42g carb. (23g sugars, 6g fiber), 15g pro.
Diabetic exchanges: 2 starch, 2 medium-fat meat, ½ fruit.

SAUSAGE-SWEET POTATO
HASH & EGGS

POACHED SALMON WITH CUCUMBER SAUCE

There's no reason to fear making fish at home with this simple recipe. Besides basil, try dill, fennel or coriander in the sauce.
—Crystal Jo Bruns, Iliff, CO

- -

Takes: 20 min. • **Makes:** 4 servings

1	cup water
½	cup dry white wine or chicken broth
1	small onion, sliced
2	sprigs fresh parsley
¼	tsp. salt
5	peppercorns
4	salmon fillets (6 oz. each)

SAUCE

½	cup sour cream
⅓	cup chopped seeded peeled cucumber
1	Tbsp. finely chopped onion
¼	tsp. salt
¼	tsp. dried basil

1. In an 11x7-in. microwave-safe dish coated with cooking spray, combine the first 6 ingredients. Microwave, uncovered, on high until mixture comes to a boil, 2-3 minutes.
2. Carefully add salmon to dish. Cover and microwave at 70% power until the fish flakes easily with a fork, 5-5½ minutes.
3. Meanwhile, in a small bowl, combine sour cream, cucumber, onion, salt and dried basil. Remove salmon from poaching liquid. Serve with sauce.

1 salmon fillet with 3 Tbsp. sauce: 361 cal., 21g fat (7g sat. fat), 105mg chol., 393mg sod., 4g carb. (2g sugars, 0 fiber), 30g pro.

TURKEY A LA KING

This delicious classic is a smart way to use up leftover turkey. You might want to make a double batch of it!
—Mary Gaylord, Balsam Lake, WI

- -

Takes: 25 min. • **Makes:** 6 servings

1	medium onion, chopped
¾	cup sliced celery
¼	cup diced green pepper
¼	cup butter, cubed
¼	cup all-purpose flour
1	tsp. sugar
1½	cups chicken broth
¼	cup half-and-half cream
3	cups cubed cooked turkey or chicken
1	can (4 oz.) sliced mushrooms, drained
6	slices bread, toasted

1. In a large skillet, saute the onion, celery and green pepper in butter until tender. Stir in flour and sugar until a paste forms.
2. Gradually stir in broth. Bring to a boil; boil until thickened, about 1 minute. Reduce heat. Add cream, cubed turkey and mushrooms; heat through. Serve with toast.

1 serving: 297 cal., 13g fat (7g sat. fat), 98mg chol., 591mg sod., 21g carb. (4g sugars, 2g fiber), 24g pro.

TURKEY A LA KING

FISH TACOS

FISH TACOS

A cool sauce with just a bit of zing tops these crispy fish tacos. This recipe is a great, guilt-free dish that doesn't break the calorie bank.

—Lena Lim, Seattle, WA

- -

Prep: 30 min. • **Cook:** 20 min.
Makes: 8 servings

- ¾ **cup reduced-fat sour cream**
- 1 **can (4 oz.) chopped green chiles**
- 1 **Tbsp. fresh cilantro leaves**
- 1 **Tbsp. lime juice**
- 4 **tilapia fillets (4 oz. each)**
- ½ **cup all-purpose flour**
- 1 **large egg white, beaten**
- ½ **cup panko bread crumbs**
- 1 **Tbsp. canola oil**
- ½ **tsp. salt**
- ½ **tsp. each white pepper, cayenne pepper and paprika**
- 8 **corn tortillas (6 in.), warmed**
- 1 **large tomato, finely chopped Additional fresh cilantro leaves, optional**

1. Place the sour cream, chiles, cilantro and lime juice in a food processor; cover and process until blended. Set aside.

2. Cut each tilapia fillet lengthwise into 2 portions. Place the flour, egg white and bread crumbs in separate shallow bowls. Dip tilapia in flour, then egg white, then crumbs.

3. In a large skillet over medium heat, cook tilapia in oil in batches until fish flakes easily with a fork, 4-5 minutes on each side. Combine seasonings; sprinkle over fish.

4. Place a portion of fish on each tortilla; top with about 2 Tbsp. of sour cream mixture. Sprinkle with tomato. If desired, top tacos with additional cilantro.

1 taco: 190 cal., 5g fat (1g sat. fat), 30mg chol., 269mg sod., 23g carb. (3g sugars, 2g fiber), 16g pro.
Diabetic exchanges: 2 lean meat, 1½ starch, ½ fat.

DENVER OMELET SALAD

This recipe is not your typical breakfast, but it has all the right elements. It's easy, healthy and fast. Turn your favorite omelet ingredients into a morning salad!
—Pauline Custer, Duluth, MN

Takes: 25 min. • **Makes:** 4 servings

- 8 **cups fresh baby spinach**
- 1 **cup chopped tomatoes**
- 2 **Tbsp. olive oil, divided**
- 1½ **cups chopped fully cooked ham**
- 1 **small onion, chopped**
- 1 **small green pepper, chopped**
- 4 **large eggs**
  Salt and pepper to taste

1. Arrange spinach and tomatoes on a platter; set aside. In a large skillet, heat 1 Tbsp. olive oil over medium-high heat. Add ham, onion and green pepper; saute until ham is heated through and vegetables are tender, 5-7 minutes. Spoon over spinach and tomatoes.

2. In same skillet, heat remaining olive oil over medium heat. Break eggs, 1 at a time, into a small cup, then gently slide into the skillet. Immediately reduce heat to low; season with salt and pepper. To prepare sunny-side up eggs, cover pan and cook until whites are completely set and yolks thicken but are not hard. Top salad with fried eggs.

1 serving: 229 cal., 14g fat (3g sat. fat), 217mg chol., 756mg sod., 7g carb. (3g sugars, 2g fiber), 20g pro.
Diabetic exchanges: 3 lean meat, 2 fat, 1 vegetable.

DENVER OMELET SALAD

FRUITY CROISSANT PUFF

FRUITY CROISSANT PUFF

I got this dish from a good friend. Sweet, tart, tender and light, it tastes like a berry cheese Danish.
—Myra Almer, Tuttle, ND

- -

Prep: 10 min. + chilling
Bake: 45 min. • **Makes:** 6 servings

- **4** large croissants, cut into 1-in. cubes (about 6 cups)
- **1½** cups mixed fresh berries
- **1** pkg. (8 oz.) cream cheese, softened
- **1** cup 2% milk
- **½** cup sugar
- **2** large eggs, room temperature
- **1** tsp. vanilla extract
  Maple syrup, optional

1. Place croissants and berries in a greased 8-in. square baking dish. In a medium bowl, beat cream cheese until smooth. Beat in milk, sugar, eggs and vanilla until blended; pour over the croissants. Refrigerate, covered, overnight.

2. Preheat oven to 350°. Remove casserole from refrigerator while oven heats. Bake, covered, for 30 minutes. Bake, uncovered, until puffed and golden and a knife inserted in the center comes out clean, 15-20 minutes. Let stand 5-10 minutes before serving. If desired, serve with syrup.

1 piece: 429 cal., 24g fat (14g sat. fat), 132mg chol., 358mg sod., 44g carb. (27g sugars, 2g fiber), 9g pro.

EVERYTHING
BAGEL CHICKEN
STRIPS

PEPPERONI &
SAUSAGE DEEP-DISH
PIZZA QUICHE

*Try this savory quiche for a hearty
change-of-pace breakfast. It's
good for lunch and dinner, too.*
—Donna Chesney, Naples, FL

- -

Prep: 20 min. • **Cook:** 40 min.
Makes: 8 servings

- 2 **cups shredded mozzarella cheese, divided**
- 1 **cup shredded sharp cheddar cheese**
- 4 **large eggs**
- 4 **oz. cream cheese, softened**
- ⅓ **cup 2% milk**
- ¼ **cup grated Parmesan cheese**
- ½ **tsp. garlic powder**
- ½ **tsp. Italian seasoning**
- ½ **lb. bulk Italian sausage**
- ½ **cup pizza sauce**
- 1 **cup chopped pepperoni**
  Fresh basil, optional

1. Preheat oven to 350°. Sprinkle
1 cup mozzarella and cheddar
cheese in a greased 13x9-in. baking
dish. In a small bowl, beat the eggs,
cream cheese, milk, Parmesan, garlic
powder and Italian seasoning; pour
into dish. Bake 30 minutes.
2. Meanwhile, in a small skillet, cook
sausage over medium heat until no
longer pink, 5-6 minutes, breaking
into crumbles; drain. Spread pizza
sauce over egg mixture; top with
sausage, pepperoni and remaining
1 cup mozzarella. Bake until golden
brown and bubbly, 10-15 minutes
longer. Let stand 5 minutes before
serving. Top with basil if desired.
1 piece: 409 cal., 34g fat (16g sat.
fat), 177mg chol., 971mg sod., 5g
carb. (2g sugars, 0 fiber), 21g pro.

EVERYTHING BAGEL
CHICKEN STRIPS

*I love the flavor of everything
bagels, so I re-created it with
baked breaded chicken fingers.
Serve theese with your favorite
chicken finger dip.*
—Cyndy Gerken, Naples, FL

- -

Takes: 30 min. • **Makes:** 4 servings

- 1 **day-old everything bagel, torn**
- ½ **cup panko bread crumbs**
- ½ **cup grated Parmesan cheese**
- ¼ **tsp. crushed red pepper flakes**
- ¼ **cup butter, cubed**
- 1 **lb. chicken tenderloins**
- ½ **tsp. salt**

1. Preheat oven to 425°. Pulse torn
bagel in a food processor until
coarse crumbs form. Place ½ cup
bagel crumbs in a shallow bowl; toss
with panko, Parmesan cheese and
pepper flakes. (Save remaining bagel
crumbs for another use.)
2. In a microwave-safe shallow bowl,
microwave the butter until melted.
Sprinkle chicken with salt. Dip in
warm butter, then coat with the
crumb mixture, patting to help
adhere. Place on a greased rack
in a 15x10x1-in. pan.
3. Bake until breading is golden
brown and chicken is no longer pink,
15-17 minutes.
1 serving: 246 cal., 12g fat (7g sat.
fat), 85mg chol., 593mg sod., 6g carb.
(0 sugars, 0 fiber), 30g pro.

BISCUITS & GRAVY BAKE

BISCUITS & GRAVY BAKE

Biscuits and gravy are usually prepared separately but served together. I created a way to bake them all at once in this scrumptious casserole.

—Nancy McInnis, Olympia, WA

- -

Prep: 20 min. + chilling
Bake: 25 min. • **Makes:** 10 servings

- 1   **lb. bulk pork sausage**
- ¼   **cup all-purpose flour**
- 3   **cups 2% milk**
- 1½ **tsp. pepper**
- 1   **tsp. paprika**
- ¼   **tsp. chili powder**
- 2¼ **cups biscuit/baking mix**
- ½   **cup sour cream**
- ¼   **cup butter, melted**

1. In a large skillet, cook sausage over medium heat until no longer pink, 6-8 minutes, breaking into crumbles. Remove with a slotted spoon; discard drippings, reserving ¼ cup in pan. Stir in flour until blended; cook and stir until golden brown (do not burn), 1-2 minutes. Gradually whisk in the milk. Bring to a boil, stirring constantly; cook and stir until thickened, 2-3 minutes. Stir in sausage, pepper, paprika and chili powder. Pour into a greased 13x9-in. baking dish. Cool completely.
2. Meanwhile, in a large bowl, mix baking mix, sour cream and melted butter until moistened. Turn onto a lightly floured surface; knead gently 8-10 times.
3. Pat or roll dough to ¾-in. thickness; cut with a floured 2½-in. biscuit cutter. Place biscuits over gravy. Refrigerate dish, covered, overnight.

4. Preheat oven to 400°. Remove casserole from refrigerator while oven heats. Bake, uncovered, until gravy is heated through and biscuits are golden brown, 22-25 minutes.
Freeze option: Cover and freeze unbaked biscuits and gravy. To use, partially thaw in the refrigerator overnight. Remove from refrigerator 30 minutes before baking. Preheat oven to 400°. Bake as directed, increasing time as needed, until gravy is heated through and biscuits are golden brown.
1 serving: 373 cal., 26g fat (11g sat. fat), 50mg chol., 640mg sod., 26g carb. (5g sugars, 1g fiber), 10g pro.

READER REVIEW
"I just made for hunting camp for the second time. Won't be the last…easy enough and good flavor. Thanks for sharing!"
—JENNY TEPOEL, TASTEOFHOME.COM

SHAKSHUKA BREAKFAST PIZZA

I turned traditional shakshuka into a fun brunch pizza. Its sweet, spicy and crunchy ingredients make it perfect for morning, noon or night.

—Phillipe Sobon,
Harwood Heights, IL

Prep: 35 min. • **Bake:** 15 min.
Makes: 6 servings

- 1 Tbsp. olive oil
- 1 large onion, thinly sliced
- 1 Tbsp. ground cinnamon
- 1 Tbsp. paprika
- 2 tsp. ground cumin
- 2 garlic cloves, minced
- ⅛ tsp. cayenne pepper
- 1 can (14½ oz.) whole plum tomatoes, undrained
- 1 tsp. hot pepper sauce
- ½ tsp. salt
- ¼ tsp. pepper
- 1 loaf (1 lb.) frozen pizza dough, thawed
- 6 large eggs
- ½ cup crumbled feta cheese

1. Preheat oven to 400°. In a large saucepan, heat oil over medium-high heat. Add onion; cook and stir until tender, 4-5 minutes. Add cinnamon, paprika, cumin, garlic and cayenne; cook 1 minute longer. Stir in plum tomatoes, hot pepper sauce, salt and pepper; cook and stir over medium heat until thickened, about 10 minutes.

2. Meanwhile, grease a 12-in. pizza pan. Roll dough to fit pan. Pinch the edge to form a rim. Bake until edge is lightly browned, 10-12 minutes.

3. Spread crust with tomato mixture. Using a spoon, make 6 indentations in tomato mixture; carefully break an egg into each. Sprinkle with feta. Bake until egg whites are completely set and yolks begin to thicken but are not hard, 12-15 minutes.

1 slice: 336 cal., 12g fat (3g sat. fat), 191mg chol., 654mg sod., 41g carb. (4g sugars, 5g fiber), 16g pro.

GRILLED LAVENDER CHICKEN

The lavender in this recipe gives off an amazing aroma while the chicken is grilling. The subtle flavor will win over even those leery of cooking with flowers!

—Colleen Duffley,
Santa Rosa Beach, FL

Prep: 15 min. + marinating
Grill: 30 min. • **Makes:** 6 servings

- ⅔ cup barbecue sauce
- ¼ cup dried lavender flowers
- ¼ cup olive oil
- 2 garlic cloves, minced
- 1 broiler/fryer chicken (3 to 4 lbs.), cut up

1. In a large bowl or shallow dish, combine the barbecue sauce, lavender, oil and garlic. Add the chicken and turn to coat. Refrigerate for up to 4 hours.

2. Drain the chicken, discarding marinade. Place chicken skin side down on grill rack. Grill, covered, over medium heat for 20 minutes. Turn; grill until juices run clear, 10-15 minutes longer.

1 serving: 315 cal., 20g fat (5g sat. fat), 88mg chol., 243mg sod., 3g carb. (2g sugars, 0 fiber), 28g pro.

SHAKSHUKA BREAKFAST PIZZA

MINI SHEPHERD'S PIES

MINI SHEPHERD'S PIES

I'm as confident serving these little freezer-friendly pies to company as to my husband and three boys. If I'm not pressed for time, I sometimes make these with homemade biscuits and mashed potatoes.

—Ellen Osborne, Clarksville, TN

- -

Prep: 30 min. • **Bake:** 20 min.
Makes: 5 servings

1	lb. ground beef
¼	cup chopped onion
1	garlic clove, minced
⅓	cup chili sauce or ketchup
1	Tbsp. cider vinegar
1¼	cups water
3	oz. cream cheese, cubed
3	Tbsp. butter
1¼	cups mashed potato flakes
2	tubes (6 oz. each) small refrigerated buttermilk biscuits
½	cup crushed potato chips
	Paprika, optional

1. Preheat oven to 375°. In a large skillet, cook and crumble beef with onion and garlic over medium heat until no longer pink, 5-7 minutes; drain. Stir in chili sauce and vinegar.

2. In a small saucepan, combine water, cream cheese and butter; bring to a boil. Remove from heat; stir in potato flakes.

3. Separate biscuits; press each onto bottom and up sides of a greased muffin cup. Fill with beef mixture; top with mashed potatoes. Sprinkle with potato chips.

4. Bake until the topping is golden brown, 20-25 minutes. If desired, sprinkle with paprika.

Freeze option: Freeze cooled pies in a single layer in freezer containers. To use, partially thaw in refrigerator overnight. Reheat on a baking sheet in a preheated 375° oven until heated through, 15-18 minutes.

2 mini shepherd's pies: 612 cal., 36g fat (15g sat. fat), 92mg chol., 1094mg sod., 49g carb. (11g sugars, 2g fiber), 24g pro.

RAMONA'S CHILAQUILES

A dear neighbor shared her from-scratch recipe. My version takes a few easy shortcuts.
—Marina Castle Kelley, Canyon Country, CA

- -

Takes: 30 min. • **Makes:** 4 servings

- ½ lb. lean ground beef (90% lean)
- ½ lb. fresh chorizo or bulk spicy pork sausage
- 1 medium onion, diced
- 1 garlic clove, minced
- 1 can (14½ oz.) diced tomatoes with mild green chiles, undrained
- 1 can (10 oz.) diced tomatoes and green chiles, undrained
- 4 cups tortilla chips (6 oz.)
- 1 cup shredded Monterey Jack cheese
  Chopped fresh cilantro
  Optional toppings: Sour cream, diced avocado and sliced red onion

1. Preheat oven to 350°. In a large skillet, cook and crumble beef and chorizo with onion and garlic over medium heat until beef is no longer pink, 5-7 minutes; drain. Stir in both cans of tomatoes; bring to a boil. In a greased 1½-qt. or 8-in. square baking dish, layer 2 cups chips, half of the meat mixture and ½ cup cheese; repeat layers.

2. Bake until the cheese is melted, 12-15 minutes. Sprinkle with cilantro. If desired, serve with toppings.

1 serving: 573 cal., 35g fat (14g sat. fat), 110mg chol., 1509mg sod., 28g carb. (5g sugars, 4g fiber), 33g pro.

RAMONA'S CHILAQUILES

TURKEY CLUB ROULADES

TURKEY CLUB ROULADES

Meals take an elegant turn when these short-prep roulades are on the menu.
—*Taste of Home* Test Kitchen

Prep: 20 min. • **Cook:** 15 min.
Makes: 8 servings

¾ lb. fresh asparagus, trimmed
8 turkey breast cutlets (about 1 lb.)
1 Tbsp. Dijon-mayonnaise blend
8 slices deli ham
8 slices provolone cheese
½ tsp. poultry seasoning
½ tsp. pepper
8 bacon strips

SAUCE

⅔ cup Dijon-mayonnaise blend
4 tsp. 2% milk
¼ tsp. poultry seasoning

1. Bring 4 cups water to a boil in a large saucepan. Add asparagus; cook, uncovered, for 3 minutes or until crisp-tender. Drain and immediately place asparagus in ice water. Drain and pat dry. Set aside.

2. Spread the turkey cutlets with Dijon-mayonnaise. Layer with ham, cheese and asparagus. Sprinkle with poultry seasoning and pepper. Roll up tightly and wrap with bacon.

3. Cook roulades in a large skillet over medium-high heat until bacon is crisp and turkey is no longer pink, turning occasionally, 12-15 minutes. Combine sauce ingredients; serve with roulades.

1 roulade with 1 Tbsp. sauce: 224 cal., 11g fat (5g sat. fat), 64mg chol., 1075mg sod., 2g carb. (1g sugars, 0 fiber), 25g pro.

SPICY BREAKFAST
LASAGNA

SPICY BREAKFAST LASAGNA

It's fun to cook up something new for family and friends—especially when it gets rave reviews. When I took this dish to our breakfast club at work, people said it really woke up their taste buds!
—Guthrie Torp Jr.,
Highland Ranch, CO

Prep: 20 min. + chilling
Bake: 35 min. • **Makes:** 16 servings

- 3 **cups 4% cottage cheese**
- ½ **cup minced chives**
- ¼ **cup sliced green onions**
- 18 **large eggs**
- ⅓ **cup 2% milk**
- ½ **tsp. salt**
- ¼ **tsp. pepper**
- 1 **Tbsp. butter**
- 8 **lasagna noodles, cooked and drained**
- 4 **cups frozen shredded hash browns, thawed**
- 1 **lb. bulk pork sausage, cooked and crumbled**
- 8 **oz. sliced Monterey Jack cheese with jalapeno peppers**
- 8 **oz. sliced Muenster cheese**

1. Combine cottage cheese, chives and onions; set aside. In another bowl, whisk eggs, milk, salt and pepper until blended. In a large skillet, heat butter over medium heat. Pour in egg mixture; cook and stir until eggs are thickened and no liquid egg remains. Remove from heat; set aside.

2. Place 4 lasagna noodles in a greased 13x9-in. baking dish. Layer with 2 cups hash browns, scrambled eggs, sausage and half the cottage cheese mixture. Cover with the Monterey Jack cheese. Top with remaining lasagna noodles, hash browns and cottage cheese mixture. Cover with sliced Muenster cheese. Refrigerate, covered, for 8 hours or overnight.

3. Remove dish from refrigerator 30 minutes before baking. Preheat oven to 350°. Bake, uncovered, until a knife inserted in center comes out clean, 35-40 minutes. Let stand 5 minutes before cutting.

1 piece: 366 cal., 23g fat (11g sat. fat), 256mg chol., 640mg sod., 16g carb. (3g sugars, 1g fiber), 23g pro.

SPICY KALE & HERB PORCHETTA

SPICY KALE & HERB PORCHETTA

Serve this classic Italian specialty as a main dish with crusty artisan bread or as a sandwich. You can add your favorite seasonings to the liquid from the slow cooker to make a customized savory sauce or gravy.

—Sandi Sheppard, Norman, OK

Prep: 30 min. + chilling **Cook:** 5 hours
Makes: 12 servings

- 1½ cups packed torn fresh kale leaves (no stems)
- ¼ cup chopped fresh sage
- ¼ cup chopped fresh rosemary
- ¼ cup chopped fresh parsley
- 2 Tbsp. kosher salt
- 1 Tbsp. crushed fennel seed
- 1 tsp. crushed red pepper flakes
- 4 garlic cloves, halved

- 1 boneless pork shoulder roast (about 6 lbs.), butterflied
- 2 tsp. grated lemon zest
- 1 large sweet onion, thickly sliced
- ¼ cup white wine or chicken broth
- 1 Tbsp. olive oil
- 3 Tbsp. cornstarch
- 3 Tbsp. water

1. In a blender or food processor, pulse the first 8 ingredients until finely chopped. In a 15x10x1-in. baking pan, open roast flat. Spread evenly over meat to within ½ in. of edges; sprinkle with lemon zest.
2. Starting at a long side, roll up jelly-roll style. Using a sharp knife, score fat on outside of roast. Tie at 2-in. intervals with kitchen string. Secure the ends with toothpicks. Refrigerate, covered, at least 4 hours or overnight.

3. In a 6-qt. slow cooker, combine onion and wine. Place porchetta seam side down on top of onion. Cook, covered, on low 5-6 hours or until tender. Remove toothpicks. Reserve cooking juices.
4. In a large skillet, heat oil over medium heat. Brown porchetta on all sides; remove from heat. Tent with foil. Let stand 15 minutes.
5. Meanwhile, strain and skim fat from cooking juices. Transfer to a large saucepan; bring to a boil. In a small bowl, mix cornstarch and water until smooth; stir into juices. Return to a boil, stirring constantly; cook and stir until thickened, 1-2 minutes. Cut string on roast and slice. Serve with gravy.

1 serving: 402 cal., 24g fat (8g sat. fat), 135mg chol., 1104mg sod., 5g carb. (1g sugars, 1g fiber), 39g pro.

PORCINI-CRUSTED PORK WITH POLENTA

Hints of rosemary and Parmesan cheese meet earthy mushroom undertones in this restaurant-quality dish you can proudly call your own.

—Casandra Rittenhouse, North Hollywood, CA

- -

Prep: 20 min. • **Bake:** 20 min.
Makes: 4 servings

- 1 pkg. (1 oz.) dried porcini mushrooms
- ¼ tsp. salt
- ¼ tsp. pepper
- 4 bone-in pork loin chops (7 oz. each)
- 2 tsp. olive oil
- 1 tube (1 lb.) polenta
- ½ cup grated Parmesan cheese
- ¼ tsp. dried rosemary, crushed

1. Process mushrooms in a food processor until coarsely chopped. Transfer to a shallow bowl; stir in salt and pepper. Press 1 side of each pork chop into mushroom mixture.
2. In a large ovenproof skillet coated with cooking spray, heat the olive oil over medium-high heat. Place chops, mushroom side down, in the skillet; cook for 2 minutes. Turn and cook 2 minutes longer. Bake pork chops, uncovered, at 375° until a thermometer inserted in pork reads 145°, 20-25 minutes. Let stand for 5 minutes before serving.
3. Prepare polenta according to package directions for soft polenta. Stir in cheese and rosemary. Serve with pork chops.

1 serving: 397 cal., 14 g fat (5 g sat. fat), 94 mg chol., 825 mg sod., 26 g carb., 3 g fiber, 38 g pro.

PORCINI-CRUSTED PORK WITH POLENTA

CHERRY-GLAZED LAMB CHOPS

An elegant sauce studded with cherries is the ideal partner for classic rosemary lamb chops. Try my recipe for a quiet dinner in with that special someone.

—Kerry Dingwall, Wilmington, NC

- -

Takes: 25 min. • **Makes:** 2 servings

- 1 tsp. dried rosemary, crushed
- ¼ tsp. salt
- ¼ tsp. pepper, divided
- 4 lamb loin chops (4 oz. each)
- 1 garlic clove, minced
- ¼ cup beef broth
- ¼ cup cherry preserves
- ¼ cup balsamic vinegar

1. Combine rosemary, salt and ⅛ tsp. pepper; rub over lamb chops. In a large skillet coated with cooking spray, cook chops over medium heat for 4-6 minutes on each side or until meat reaches desired doneness (for medium-rare, a thermometer should read 135°; medium, 140°; medium-well, 145°). Remove and keep warm.
2. Add garlic to the pan; cook for 1 minute. Stir in broth, preserves, vinegar and remaining pepper; cook until thickened, 2-4 minutes. Return chops to pan; turn to coat.
2 lamb chops with 2 Tbsp. sauce: 331 cal., 9g fat (3g sat. fat), 90mg chol., 495mg sod., 32g carb. (28g sugars, 0 fiber), 29g pro.

KIMCHI
CAULIFLOWER
FRIED RICE

KIMCHI CAULIFLOWER FRIED RICE

This is one of my favorite recipes, because it is customizable. If there's a vegetarian in the family, leave out the bacon. You can also add your favorite veggies.
—Stefanie Schaldenbrand, Los Angeles, CA

- -

Takes: 30 min. • **Makes:** 2 servings

- 2 **bacon strips, chopped**
- 1 **green onion, chopped**
- 2 **garlic cloves, minced**
- 1 **cup kimchi, chopped**
- 3 **cups frozen riced cauliflower**
- 2 **large eggs**
- 1 **to 3 Tbsp. kimchi juice**
  Optional: Sesame oil and sesame seeds

1. In a large skillet, cook bacon over medium heat until partially cooked but not crisp, stirring occasionally. Add onion and garlic; cook 1 minute longer. Stir in kimchi; heat through, 2-3 minutes. Add cauliflower; cook and stir until tender, 8-10 minutes.
2. Meanwhile, heat a large nonstick skillet over medium-high heat. Break eggs, 1 at a time, into pan; reduce heat to low. Cook until whites are set and yolks begin to thicken, turning once if desired. Stir enough kimchi juice into cauliflower mixture to moisten. Divide between 2 bowls. Top with fried eggs, additional onion and, if desired, sesame seeds and oil.
1 serving: 254 cal., 17g fat (5g sat. fat), 204mg chol., 715mg sod., 13g carb. (6g sugars, 6g fiber), 15g pro.
Diabetic exchanges: 2 high-fat meat, 2 vegetable.

CHILI-TOPPED CORNBREAD WAFFLES

CHILI-TOPPED CORNBREAD WAFFLES

Everyone in my family loves chili except my daughter, but she loves cornbread. One day she asked if she could have mostly cornbread, with just a little chili. Then we had a great idea—cornbread waffles topped with chili and all of the fixings! It was a hit.
—Courtney Stultz, Weir, KS

- -

Takes: 20 min. • **Makes:** 8 servings

- 1½ **cups gluten-free all-purpose baking flour**
- 1½ **cups cornmeal**
- 2 **tsp. baking powder**
- 1 **tsp. sea salt**
- 2 **large eggs, room temperature**
- 2 **cups 2% milk**
- ½ **cup olive oil**
- 2 **cans (15 oz.) chili with beans or 4 cups leftover chili, warmed**
  Jalapeno slices, shredded cheddar cheese, sour cream, cubed avocado and minced fresh cilantro

1. Preheat waffle maker. In a large bowl, whisk flour, cornmeal, baking powder and salt. In another bowl, whisk eggs, milk and olive oil until blended. Add to dry ingredients; stir just until moistened. Bake waffles according to manufacturer's directions until golden brown.
2. Serve with chili and toppings of your choice.
1 serving: 464 cal., 20g fat (4g sat. fat), 64mg chol., 796mg sod., 57g carb. (6g sugars, 6g fiber), 15g pro.

GREEN TEA SALMON WITH GRAPEFRUIT SALSA

Family and friends often request this recipe when they know they'll be dining with me. I gladly fill their requests because this is so easy, and the dish is delicious—and it especially pleases any diners who are counting calories.
—Patricia Nieh, Portola Valley, CA

Takes: 30 min. • **Makes:** 4 servings

- 5 cups strong brewed green tea
- 4 fresh basil sprigs
- 4 fresh thyme sprigs
- 4 fresh cilantro sprigs
- 3 Tbsp. lemon juice
- 3 Tbsp. minced fresh gingerroot
- 4 salmon fillets (4 oz. each)

SALSA
- 1 large pink grapefruit, sectioned and chopped
- 4 green onions, thinly sliced
- 1 Tbsp. minced fresh cilantro
- 1 Tbsp. finely chopped crystallized ginger
- ¼ tsp. salt

1. In a large skillet, combine the first 6 ingredients. Bring to a boil. Reduce heat; add salmon fillets and poach, uncovered, for 8-10 minutes or until fish flakes easily with a fork.
2. Meanwhile, in a small bowl, combine the salsa ingredients. Remove salmon with a slotted spoon. Serve with salsa.
1 serving: 220 cal., 11g fat (2g sat. fat), 57mg chol., 209mg sod., 11g carb. (7g sugars, 1g fiber), 20g pro.
Diabetic exchanges: 3 lean meat, 1 starch.

NICOISE SALAD

My garden-fresh salad is a feast for the eyes as well as the palate. Add some crusty bread and you have a mouthwatering meal.
—Marla Fogderud, Mason, MI

Prep: 40 min. + cooling
Makes: 2 servings

- ⅓ cup olive oil
- 3 Tbsp. white wine vinegar
- 1½ tsp. Dijon mustard
- ⅛ tsp. each salt, onion powder and pepper

SALAD
- 2 small red potatoes
- ½ cup cut fresh green beans
- 3½ cups torn Bibb lettuce
- ½ cup cherry tomatoes, halved
- 10 Greek olives, pitted and halved
- 2 hard-boiled large eggs, quartered
- 1 can (5 oz.) albacore white tuna in water, drained and flaked

1. In a small bowl, whisk the olive oil, vinegar, mustard, salt, onion powder and pepper; set aside.
2. Place potatoes in a small saucepan and cover with water. Bring to a boil. Reduce heat; cover and simmer until tender, 15-20 minutes. Drain and cool; cut into quarters.
3. Place the green beans in another saucepan and cover with water. Bring to a boil. Cover and cook until crisp-tender, 3-5 minutes; drain and rinse in cold water.
4. Divide lettuce between 2 salad plates; top with potatoes, beans, tomatoes, olives, eggs and tuna. Drizzle with dressing.
1 serving: 613 cal., 49g fat (8g sat. fat), 242mg chol., 886mg sod., 18g carb. (3g sugars, 3g fiber), 26g pro.

NICOISE SALAD

AIR-FRYER SWEET
POTATO-CRUSTED
CHICKEN NUGGETS

AIR-FRYER SWEET POTATO-CRUSTED CHICKEN NUGGETS

I was looking for ways to spice up traditional chicken nuggets and came up with this recipe. The chips add a crunchy texture and flavor, while the meat is tender on the inside.
—Kristina Segarra, Yonkers, NY

- -

Prep: 15 min. • **Cook:** 10 min./batch
Makes: 4 servings

- 1   **cup sweet potato chips**
- ¼   **cup all-purpose flour**
- 1   **tsp. salt, divided**
- ½   **tsp. coarsely ground pepper**
- ¼   **tsp. baking powder**
- 1   **Tbsp. cornstarch**
- 1   **lb. chicken tenderloins, cut into 1½-in. pieces**
-     **Cooking spray**

1. Preheat air fryer to 400°. Place chips, flour, ½ tsp. salt, pepper and baking powder in a food processor; pulse until ground. Transfer to a shallow dish.

2. Mix cornstarch and remaining ½ tsp. salt; toss with chicken. Toss chicken with potato chip mixture, pressing to coat.

3. In batches, arrange chicken in a single layer on greased tray in air-fryer basket; spritz with cooking spray. Cook until golden brown, 3-4 minutes. Turn; spritz with cooking spray. Cook until golden brown and chicken is no longer pink, 3-4 minutes longer.

3 oz. cooked chicken: 190 cal., 4g fat (0 sat. fat), 56mg chol., 690mg sod., 13g carb. (1g sugars, 1g fiber), 28g pro.
Diabetic exchanges: 3 lean meat, 1 starch.

CAPRESE CHICKEN
WITH BACON

CAPRESE CHICKEN
WITH BACON

*Smoky bacon, fresh basil, ripe
tomatoes and gooey mozzarella
top these tasty, appealing chicken
breasts. The aroma as the chicken
bakes is irresistible!*
—Tammy Hayden, Quincy, MI

- -

Prep: 20 min. • **Bake:** 20 min.
Makes: 4 servings

- 8 bacon strips
- 4 boneless skinless chicken
     breast halves (6 oz. each)
- 1 Tbsp. olive oil
- ½ tsp. salt
- ¼ tsp. pepper
- 2 plum tomatoes, sliced
- 6 fresh basil leaves, thinly sliced
- 4 slices part-skim mozzarella
     cheese

1. Place bacon in an ungreased
15x10x1-in. baking pan. Bake at 400°
until partially cooked but not crisp,
8-10 minutes. Remove to paper
towels to drain.
2. Place chicken in an ungreased
13x9-in. baking pan; brush with oil
and sprinkle with salt and pepper.
Top with tomatoes and basil. Wrap
each in 2 bacon strips, arranging
bacon in a crisscross.
3. Bake, uncovered, at 400° until
a thermometer inserted in chicken
reads 170°, 20-25 minutes. Top
with mozzarella; bake until melted,
about 1 minute longer.

1 chicken breast half: 373 cal., 18g
fat (7g sat. fat), 123mg chol., 821mg
sod., 3g carb. (1g sugars, 0 fiber),
47g pro.

BACON BREAKFAST PIZZA

BACON BREAKFAST PIZZA

Pizza for breakfast? Yes, please! I used to make this rise-and-shine recipe for my morning drivers when I worked at a pizza delivery place. It's a quick and easy eye-opener that rapidly became a hit!

—Cathy Shortall, Easton, MD

- -

Takes: 30 min. • **Makes:** 8 servings

1 tube (13.8 oz.) refrigerated
   pizza crust
2 Tbsp. olive oil, divided
6 large eggs
2 Tbsp. water
1 pkg. (3 oz.) bacon bits
1 cup shredded Monterey Jack
   cheese
1 cup shredded cheddar
   cheese

1. Preheat oven to 400°. Unroll and press dough onto bottom and ½ in. up sides of a greased 15x10x1-in. pan. Prick thoroughly with a fork; brush with 1 Tbsp. oil. Bake until lightly browned, 7-8 minutes.
2. Meanwhile, whisk together eggs and water. In a nonstick skillet, heat remaining 1 Tbsp. oil over medium heat. Add eggs; cook and stir just until thickened and no liquid egg remains. Spoon over crust. Sprinkle with bacon bits and cheeses.
3. Bake until the cheese is melted, 5-7 minutes.
1 piece: 352 cal., 20g fat (8g sat. fat), 169mg chol., 842mg sod., 24g carb. (3g sugars, 1g fiber), 20g pro.

PROSCIUTTO-PESTO
BREAKFAST STRATA

PROSCIUTTO-PESTO BREAKFAST STRATA

I'd never tried prosciutto before this recipe, and it instantly made me a big-time fan! The layers of flavor in this dish are brilliant, making it well worth the time and a must for your recipe box.
—Vicki Anderson, Farmington, MN

Prep: 25 min. + chilling
Cook: 50 min. • **Makes:** 10 servings

- 2 **cups 2% milk**
- 1 **cup white wine or chicken broth**
- 1 **loaf (1 lb.) French bread, cut into ½-in. slice**
- ¼ **cup minced fresh basil**
- ¼ **cup minced fresh parsley**
- 3 **Tbsp. olive oil**
- ½ **lb. thinly sliced smoked Gouda cheese**
- ½ **lb. thinly sliced prosciutto**
- 3 **medium tomatoes, thinly sliced**
- ½ **cup prepared pesto**
- 4 **large eggs**
- ½ **cup heavy whipping cream**
- ½ **tsp. salt**
- ¼ **tsp. pepper**

1. In a shallow bowl, combine milk and wine. Dip both sides of bread in the milk mixture; squeeze gently to remove excess liquid. Layer the bread slices in a greased 13x9-in. baking dish.

2. Sprinkle with basil and parsley; drizzle with oil. Layer with half of the cheese, half of the prosciutto and all of the tomatoes; drizzle with half of the pesto. Top with remaining cheese, prosciutto and pesto.

3. In a small bowl, whisk eggs, cream, salt and pepper until blended; pour over top. Refrigerate, covered, for several hours or overnight.

4. Preheat oven to 350°. Remove strata from refrigerator while the oven heats. Bake, uncovered, until top is golden brown and a knife inserted in the center comes out clean, 50-60 minutes. Let stand for 5-10 minutes before serving.

1 piece: 440 cal., 26g fat (10g sat. fat), 138mg chol., 1215mg sod., 30g carb. (7g sugars, 2g fiber), 22g pro.

SHEPHERD'S INN BREAKFAST PIE

Running a bed-and-breakfast keeps us busy. Once in a while I get creative and try to improve on an already good dish. That's how I came up with this one. It's a favorite among our guests as well as with family.
—Ellen Berdan, Salkum, WA

- -

Prep: 15 min. • **Bake:** 50 min.
Makes: 6 servings

1½	**lbs. bulk pork sausage**
4	**cups frozen Tater Tots**
1	**cup shredded cheddar cheese**
4	**large eggs**
½	**cup 2% milk**
1	**Tbsp. minced green onion**
⅛	**tsp. pepper**
	Dash garlic powder
2	**tomatoes, sliced and quartered**
	Minced chives

1. In a large skillet, cook the sausage over medium heat until no longer pink; drain. Spread in an ungreased 11x7-in. baking dish. Top with Tater Tots; sprinkle with cheese.

2. In a large bowl, beat the eggs, milk, onion, pepper and garlic powder just until blended. Pour over cheese.

3. Cover and bake at 350° for 30 minutes. Uncover; bake for another 20-25 minutes. Top with tomato. Sprinkle with chives.

1 cup: 632 cal., 45g fat (15g sat. fat), 206mg chol., 1425mg sod., 32g carb. (4g sugars, 3g fiber), 24g pro.

SHEPHERD'S INN
BREAKFAST PIE

BBQ CHICKEN POLENTA WITH FRIED EGG

When I was in college, I'd make this in the morning before I left for classes and it kept me full until I got home in the evening. I cook it now when I have friends or family over for Sunday brunch.
—Evan Janney, Los Angeles, CA

- -

Takes: 25 min. • **Makes:** 4 servings

- 2 **cups shredded cooked chicken breast**
- ¾ **cup barbecue sauce**
- 1 **Tbsp. minced fresh cilantro**
- 2 **Tbsp. olive oil, divided**
- 1 **tube (1 lb.) polenta, cut into 8 slices**
- 1 **small garlic clove, minced**
- 4 **large eggs**

1. In a small saucepan, combine chicken, barbecue sauce and minced cilantro; heat through over medium heat, stirring occasionally.
2. In a large skillet, heat 1 Tbsp. olive oil over medium-high heat. Add polenta; cook until lightly browned, 2-3 minutes on each side. Transfer to a plate; keep warm.
3. In same pan, heat remaining oil over medium-high heat. Add garlic; cook and stir 1 minute. Break eggs, 1 at a time, into pan. Reduce heat to low. Cook to desired doneness, turning after whites are set, if desired. Serve over polenta with chicken mixture.
2 polenta slices with ½ cup chicken mixture and 1 egg: 367 cal., 15g fat (3g sat. fat), 265mg chol., 923mg sod., 27g carb. (8g sugars, 1g fiber), 29g pro.

BUFFET BRUNCH BURRITOS

I like to use a second slow cooker to keep the tortillas warm and pliable when I serve these yummy burritos. Just place a clean wet cloth in the bottom, then cover it with foil and add your tortillas.
—Beth Osburn, Levelland, TX

- -

Prep: 30 min. • **Cook:** 4 hours
Makes: 10 servings

- 1 **lb. bulk pork sausage, cooked and drained**
- ½ **lb. bacon strips, cooked and crumbled**
- 18 **large eggs, lightly beaten**
- 2 **cups frozen shredded hash brown potatoes, thawed**
- 1 **large onion, chopped**
- 1 **can (10¾ oz.) condensed cheddar cheese soup, undiluted**
- 1 **can (4 oz.) chopped green chiles**
- 1 **tsp. garlic powder**
- ½ **tsp. pepper**
- 2 **cups shredded cheddar cheese**
- 10 **flour tortillas (10 in.), warmed**
  Optional toppings: Jalapeno peppers, salsa and hot pepper sauce

1. In a large bowl, combine the first 9 ingredients. Pour half of the egg mixture into a 4- or 5-qt. slow cooker coated with cooking spray. Top with half of the cheese. Repeat layers.
2. Cook, covered, on low 4-5 hours or until the center is set and a thermometer reads 160°.
3. Spoon ¾ cup egg mixture across center of each tortilla. Fold bottom and sides of tortilla over filling and roll up. Add toppings of your choice.
1 burrito: 683 cal., 38g fat (15g sat. fat), 449mg chol., 1650mg sod., 41g carb. (3g sugars, 7g fiber), 35g pro.

BUFFET BRUNCH BURRITOS

CHICKEN POTPIE GALETTE WITH CHEDDAR-THYME CRUST

CHICKEN POTPIE GALETTE WITH CHEDDAR-THYME CRUST

This gorgeous galette takes traditional chicken potpie and gives it a fun open-faced spin. The flaky cheddar-flecked pie crust and rich filling make it taste so homey.
—Elisabeth Larsen, Pleasant Grove, UT

Prep: 45 min. + chilling
Bake: 30 min. + cooling
Makes: 8 servings

- 1¼ cups all-purpose flour
- ½ cup shredded sharp cheddar cheese
- 2 Tbsp. minced fresh thyme
- ¼ tsp. salt
- ½ cup cold butter, cubed
- ¼ cup ice water

FILLING
- 3 Tbsp. butter
- 2 large carrots, sliced
- 1 celery rib, diced
- 1 small onion, diced
- 8 oz. sliced fresh mushrooms
- 3 cups julienned Swiss chard
- 3 garlic cloves, minced
- 1 cup chicken broth
- 3 Tbsp. all-purpose flour
- ½ tsp. salt
- ¼ tsp. pepper
- 2 cups shredded cooked chicken
- ½ tsp. minced fresh oregano
- 2 Tbsp. minced fresh parsley

1. Combine flour, cheese, thyme and salt; cut in butter until crumbly. Gradually add ice water, tossing with a fork until dough holds together when pressed. Shape into a disk; refrigerate 1 hour.

2. For filling, melt butter in a large saucepan over medium-high heat. Add carrots, celery and onion; cook and stir until slightly softened, for 5-7 minutes. Add mushrooms; cook 3 minutes longer. Add Swiss chard and minced garlic; cook until wilted, 2-3 minutes.

3. Whisk together chicken broth, flour, salt and pepper; slowly pour over vegetables, stirring constantly. Cook until thickened, 2-3 minutes. Stir in chicken and oregano.

4. Preheat oven to 400°. On a floured sheet of parchment, roll dough into a 12-in. circle. Transfer to a baking sheet. Spoon filling over crust to within 2 in. of edge. Fold crust edge over filling, pleating as you go, leaving center uncovered. Bake on a lower oven rack until crust is golden brown and filling bubbly, 30-35 minutes. Cool 15 minutes before slicing. Sprinkle with parsley.

1 piece: 342 cal., 21g fat (12g sat. fat), 81mg chol., 594mg sod., 22g carb. (2g sugars, 2g fiber), 16g pro.

HAM STEAKS WITH GRUYERE, BACON & MUSHROOMS

This meat lover's breakfast has a big wow factor. The Gruyere, bacon and fresh mushrooms in the topping are a great combination.
—Lisa Speer, Palm Beach, FL

Takes: 25 min. • **Makes:** 4 servings

- 2   **Tbsp. butter**
- ½   **lb. sliced fresh mushrooms**
- 1   **shallot, finely chopped**
- 2   **garlic cloves, minced**
- ⅛   **tsp. coarsely ground pepper**
- 1   **fully cooked boneless ham steak (about 1 lb.), cut into 4 pieces**
- 1   **cup shredded Gruyere cheese**
- 4   **bacon strips, cooked and crumbled**
- 1   **Tbsp. minced fresh parsley, optional**

1. In a large nonstick skillet, heat the butter over medium-high heat. Add mushrooms and shallot; cook and stir 4-6 minutes or until tender. Add garlic and pepper; cook 1 minute longer. Remove from pan; keep warm. Wipe skillet clean.

2. In same skillet, cook ham over medium heat 3 minutes. Turn; sprinkle with cheese and bacon. Cook, covered, 2-4 minutes longer or until cheese is melted and ham is heated through. Serve with the mushroom mixture. If desired, sprinkle with parsley.

1 serving: 352 cal., 22g fat (11g sat. fat), 113mg chol., 1576mg sod., 5g carb. (2g sugars, 1g fiber), 34g pro.

HAM STEAKS WITH
GRUYERE, BACON
& MUSHROOMS

SLOW-COOKER CHORIZO BREAKFAST CASSEROLE

My kids ask for this slow-cooked casserole for both breakfast and dinner. I've served it with white country gravy or salsa— it's delightful either way.
—Cindy Pruitt, Grove, OK

- -

Prep: 25 min.
Cook: 4 hours + standing
Makes: 8 servings

1	**lb. fresh chorizo or bulk spicy pork sausage**
1	**medium onion, chopped**
1	**medium sweet red pepper, chopped**
2	**jalapeno peppers, seeded and chopped**
1	**pkg. (30 oz.) frozen shredded hash brown potatoes, thawed**
1½	**cups shredded Mexican cheese blend**
12	**large eggs**
1	**cup 2% milk**
½	**tsp. pepper**
	Optional: Chopped avocado and tomato

1. In a large skillet, cook chorizo, onion, red pepper and jalapenos over medium heat until cooked through and vegetables are tender, 7-8 minutes, breaking chorizo into crumbles; drain. Cool slightly.

2. In a greased 5-qt. slow cooker, layer a third of the potatoes, chorizo mixture and cheese. Repeat layers twice. In a large bowl, whisk eggs, milk and pepper until blended; pour over top.

3. Cook, covered, on low for 4-4½ hours or until the eggs are set and a thermometer reads 160°. Uncover and let stand 10 minutes before serving. If desired, top with chopped avocado and tomato.

1½ cups: 512 cal., 32g fat (12g sat. fat), 350mg chol., 964mg sod., 25g carb. (4g sugars, 2g fiber), 30g pro.

Jelly Cupboard

Homemade jams, syrups and spreads are sure to take your gathering right over the top.

HONEY CINNAMON BUTTER

This is a simple but special spread for toast and muffins.
—Sue Seymour, Valatie, NY

Takes: 5 min.
Makes: about 1⅓ cups

- 1 **cup butter, softened**
- ½ **cup honey**
- 1 **tsp. ground cinnamon**

Beat all ingredients until smooth. Store, tightly covered, in the refrigerator.

1 Tbsp.: 107 cal., 9g fat (6g sat. fat), 24mg chol., 73mg sod., 7g carb. (7g sugars, 0 fiber), 0 pro.

DUTCH HONEY

I grew up on a farm where a big breakfast was an everyday occurrence. Still, it was a special treat when Mom served this syrup with our pancakes.
—Kathy Scott, Lingle, WY

Takes: 15 min. • **Makes:** 2 cups

- 1 **cup sugar**
- 1 **cup corn syrup**
- 1 **cup heavy whipping cream**
- 1 **tsp. vanilla extract**

In a saucepan, bring sugar, corn syrup and cream to a boil over medium heat. Cook 5 minutes or until slightly thickened, stirring occasionally. Add vanilla. Serve warm over pancakes or waffles.

2 Tbsp.: 158 cal., 6g fat (3g sat. fat), 20mg chol., 31mg sod., 29g carb. (23g sugars, 0 fiber), 0 pro.

OLD-FASHIONED FRUIT COMPOTE

A perfect partner to any holiday spread, this warm and fruity, lightly spiced condiment can simmer while you prepare the rest of your menu. Or make it ahead and reheat before serving.
—Shirley Glaab, Hattiesburg, MS

Prep: 15 min. • **Cook:** 1 hour
Makes: 8 cups

- 1 **can (20 oz.) pineapple chunks**
- 1 **can (15¼ oz.) sliced peaches**
- 1 **can (11 oz.) mandarin oranges**
- 1 **pkg. (18 oz.) pitted dried plums**
- 2 **pkg. (3½ oz. each) dried blueberries**
- 1 **pkg. (6 oz.) dried apricots**
- ½ **cup golden raisins**
- 4 **lemon zest strips**
- 1 **cinnamon stick (3 in.)**
- 1 **jar (10 oz.) maraschino cherries, drained**

Drain the pineapple, peaches and oranges, reserving the juices; set drained fruit aside. In a Dutch oven, combine fruit juices, dried fruits, lemon zest strips and cinnamon. Bring to a boil. Reduce heat; cover and simmer until the fruit is tender, about 30 minutes. Add the canned fruit and cherries; heat through. Serve the fruit compote warm or at room temperature.

¼ cup: 126 cal., 0 fat (0 sat. fat), 0 chol., 4mg sod., 31g carb. (22g sugars, 2g fiber), 1g pro.

OLD-FASHIONED FRUIT COMPOTE

BERRY CURD

I've always loved strawberries. Each time they're in season, I think of new and interesting ways to use them. I spoon this curd over just about everything, from waffles to cake and ice cream.
—Margo Zoerner,
Pleasant Prairie, WI

- -

Prep: 5 min. • **Cook:** 10 min. + chilling
Makes: ¾ cup

- 1 **cup chopped fresh strawberries**
- 1 **cup fresh raspberries**
- ⅓ **cup sugar**
- 1 **Tbsp. cornstarch**
- 3 **large egg yolks**
- 2 **Tbsp. butter**
- 1 **tsp. vanilla extract**

1. Place strawberries and raspberries in a blender; cover and process until almost smooth. Press through a fine-mesh strainer into a bowl; reserve ½ cup plus 1 Tbsp. juice. Discard seeds.

2. In a small heavy saucepan, mix sugar and cornstarch. Whisk in egg yolks and berry puree until blended. Add butter; cook over medium heat, whisking constantly, until mixture is just thick enough to coat a metal spoon and a thermometer reads at least 170°. Do not allow to boil. Remove from heat immediately; stir in vanilla.

3. Transfer to a bowl; cool. Press plastic wrap onto surface of curd; refrigerate until cold. Serve or transfer to covered jars and refrigerate up to 2 weeks.

2 Tbsp.: 66 cal., 3g fat (2g sat. fat), 51mg chol., 18mg sod., 9g carb. (7g sugars, 1g fiber), 1g pro.

BERRY CURD

FRESH HERB BUTTER

I love impressing guests with flavored butter. I mix up a big batch, and then freeze it so when company comes, this special spread is ready to go. Cut them in different shapes for a little fun.
—Pam Duncan, Summers, AR

- -

Prep: 25 min. + freezing
Makes: 24 servings

1	**cup butter, softened**
2	**Tbsp. minced fresh chives**
2	**Tbsp. minced fresh parsley**
1	**Tbsp. minced fresh tarragon**
1	**Tbsp. lemon juice**
¼	**tsp. pepper**

1. In a small bowl, beat all ingredients until blended. Spread onto a baking sheet to ½-in. thickness. Freeze, covered, until firm.

2. Cut butter with a 1-in. cookie cutter. Store, layered between waxed paper, in an airtight container in the refrigerator up to 1 week or in the freezer up to 3 months.

About 1 Tbsp.: 68 cal., 8g fat (5g sat. fat), 20mg chol., 61mg sod., 0 carb. (0 sugars, 0 fiber), 0 pro.

HOW-TO

Prepare & Freeze Compound Butter

- Place butter on a square of parchment paper, mounding butter into a rough log shape.

- Fold paper toward you, enclosing the butter. Press butter with a ruler to form a log, holding the edges of paper securely with the other hand. Twist edges to seal. Wrap butter in plastic and freeze. Slice off the desired portions when ready to use, then rewrap butter and return to the freezer.

- You can also freeze scoops or rosettes of flavored butter on a parchment-lined baking sheet. Once frozen, arrange butter portions on layers of paper in a freezer container. Remove desired number of portions when needed.

FRESH HERB BUTTER

⏱ 5i

PEACH WAFFLE SYRUP

I make this sweet and chunky syrup on Saturday mornings when my husband and I have extra time for a nice breakfast. You can substitute fresh or canned peaches.
—Kristina Dalton, Coker, AL

- -

Takes: 30 min.
Makes: about 3½ cups

- 1 pkg. (20 oz.) frozen unsweetened peach slices, thawed and chopped
- 2 cups water
- ½ to ⅔ cup confectioners' sugar
- ⅛ tsp. ground cinnamon
- 1 Tbsp. cornstarch
- 2 Tbsp. cold water

1. In a large saucepan, combine the peaches, water, confectioners' sugar and cinnamon. Bring to a boil. Reduce heat; simmer, uncovered, for 20 minutes.

2. Combine the cornstarch and cold water until smooth; gradually add to the peach mixture. Bring mixture to a boil; cook and stir 2 minutes or until thickened.

¼ cup: 54 cal., 1g fat (1g sat. fat), 0 chol., 3mg sod., 14g carb. (0 sugars, 1g fiber), 1g pro.
Diabetic exchanges: 1 fruit.

ROSE PETAL
HONEY

MAKE AHEAD 5i

ROSE PETAL HONEY

This recipe is a perfect topping for toast or English muffins. It is so simple to make and such a pretty color. Nice for a tea.
—Mary Kay Dixson, Decatur, AL

Prep: 5 min. • **Cook:** 35 min. + cooling
Makes: about 1 cup

1	cup packed rose petals (about 6 medium roses)
1	cup water
2	Tbsp. lemon juice
6	Tbsp. sugar
1	pouch (3 oz.) liquid fruit pectin

1. In a large saucepan, combine rose petals, water and lemon juice; bring to a boil. Reduce the heat; simmer, uncovered, until petals lose their color. Strain, reserving liquid and discarding petals. Return liquid to the saucepan.

2. Stir in sugar. Bring mixture to a full rolling boil over high heat, stirring constantly. Stir in pectin. Continue to boil 1 minute, stirring constantly. Pour into a jar and cool to room temperature. Cover and refrigerate up to 3 weeks.

2 Tbsp.: 39 cal., 0 fat (0 sat. fat), 0 chol., 2mg sod., 10g carb. (9g sugars, 0 fiber), 0 pro.

MAKE AHEAD 5i

STRAWBERRY BUTTER

There are several farms in our community where families can go pick their own strawberries. We usually pick a big bucketful and can't resist sampling some in the car on the way home. But we make sure to save enough for this delicious spread.
—Kim Hammond, Watsonville, CA

Prep: 10 min. + chilling
Makes: 2 cups

1	pkg. (8 oz.) cream cheese, softened
½	cup butter, softened
1	cup confectioners' sugar
1	tsp. vanilla extract
1	cup fresh strawberries, pureed

In a bowl, beat cream cheese and butter until smooth. Gradually add sugar and vanilla; mix well. Stir in strawberries. Cover tightly and refrigerate for several hours or overnight. May be stored in the refrigerator up to 1 week. Serve butter with English muffins, toast, waffles or pancakes.

2 Tbsp.: 132 cal., 11g fat (7g sat. fat), 31mg chol., 100mg sod., 8g carb. (8g sugars, 0 fiber), 1g pro.

STRAWBERRY
BUTTER

CHRISTMAS JAM

CHRISTMAS JAM

I have a passion for cooking, and I can probably thank my grandmother for it. She was a marvelous cook who could really stretch a food dollar.

—Jo Talvacchia, Lanoka Harbor, NJ

Prep: 25 min. • **Process:** 10 min.
Makes: about 14 half-pints

1   **pkg. (40 oz.) frozen unsweetened strawberries, thawed or 2½ qt. fresh strawberries, hulled**
1   **lb. fresh or frozen cranberries, thawed**
5   **lbs. sugar**
2   **pouches (3 oz. each) liquid fruit pectin**

1. Grind the strawberries and cranberries in a food processor or grinder; place in a Dutch oven. Add sugar. Bring to a full rolling boil; boil for 1 minute. Remove from heat; stir in pectin and return to a full rolling boil. Boil for 1 minute, stirring constantly. Remove from the heat.
2. Cool for 5 minutes; skim off foam. Carefully ladle hot mixture into hot half-pint jars, leaving ¼-in. headspace. Remove air bubbles; wipe rims and adjust lids. Process for 10 minutes in a boiling-water canner.
2 Tbsp.: 84 cal., 0 fat (0 sat. fat), 0 chol., 0 sod., 22g carb. (21g sugars, 0 fiber), 0 pro.
Note: The processing time listed is for altitudes of 1,000 feet or less. Add 1 minute to the processing time for each 1,000 feet of additional altitude.

PUMPKIN BUTTER

Biting into this spiced butter on a hot biscuit is absolutely heavenly. Add a dash of whipped cream and you just might think you were eating pumpkin pie!

—June Barrus, Springville, UT

- -

Prep: 5 min. • **Cook:** 20 min. + cooling
Makes: 6 cups

- 3 **cans (15 oz. each) pumpkin**
- 2 **cups sugar**
- 1½ **cups water**
- 3 **Tbsp. lemon juice**
- 1 **Tbsp. grated lemon zest**
- 3 **tsp. ground cinnamon**
- ¾ **tsp. salt**
- ¾ **tsp. ground nutmeg**
- ¾ **tsp. ground ginger**

1. In a large saucepan, combine all ingredients. Bring to a boil, stirring frequently. Reduce heat; cover and simmer for 20 minutes to allow flavors to blend.

2. Cool. Spoon into jars. Cover and store in the refrigerator for up to 3 weeks.

2 Tbsp.: 42 cal., 0 fat (0 sat. fat), 0 chol., 38mg sod., 11g carb. (9g sugars, 1g fiber), 0 pro.

PUMPKIN BUTTER

GINGERBREAD-SPICED SYRUP

Here's a wonderful treat for the winter months. Stir a tablespoon of this syrup into coffee, tea or cider. Drizzle it over pancakes, hot cereal or yogurt. Or use it as a glaze for roast chicken or chops!

—Darlene Brenden, Salem, OR

- -

Prep: 20 min.
Cook: 35 min. + cooling
Makes: 2 cups

- 2 **cinnamon sticks (3 in.), broken into pieces**
- 16 **whole cloves**
- 3 **Tbsp. coarsely chopped fresh gingerroot**
- 1 **tsp. whole allspice**
- 1 **tsp. whole peppercorns**
- 2 **cups sugar**
- 2 **cups water**
- 2 **Tbsp. honey**
- 1 **tsp. ground nutmeg**

1. Place the first 5 ingredients on a double thickness of cheesecloth; bring up corners of cloth and tie with string to form a bag.

2. In a large saucepan, combine the sugar, water, honey, nutmeg and spice bag; bring to a boil. Reduce heat; simmer, uncovered, until syrup reaches desired consistency, 30-45 minutes.

3. Remove from the heat; cool to room temperature. Discard spice bag; transfer the syrup to airtight containers. Store in the refrigerator for up to 1 month.

2 Tbsp.: 108 cal., 0 fat (0 sat. fat), 0 chol., 0 sod., 28g carb. (27g sugars, 0 fiber), 0 pro.

BANANA RUM SAUCE

This sweet treat is very appealing and versatile! It's an impressive ending to everyday meals as a dessert with ice cream, or with waffles for an amazing brunch.
—*Taste of Home* Test Kitchen

- -

Takes: 15 min. • **Makes:** 4 servings

¼ cup butter, cubed
¾ cup packed brown sugar
¼ tsp. ground cinnamon
⅛ tsp. ground nutmeg
  Dash ground cloves
¼ cup heavy whipping cream
3 medium firm bananas, halved lengthwise and cut into thirds
¼ tsp. rum extract
  Optional: Waffles, pancakes or vanilla ice cream

In a large skillet, melt butter. Stir in the brown sugar, cinnamon, nutmeg and cloves. Cook and stir until sugar is dissolved, about 2 minutes. Stir in the cream. Add bananas and extract. Serve warm, with waffles, pancakes or vanilla ice cream if desired.

½ cup: 589 cal., 28g fat (17g sat. fat), 95mg chol., 218mg sod., 85g carb. (74g sugars, 2g fiber), 5g pro.

READER REVIEW

"Quick and easy. You can serve this over ice cream, but we had it over pancakes. I made the pancakes first and then kept them warm in the oven while I made the bananas."
— MARTINELLI13, TASTEOFHOME.COM

BANANA RUM SAUCE

**HOMEMADE
LEMON CURD**

MAKE AHEAD 5i

HOMEMADE
LEMON CURD

*Lemon curd is a scrumptious
spread for scones, biscuits or
other baked goods. You can
find it in larger grocery stores
alongside the jams and jellies or
with the baking supplies, but we
like making it from scratch.*
—Mark Hagen, Milwaukee, WI

- -

Prep: 20 min. + chilling
Makes: 1⅔ cups

- 3 large eggs
- 1 cup sugar
- ½ cup lemon juice (about
  2 lemons)
- ¼ cup butter, cubed
- 1 Tbsp. grated lemon zest

In a small heavy saucepan over
medium heat, whisk eggs, sugar and
lemon juice until blended. Add butter
and lemon zest; cook, whisking
constantly, until mixture is thickened
and coats the back of a metal spoon.

Transfer to a small bowl; cool
10 minutes. Refrigerate, covered,
until cold.
2 Tbsp.: 110 cal., 5g fat (3g sat. fat),
52mg chol., 45mg sod., 16g carb.
(16g sugars, 0 fiber), 2g pro.

HOW-TO

Test Lemon Curd
To know when the curd
is ready, coat the back
of a spoon and run your
finger through it. If it
leaves a path, the curd is
ready. Curd will thicken
slightly as it cools.

ALL-DAY APPLE BUTTER

I make several batches of this simple and delicious apple butter to freeze in jars. Depending on the sweetness of the apples used, you can adjust the sugar to taste.

—Betty Ruenholl, Syracuse, NE

Prep: 20 min. • **Cook:** 11 hours
Makes: 4 pints

- 5½ lbs. apples, peeled, cored and finely chopped
- 4 cups sugar
- 2 to 3 tsp. ground cinnamon
- ¼ tsp. ground cloves
- ¼ tsp. salt

1. Place apples in a 3-qt. slow cooker. Combine sugar, cinnamon, cloves and salt; pour over apples and mix well. Cover and cook on high for 1 hour.

2. Reduce heat to low; cover and cook for 9-11 hours or until thickened and dark brown, stirring occasionally (stir more frequently as it thickens to prevent sticking).

3. Uncover and cook on low 1 hour longer. If desired, stir with a wire whisk until smooth. Spoon into freezer containers, leaving ½-in. heads pace. Cool. Cover and refrigerate or freeze.

2 Tbsp.: 68 cal., 0 fat (0 sat. fat), 0 chol., 9mg sod., 17g carb. (16g sugars, 1g fiber), 0 pro.

SPICED PEAR JAM

Years ago, I canned plenty of pears from my in-laws. Then a neighbor passed along this recipe, and it became a favorite.

—Karen Bockelman, Portland, OR

Prep: 1¾ hours • **Process:** 10 min.
Makes: 6 half-pints

- 8 cups chopped or coarsely ground peeled pears (about 5½ lbs.)
- 4 cups sugar
- 1 tsp. ground cinnamon
- ¼ tsp. ground cloves

1. Combine all the ingredients in a Dutch oven. Simmer, uncovered, for 1½-2 hours or until thick, stirring occasionally. Stir more frequently as the mixture thickens.

2. Remove from the heat; skim off foam. Carefully ladle into hot half-pint jars, leaving ¼-in. headspace. Remove air bubbles; wipe rims and adjust lids. Process for 10 minutes in a boiling-water canner.

2 Tbsp.: 81 cal., 0 fat (0 sat. fat), 0 chol., 0 sod., 21g carb. (19g sugars, 1g fiber), 0 pro.

Note: The processing time listed is for altitudes of 1,000 feet or less. Add 1 minute to the processing time for each 1,000 feet of additional altitude.

SPICED PEAR JAM

FRESH STRAWBERRY SYRUP

One summer, our garden yielded 80 quarts of strawberries! A good portion of that was preserved as strawberry syrup. We treat ourselves to this sweet, warm mixture over waffles or pancakes.
—Heather Biedler, Martinsburg, WV

- -

Takes: 15 min. • **Makes:** 2 cups

¼   **cup sugar**
2   **tsp. cornstarch**
     Dash salt
2   **cups chopped fresh
     strawberries**
½   **cup water**
½   **tsp. lemon juice**

In a small saucepan, combine sugar, cornstarch and salt. Stir in chopped strawberries, water and lemon juice until blended. Bring to a boil. Reduce heat; simmer, uncovered, until the mixture is thickened and berries are tender, 2-3 minutes.

¼ cup: 40 cal., 0 fat (0 sat. fat), 0 chol., 19mg sod., 10g carb. (8g sugars, 1g fiber), 0 pro.

BRIGHT IDEA

Treat the kids to old-fashioned ice cream sodas: Layer vanilla ice cream scoops and the homemade syrup in a tall glass, then pour in chilled strawberry soda.

FRESH
STRAWBERRY
SYRUP

The Bakery

Nothing encourages folks to linger just a little bit longer like a sweet homemade bite.

MAKE AHEAD

COFFEE LOVER'S MINI CHEESECAKES

Everyone in my family knows how much I adore cheesecake. But I was getting bored with my standard go-to flavors, chocolate or cherry. And then I had an idea—mocha cheesecake! After lots of experiments, I came up with this fun version.

—Holly Sharp, Warren, ON

Prep: 30 min.
Bake: 20 min. + chilling
Makes: 2 dozen

- 30 **chocolate wafers, finely crushed (about 1⅔ cups crumbs)**
- ¼ **cup sugar**
- 2 **Tbsp. butter, melted**
- 2 **Tbsp. brewed espresso**
  FILLING
- 8 **oz. semisweet chocolate**
- 2 **Tbsp. brewed espresso**
- 3 **pkg. (8 oz. each) cream cheese, softened**
- 1 **can (14 oz.) sweetened condensed milk**
- 4 **large eggs, room temperature, lightly beaten**
- 2 **cups frozen whipped topping, thawed**
- 24 **chocolate-covered coffee beans**
  Baking cocoa, optional

1. Preheat the oven to 325°. Line 24 muffin cups with foil liners. Mix wafer crumbs and sugar; stir in butter and espresso. Press by tablespoonfuls onto bottoms of liners.

2. For filling, melt chocolate in a microwave; stir in espresso until blended. In a large bowl, beat cream cheese until smooth; slowly stir in condensed milk until blended. Stir chocolate mixture into cream cheese mixture until combined. Add eggs; beat just until blended.

3. Fill prepared cups with ¼ cup cheesecake batter. Bake until centers are almost set, 17-20 minutes. Cool in pans 10 minutes before removing to wire racks to cool completely. Refrigerate overnight, covering when completely cooled.

4. Garnish with whipped topping and chocolate-covered coffee beans; if desired, dust with baking cocoa.

1 mini cheesecake: 308 cal., 19g fat (11g sat. fat), 70mg chol., 181mg sod., 25g carb. (21g sugars, 1g fiber), 6g pro.

LEMON CHEESECAKE TARTS

To make these cute tarts even more quickly, add the filling to store-bought phyllo tart shells.
—Sarah Gilbert, Beaverton, OR

Prep: 30 min.
Bake: 10 min. + cooling
Makes: 2 dozen

- 2 **sheets refrigerated pie crust**
  FILLING
- 1 **pkg. (8 oz.) cream cheese, softened**
- 1 **tsp. vanilla extract**
- 1 **jar (10 oz.) lemon curd, divided**
- 1 **container (8 oz.) frozen whipped topping, thawed**
- 1 **cup fresh blueberries**
  Confectioners' sugar, optional

1. Preheat oven to 450°. On a work surface, unroll crusts. Cut 24 circles with a floured 3-in. scalloped round cookie cutter, rerolling scraps as necessary. Press the circles onto bottoms and partway up sides of ungreased muffin cups, smoothing edges. Prick bottoms generously with a fork.

2. Bake until light golden brown, 5-7 minutes. Remove from pans to wire racks to cool completely.

3. In a large bowl, beat cream cheese and vanilla until blended; beat in ¼ cup lemon curd. Fold in a third of the whipped topping, then fold in remaining topping.

4. Spoon 2 Tbsp. cream cheese mixture into each tart shell; top each with 1 tsp. lemon curd. Top with blueberries; refrigerate until serving. If desired, sprinkle tarts with confectioners' sugar.

1 tart: 166 cal., 9g fat (5g sat. fat), 22mg chol., 95mg sod., 18g carb. (10g sugars, 0 fiber), 1g pro.

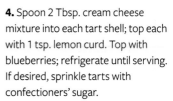

MAKE AHEAD
HOMEMADE BUTTER MINTS

These creamy mints are smooth as silk and melt in your mouth! As a wife and mother of three youngsters, I treasure treats like these that come together quickly but taste terrific.
—Bev Schloneger, Dalton, OH

Prep: 20 min. + chilling
Makes: about 8 dozen

- ½ **cup butter, softened**
- 3¾ **cups confectioners' sugar**
- 1 **Tbsp. half-and-half cream or whole milk**
- 1 **tsp. vanilla extract**
- ¼ **tsp. peppermint extract**
  Paste food coloring, optional

1. In a large bowl, beat the butter, confectioners' sugar, cream and extracts. If desired, divide dough into portions and knead in food coloring.

2. Form into balls by teaspoonfuls; flatten into patties, or roll between 2 pieces of waxed paper to ⅛-in. thickness. Cut mints into desired shapes. Cover and refrigerate for several hours or overnight. Store in the refrigerator.

1 mint: 27 cal., 1g fat (1g sat. fat), 3mg chol., 8mg sod., 5g carb. 5g sugars, 0 fiber), 0 pro.

LEMON CHEESECAKE TARTS

RASPBERRY CUSTARD KUCHEN

Back where I grew up in Wisconsin, people have been baking this German treat for generations. We love it for breakfast or as a special dessert. It's no fuss to fix and impressive to serve.

—Virginia Arndt, Sequim, WA

- -

Prep: 20 min. • **Bake:** 40 min.
Makes: 12 servings

- 1½ cups all-purpose flour, divided
- ½ tsp. salt
- ½ cup cold butter
- 2 Tbsp. heavy whipping cream
- ½ cup sugar

FILLING

- 3 cups fresh raspberries
- 1 cup sugar
- 1 Tbsp. all-purpose flour
- 2 large eggs, beaten
- 1 cup heavy whipping cream
- 1 tsp. vanilla extract

1. In a bowl, combine 1 cup flour and salt; cut in butter until the mixture resembles coarse crumbs. Stir in cream; pat onto the bottom of a greased 13x9-in. baking dish. Combine the sugar and remaining flour; sprinkle over crust.

2. Arrange raspberries over crust. In a large bowl, combine sugar and flour. Stir in eggs, cream and vanilla; pour over berries.

3. Bake at 375° for 40-45 minutes or until lightly browned. Serve warm or cold. Store in refrigerator.

1 piece: 328 cal., 17g fat (10g sat. fat), 86mg chol., 195mg sod., 42g carb. (27g sugars, 3g fiber), 4g pro.

SPARKLING CIDER POUND CAKE

This cake reminds me of fall with every bite. Using sparkling apple cider in the batter and the glaze gives it a delicious and unique flavor. I love everything about it!

—Nikki Barton, Providence, UT

- -

Prep: 20 min.
Bake: 40 min. + cooling
Makes: 12 servings

- ¾ cup butter, softened
- 1½ cups sugar
- 3 large eggs, room temperature
- 1½ cups all-purpose flour
- ¼ tsp. baking powder
- ¼ tsp. salt
- ½ cup sparkling apple cider

GLAZE

- ¾ cup confectioners' sugar
- 3 to 4 tsp. sparkling apple cider

1. Preheat oven to 350°. Line bottom of a greased 9x5-in. loaf pan with parchment paper; grease paper.

2. In a large bowl, cream butter and sugar 5-7 minutes or until light and fluffy. Add the eggs, 1 at a time, beating well after each addition. Whisk the flour, baking powder and salt; add to the creamed mixture alternately with cider, beating well after each addition.

3. Transfer batter to prepared pan. Bake 40-50 minutes or until a toothpick inserted in center comes out clean. Cool in pan 10 minutes before removing to a wire rack to cool completely.

4. Mix glaze ingredients until smooth; spoon over top of cake, allowing it to flow over sides.

1 slice: 308 cal., 13g fat (8g sat. fat), 77mg chol., 169mg sod., 46g carb. (34g sugars, 0 fiber), 3g pro.

SPARKLING CIDER POUND CAKE

PEANUT BUTTER-BANANA MUFFINS

PEANUT BUTTER-BANANA MUFFINS

These bite-sized muffins make a great treat. Banana and peanut butter are ideal partners and taste terrific with chocolate.

—Patty Putter, Marion, KS

- -

Prep: 25 min. • **Bake:** 10 min./batch
Makes: 4 dozen

- 1   cup old-fashioned oats
- 1   cup whole wheat flour
- ½   cup all-purpose flour
- ½   cup sugar
- 1   tsp. baking powder
- ½   tsp. baking soda
- ½   tsp. salt
- 1   large egg, room temperature
- ¾   cup fat-free milk
- ¾   cup mashed ripe bananas
- ½   cup creamy peanut butter
- ⅓   cup unsweetened applesauce
- ½   tsp. vanilla extract
- ¾   cup miniature semisweet chocolate chips

TOPPING
- ⅓   cup packed brown sugar
- ⅓   cup dry roasted peanuts, coarsely chopped
- ⅓   cup miniature semisweet chocolate chips

1. In a large bowl, combine the first 7 ingredients. In a small bowl, combine the egg, milk, bananas, peanut butter, applesauce and vanilla. Stir into dry ingredients just until moistened. Fold in the chocolate chips.

2. Fill greased or paper-lined miniature muffin cups three-fourths full. For topping, in a small bowl, combine the brown sugar, peanuts and chocolate chips. Sprinkle over the muffins. Bake at 350° until a toothpick inserted in the center comes out clean, 10-13 minutes.

3. Cool for 5 minutes before removing from pans to wire racks. Serve warm.

1 miniature muffin: 80 cal., 3g fat (1g sat. fat), 4mg chol., 71mg sod., 12g carb. (7g sugars, 1g fiber), 2g pro.
Diabetic exchanges: 1 starch.

VANILLA CHEESECAKE

To me, there is nothing better than a simple, elegant cheesecake where the creamy vanilla flavor takes center stage. When I'm feeling decadent, I'll add a rich chocolate ganache topping.
—Ellen Riley, Murfreesboro, TN

- -

Prep: 30 min. • **Bake:** 1 hour + chilling
Makes: 12 servings

2	**cups graham cracker crumbs**
½	**cup butter, melted**
¼	**cup sugar**

FILLING

4	**pkg. (8 oz. each) cream cheese, softened**
1½	**cups sugar**
3	**Tbsp. vanilla extract**
⅛	**tsp. salt**
4	**large eggs, room temperature, lightly beaten**

1. Preheat oven to 325°. Mix cracker crumbs, butter and sugar; press onto bottom and 1 in. up sides of a greased 9-in. springform pan.
2. In a large bowl, beat cream cheese and sugar until smooth. Beat in vanilla and salt. Add eggs; beat on low speed just until blended. Pour into crust. Place on a baking sheet.
3. Bake until center is almost set, 55-60 minutes. Cool on a wire rack 10 minutes. Loosen sides from pan with a knife. Cool 1 hour longer. Refrigerate overnight, covering when completely cooled.
1 slice: 551 cal., 37g fat (21g sat. fat), 159mg chol., 424mg sod., 47g carb. (37g sugars, 1g fiber), 8g pro.

HOW-TO

Plate Like a Pro

A hot knife is the secret to cutting nice tidy slices of cake and cheesecake. You'll need a sharp knife, some hot water and a towel. Dip the blade in water to heat, then wipe dry and cut. Repeat each time for pretty slices with a clean edge.

**FUNFETTI ICE
CREAM CAKE**

FUNFETTI ICE
CREAM CAKE

*When we were young, Mom
made birthday cakes with a small
toy on top, chosen just for us.
Now that I'm a parent, I go with
colorful sprinkles.*
—Becky Herges, Fargo, ND

- -

Prep: 50 min. + freezing
Makes: 12 servings

4 cups birthday cake-flavored
    ice cream or flavor of your
    choice, softened if necessary
1 funfetti cake mix (regular
    size)
1 carton (8 oz.) frozen
    whipped topping, thawed
    Sprinkles

1. Line a 9-in. round pan with plastic
wrap. Spread ice cream into pan.
Freeze 2 hours or until firm.
2. Prepare and bake cake mix
according to package directions,
using two 9-in. round baking
pans. Cool in pans 10 minutes
before removing to wire racks
to cool completely.
3. Using a serrated knife, trim tops of
cakes if domed. Place 1 cake layer on
a serving plate. Invert ice cream onto
cake layer; remove plastic wrap. Top
with remaining cake layer. Spread
whipped topping over top and sides
of cake. Decorate with sprinkles as
desired. Freeze 2 hours longer or
until firm.
1 slice: 374 cal., 19g fat (8g sat. fat),
66mg chol., 315mg sod., 45g carb.
(27g sugars, 1g fiber), 5g pro.

GRANDMA'S POPOVERS

Still warm from the oven, popovers are always a fun accompaniment to a homey meal. I was raised on these—my grandmother often made them for our Sunday dinners. The recipe couldn't be simpler.
—Debbie Terenzini, Lusby, MD

- -

Prep: 10 min. + standing
Bake: 30 min.
Makes: 6 popovers

- 1 cup all-purpose flour
- ⅛ tsp. salt
- 3 large eggs
- 1 cup 2% milk

1. In a large bowl, combine flour and salt. Beat eggs and milk; whisk into dry ingredients just until combined. Cover and let stand at room temperature for 45 minutes. Grease cups of a popover pan well with butter or oil; fill cups of two-thirds full with batter.

2. Bake at 450° for 15 minutes. Reduce heat to 350° (do not open the oven door). Bake 15 minutes longer or until deep golden brown (do not underbake).

3. Run a table knife or small metal spatula round edges of cups to loosen if necessary. Immediately remove popovers from pan; prick with a small sharp knife to allow steam to escape. Serve immediately.

1 popover: 132 cal., 3g fat (1g sat. fat), 109mg chol., 105mg sod., 18g carb. (2g sugars, 1g fiber), 7g pro.

SOUR CREAM STREUSEL COFFEE CAKE

I like that I can use delicious Wisconsin sour cream in this recipe. This coffee cake tastes wonderful and feeds a crowd, so it's perfect for a morning meeting or for breakfast or brunch.
—Sandra Munyon, Watertown, WI

- -

Prep: 15 min. • **Bake:** 40 min.
Makes: 12 servings

- ½ cup butter, softened
- 1 cup sugar
- 2 large eggs, room temperature
- 1 cup sour cream
- 1 tsp. vanilla extract
- 2 cups all-purpose flour
- 1 tsp. baking powder
- 1 tsp. baking soda
- ¼ tsp. salt

TOPPING

- ¼ cup sugar
- ⅓ cup packed brown sugar
- 2 tsp. ground cinnamon
- ½ cup chopped pecans

1. In a large bowl, cream butter and sugar 5-7 minutes or until light and fluffy. Beat in the eggs, sour cream and vanilla. Combine the flour, baking powder, baking soda and salt; add to creamed mixture and beat until combined. Spread half the batter into a greased 13x9-in. baking pan or dish.

2. In a small bowl, combine topping ingredients; sprinkle half the topping over batter. Dollop with remaining batter and sprinkle with topping. Bake at 325° for 40 minutes or until a knife inserted in the center comes out clean. Cool on a wire rack.

1 piece: 268 cal., 12g fat (6g sat. fat), 55mg chol., 230mg sod., 36g carb. (22g sugars, 1g fiber), 4g pro.

SOUR CREAM STREUSEL COFFEE CAKE

SAVORY COCKTAIL SCONES

SAVORY COCKTAIL SCONES

Scones are comfort food to me, and I wanted to make a savory version with roasted garlic butter. The addition of bacon seemed natural. They're fantastic for a brunch buffet.

—Donna-Marie Ryan, Topsfield, MA

- -

Prep: 55 min. • **Bake:** 15 min.
Makes: 16 servings

- 1 whole garlic bulb
- 2 tsp. olive oil
- ½ cup butter, softened

SCONES

- 2 bacon strips, chopped
- ⅓ cup chopped onion
- 2 cups all-purpose flour
- 3 tsp. baking powder
- ½ tsp. baking soda
- ½ tsp. salt
- ½ cup cold butter
- 1 large egg, room temperature
- ½ cup sherry
- ⅓ cup heavy whipping cream
- ¼ cup 2% milk

1. Remove papery outer skin from garlic (do not peel or separate cloves). Cut top off of garlic bulb. Brush with oil. Wrap the bulb in heavy-duty foil. Bake at 400° for 40-45 minutes or until softened. Cool for 10-15 minutes. Squeeze softened garlic into a small bowl; mash with fork. Stir in the butter; set aside.

2. In a small skillet, cook bacon over medium heat until crisp. Remove to paper towels with a slotted spoon; drain, reserving 1 Tbsp. drippings. In the same skillet, cook and stir onion in the drippings until softened. Reduce heat to medium-low; cook, stirring occasionally, until deep golden brown, about 30 minutes. Set aside.

3. In a large bowl, combine the flour, baking powder, baking soda and salt. Cut in butter until mixture resembles coarse crumbs. Whisk egg, sherry and cream; stir into crumb mixture just until moistened. Fold in onion and bacon.

4. Turn onto a floured surface; knead 10 times. Pat into a 10x5-in. rectangle. Using a floured knife, cut into eight 2½-in. squares; cut each square diagonally in half.

5. Place on a parchment-lined baking sheet; brush with milk. Bake at 400° for 12-15 minutes or until golden brown. Serve scones warm, with garlic butter.

1 scone: 204 cal., 15g fat (9g sat. fat), 52mg chol., 297mg sod., 13g carb. (1g sugars, 1g fiber), 3g pro.

CINNAMON DOUGHNUT MUFFINS

ONE-BOWL CHOCOLATE CHIP BREAD

My family of chocoholics hops out of bed on Valentine's Day because they know I'm baking this indulgent quick bread for breakfast. But don't wait for a special occasion to enjoy it. It hits the spot any time of year.
—Angela Lively, Conroe, TX

- -

Prep: 20 min. • **Bake:** 65 minutes
Makes: 1 loaf (16 slices)

- 3 **large eggs, room temperature**
- 1 **cup sugar**
- 2 **cups sour cream**
- 3 **cups self-rising flour**
- 2 **cups semisweet chocolate chips**

1. Preheat oven to 350°. Beat the eggs, sugar and sour cream until well blended. Gradually stir in flour. Fold in chocolate chips. Transfer to a greased 9x5-in. loaf pan.
2. Bake until a toothpick comes out clean, 65-75 minutes. Cool in pan 5 minutes before removing to a wire rack to cool.

1 slice: 306 cal., 13g fat (8g sat. fat), 42mg chol., 305mg sod., 44g carb. (25g sugars, 2g fiber), 5g pro.

CINNAMON DOUGHNUT MUFFINS

Back when my children were youngsters, they loved these doughnut muffins as after-school treats or with Sunday brunch.
—Sharon Pullen, Alvinston, ON

- -

Prep: 15 min. • **Bake:** 20 min.
Makes: 10 muffins

- 1¾ **cups all-purpose flour**
- 1½ **tsp. baking powder**
- ½ **tsp. salt**
- ½ **tsp. ground nutmeg**
- ¼ **tsp. ground cinnamon**
- ¾ **cups sugar**
- ⅓ **cup canola oil**
- 1 **large egg, room temperature, lightly beaten**
- ¾ **cup 2% milk**
- 10 **tsp. seedless strawberry or other jam**

TOPPING
- ¼ **cup butter, melted**
- ⅓ **cup sugar**
- 1 **tsp. ground cinnamon**

1. In a large bowl, combine flour, baking powder, salt, nutmeg and cinnamon. In a small bowl, combine sugar, oil, egg and milk; stir into dry ingredients just until moistened.
2. Fill greased or paper-lined muffin cups half full; place 1 tsp. jam on top. Cover jam with enough batter to fill muffin cups three-fourths full. Bake at 350° for 20-25 minutes or until a toothpick comes out clean.
3. Place melted butter in a small bowl; combine sugar and cinnamon in another bowl. Immediately after removing muffins from the oven, dip tops in butter, then in cinnamon sugar. Serve warm.

1 muffin: 288 cal., 13g fat (4g sat. fat), 36mg chol., 240mg sod., 40g carb. (22g sugars, 1g fiber), 4g pro.

Warm Eggs for Better Baking

Many recipes benefit from room-temperature eggs, and it's an easy thing to do. Just place eggs in hot water while you prep your recipe. They'll be ready when it's time to get cracking.

ONE-BOWL
CHOCOLATE CHIP
BREAD

RASPBERRY BREAKFAST BRAID

We also like using blackberries, marionberries, a mixture of raspberries and blackberries, or all three in this quick and versatile pastry.

—Tressa Nicholls, Sandy, OR

- -

Prep: 20 min. • **Bake:** 15 min.
Makes: 12 servings

   2   **cups biscuit/baking mix**
   3   **oz. cream cheese, cubed**
   ¼   **cup cold butter, cubed**
   ⅓   **cup 2% milk**
   1¼   **cups fresh raspberries**
   3   **Tbsp. sugar**
   ¼   **cup vanilla frosting**

1. Preheat oven to 425°. Place biscuit mix in a large bowl. Cut in the cream cheese and butter until the mixture resembles coarse crumbs. Stir in milk just until moistened. Turn onto a lightly floured surface; knead gently 8-10 times.

2. On a greased baking sheet, roll dough into an 18x12-in. rectangle. Spoon raspberries down center third of dough; sprinkle with sugar.

3. On each long side, cut 1-in.-wide strips about 2½ in. into the center. Starting at 1 end, fold alternating strips at an angle across raspberries; seal ends.

4. Bake 15-20 minutes or until golden brown. Remove to a wire rack to cool slightly. In a microwave-safe dish, microwave frosting on high until it reaches desired consistency, 5-10 seconds; drizzle over pastry.

1 slice: 185 cal., 10g fat (5g sat. fat), 19mg chol., 319mg sod., 22g carb. (8g sugars, 1g fiber), 2g pro.

RASPBERRY BREAKFAST BRAID

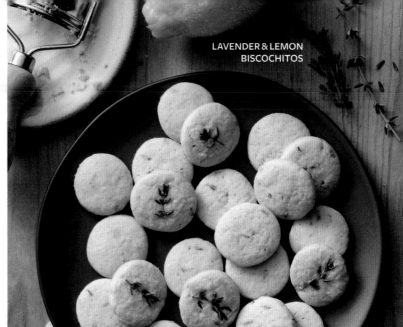

LAVENDER & LEMON
BISCOCHITOS

MAKE AHEAD

LAVENDER & LEMON BISCOCHITOS

Biscochitos are the state cookie for our home state of New Mexico. They are traditionally made with anise seeds, but I substituted lavender and lemon zest for this biscochitos recipe. The result is intriguing and delicious! I have also made these with lemon and dried thyme and they were scrumptious.

—Marla Clark, Albuquerque, NM

- -

Prep: 30 min. + chilling
Bake: 10 min./batch • **Makes:** 6 dozen

½	cup unsalted butter, softened
⅔	cup sugar
1	large egg, room temperature
1	Tbsp. dried lavender flowers
1	Tbsp. grated lemon zest
1½	cups all-purpose flour
1	tsp. baking powder
¼	tsp. salt

1. In a large bowl, cream butter and sugar until light and fluffy, 5-7 minutes. Beat in egg, lavender and lemon zest. In another bowl, whisk flour, baking powder and salt; gradually beat into creamed mixture. Divide dough in half. Shape each into a disk; cover and refrigerate for 30 minutes or until firm enough to roll.

2. Preheat oven to 350°. On a lightly floured surface, roll each portion of dough to ¼-in. thickness. Cut with a floured 1-in. round cookie cutter. Place 1 in. apart on parchment-lined baking sheets. Sprinkle cookies with additional sugar.

3. Bake until the bottoms are light brown, 9-11 minutes. Remove from pans to wire racks to cool. Store in airtight containers.

Freeze option: Freeze in freezer containers, separating layers with waxed paper. Thaw before serving.

1 cookie: 29 cal., 1g fat (1g sat. fat), 6mg chol., 16mg sod., 4g carb. (2g sugars, 0 fiber), 0 pro.

CHERRY DANISH

CHERRY DANISH

I won an award when I first made these delicious danishes for a 4-H competition years ago.
—Christie Cochran, Canyon, TX

- -

Prep: 30 min. + rising • **Bake:** 15 min.
Makes: 40 servings

- 1 pkg. (¼ oz.) active dry yeast
- ¼ cup warm water (110° to 115°)
- 1 cup warm 2% milk (110° to 115°)
- ¾ cup shortening, divided
- ⅓ cup sugar
- 3 large eggs, room temperature, divided use
- 1 tsp. salt
- ¼ tsp. each ground mace, lemon extract and vanilla extract
- 4 to 4½ cups all-purpose flour
- 1 can (21 oz.) cherry pie filling

GLAZE
- 1½ cups confectioners' sugar
- ½ tsp. vanilla extract
- 2 to 3 Tbsp. 2% milk
- ⅓ cup chopped almonds

1. In a large bowl, dissolve the yeast in water. Add the milk, ¼ cup shortening, sugar, 2 eggs, salt, mace, extracts and 2 cups of flour; beat until smooth. Add enough remaining flour to form a soft dough.

2. Turn onto a floured surface; knead until smooth and elastic, 6-8 minutes. Place in a greased bowl, turning once to grease top. Cover and let rise in a warm place until doubled, about 1 hour.

3. Punch dough down. On a large floured surface, roll dough out to a 24x16-in. rectangle. Dot half of the dough with ¼ cup shortening; fold dough lengthwise. Fold the dough 3 times lengthwise, then 2 times

widthwise, each time dotting with some of the remaining shortening. Place dough in a greased bowl; cover and let rise 20 minutes.

4. On a floured surface, roll dough into a 16x15-in. rectangle. Cut into 8x¾-in. strips; coil into spiral shapes, tucking ends underneath. Place in 2 greased 15x10x1-in. baking pans. Cover and let rise in a warm place until doubled, about 1 hour.

5. Beat the remaining egg. Make a depression in the center of each roll; brush with egg. Fill with 1 Tbsp. pie filling. Bake at 375° for 15-18 minutes or until golden brown. Cool on a wire rack. Combine confectioners' sugar, vanilla and milk; drizzle over rolls. Sprinkle with almonds.

1 pastry: 137 cal., 5g fat (1g sat. fat), 17mg chol., 70mg sod., 21g carb. (10g sugars, 1g fiber), 2g pro.

BANANA NUT CAKE

I'm a pastor's wife, and it's so helpful to have something to serve when friends drop in unexpectedly. Because this banana nut cake can be frozen and also keeps well in the refrigerator, I try to have one on hand—just in case.
—Gloria Barkley, Wilmington, NC

- -

Prep: 10 min. • **Bake:** 1 hour + cooling
Makes: 16 servings

3 cups all-purpose flour
2 cups sugar
1 tsp. salt
1 tsp. baking powder
1 tsp. baking soda
1 tsp. ground cinnamon
1 tsp. ground nutmeg
4 large eggs, room temperature
2 cups mashed ripe bananas (3 to 4 medium)
1⅓ cups canola oil
1 can (8 oz.) crushed pineapple, undrained
1½ tsp. vanilla extract
1½ cups chopped walnuts
Optional toppings: Confectioners' sugar and whipped cream

1. Preheat oven to 350°. Grease and flour a 10-in. tube pan. In a large bowl, whisk flour, sugar, salt, baking powder, baking soda, cinnamon and nutmeg. In another bowl, combine eggs, bananas, oil, pineapple and vanilla. Add to flour mixture; stir just until moistened. Fold in nuts.
2. Pour into prepared pan. Bake until a toothpick inserted in center comes out clean, 60-65 minutes. Cool in pan 15 minutes before removing to a wire rack to cool completely. If desired, dust with confectioners' sugar and serve with whipped cream and additional bananas.
Freeze option: Securely wrap cooled cake in foil, then freeze. To use, thaw at room temperature.
1 slice: 468 cal., 26g fat (3g sat. fat), 53mg chol., 268mg sod., 53g carb. (32g sugars, 2g fiber), 7g pro.

BANANA NUT CAKE

BRIGHT IDEA

To remove cakes easily, use solid shortening to grease plain and fluted tube pans.

PENNSYLVANIA DUTCH DOUGHNUTS

The potatoes keep these tasty doughnuts moist, and the glaze provides just the right amount of sweetness.

—Marlene Reichart, Leesport, PA

- -

Prep: 20 min. + chilling
Cook: 50 min.
Makes: about 4 dozen

2½ cups mashed potatoes or riced potatoes (without added milk, butter or seasonings)
1 cup whole milk
3 large eggs, lightly beaten
2 Tbsp. butter, melted
2 cups sugar
2 Tbsp. baking powder
5 to 6 cups all-purpose flour
Oil for deep-fat frying

GLAZE

2 cups confectioners' sugar
5 Tbsp. half-and-half cream
½ tsp. vanilla extract

Optional: Food coloring and sprinkles

1. In a large bowl, combine the potatoes, milk, eggs and butter. Combine the sugar, baking powder and 2 cups flour; stir into potato mixture. Add enough remaining flour to form a soft dough. Refrigerate, covered, 1 hour.

2. Divide dough in half. Turn each half onto a lightly floured surface; roll to ½-in. thickness. Cut with a 2¾-in. doughnut cutter.

3. In an electric skillet or deep-fat fryer, heat oil to 375°. Fry the doughnuts, a few at a time, until golden brown on both sides. Drain on paper towels.

4. In a small bowl, mix the glaze ingredients until smooth. Color glaze if desired. Dip doughnuts in glaze and sprinkles as desired.

1 doughnut: 163 cal., 6g fat (1g sat. fat), 14mg chol., 74mg sod., 25g carb. (14g sugars, 1g fiber), 2g pro.

HOW-TO

Decorate Doughnuts

- To make decorating easy, use small bowls for different icing colors and sprinkles.

- Dip doughnuts into glaze, then place on a wire rack and let stand until set. Or dip the just-glazed doughnuts into sprinkles.

VERMONT MAPLE OATMEAL PIE

VERMONT MAPLE OATMEAL PIE

This pie has an old-fashioned feel, but it's so easy to prepare. Serve it with ice cream and maple syrup or top it with whipped cream and a dash of cinnamon.

—Barbara J. Miller, Oakdale, MN

- -

Prep: 20 min.
Bake: 50 min.
Makes: 8 servings

1   **sheet refrigerated pie crust**
4   **large eggs**
1   **cup sugar**
3   **Tbsp. all-purpose flour**
1   **tsp. ground cinnamon**
½   **tsp. salt**
1   **cup quick-cooking oats**
¾   **cup corn syrup**
½   **cup maple syrup**
¼   **cup butter, melted**
3   **tsp. vanilla extract**
1   **cup sweetened shredded coconut**
  Vanilla ice cream, optional

1. On a lightly floured surface, roll dough to a ⅛-in.-thick circle; transfer to a 9-in. pie plate. Trim to ½ in. beyond rim of plate; flute edge.
2. In a large bowl, combine eggs, sugar, flour, cinnamon and salt. Stir in oats, syrups, butter and vanilla; pour into crust. Top with coconut.
3. Bake at 350° for 50-60 minutes or until set. Cover edge with foil during the last 15 minutes to prevent overbrowning if necessary. Cool on a wire rack. Serve with ice cream if desired. Refrigerate leftovers.
1 piece: 612 cal., 25g fat (15g sat. fat), 138mg chol., 438mg sod., 94g carb. (68g sugars, 2g fiber), 7g pro.

MAKEOVER FRUIT PIZZA

We skimmed the calories and fat from a traditional fruit pizza and created this delightful treat. It has only half the calories, fat and cholesterol of the fruit pizzas you'd find at a bakery.
—*Taste of Home* Test Kitchen

- -

Prep: 25 min. + chilling
Bake: 10 min. + cooling
Makes: 16 servings

1	cup all-purpose flour
¼	cup confectioners' sugar
½	cup cold butter, cubed

GLAZE

5	tsp. cornstarch
1¼	cups unsweetened pineapple juice
1	tsp. lemon juice

TOPPINGS

1	pkg. (8 oz.) reduced-fat cream cheese
⅓	cup sugar
1	tsp. vanilla extract
2	cups halved fresh strawberries
1	cup fresh blueberries
1	can (11 oz.) mandarin oranges, drained

1. Preheat oven to 350°. In a large bowl, mix flour and confectioners' sugar; cut in butter until crumbly. Press onto an ungreased 12-in. pizza pan. Bake until very lightly browned, 10-12 minutes. Cool completely on a wire rack.

2. In a small saucepan, mix glaze ingredients until smooth; bring to a boil. Cook and stir until thickened, about 2 minutes. Cool slightly.

3. In a bowl, beat cream cheese, sugar and vanilla until smooth. Spread over crust. Top with berries and mandarin oranges. Drizzle with glaze. Refrigerate until cold.

1 slice: 170 cal., 9g fat (6g sat. fat), 25mg chol., 120mg sod., 20g carb. (13g sugars, 1g fiber), 3g pro.
Diabetic exchanges: 1½ fat, 1 starch, ½ fruit.

MAKEOVER FRUIT PIZZA

OVERNIGHT CINNAMON ROLLS

OVERNIGHT CINNAMON ROLLS

I like to try different fun fillings in these soft rolls, and each one is packed with cinnamon flavor. They are definitely worth the overnight wait.
—Chris O'Connell, San Antonio, TX

- -

Prep: 35 min. + chilling
Bake: 20 min. • **Makes:** 2 dozen

- **2** pkg. (¼ oz. each) active dry yeast
- **1½** cups warm water (110° to 115°)
- **2** large eggs, room temperature
- **½** cup butter, softened
- **½** cup sugar
- **2** tsp. salt
- **5¾** to 6¼ cups all-purpose flour

CINNAMON FILLING

- **1** cup packed brown sugar
- **4** tsp. ground cinnamon
- **½** cup softened butter, divided

GLAZE

- **2** cups confectioners' sugar
- **¼** cup half-and-half cream
- **2** tsp. vanilla extract

1. In a small bowl, dissolve yeast in warm water. In a large bowl, combine eggs, butter, sugar, salt, yeast mixture and 3 cups flour; beat on medium speed until smooth. Stir in enough remaining flour to form a very soft dough (dough will be sticky). Do not knead. Cover; refrigerate overnight.

2. In a small bowl, mix brown sugar and cinnamon. Turn dough onto a floured surface; divide dough in half. Roll 1 portion into an 18x12-in. rectangle. Spread with ¼ cup butter to within ½ in. of edges; sprinkle the butter evenly with half of the brown sugar mixture.

3. Roll up jelly-roll style, starting with a long side; pinch seam to seal. Cut into 12 slices. Place in a greased 13x9-in. baking pan, cut side down. Repeat with the remaining dough and filling.

4. Cover with kitchen towels; let rise in a warm place until doubled, about 1 hour. Preheat oven to 375°.

5. Bake 20-25 minutes or until lightly browned. In a small bowl, mix confectioners' sugar, cream and vanilla; spread over warm rolls.

1 roll: 278 cal., 9g fat (5g sat. fat), 39mg chol., 262mg sod., 47g carb. (23g sugars, 1g fiber), 4g pro.

WINNIE'S MINI
RHUBARB &
STRAWBERRY PIES

WINNIE'S MINI RHUBARB & STRAWBERRY PIES

Every spring, we had strawberries and rhubarb on our farm outside Seattle. These fruity hand pies remind me of those times and of Grandma Winnie's baking.
—Shawn Carleton, San Diego, CA

- -

Prep: 25 min. + chilling
Bake: 15 min.
Makes: 18 mini pies

- 3   Tbsp. quick-cooking tapioca
- 4   cups sliced fresh strawberries
- 2   cups sliced fresh rhubarb
- ¾   cup sugar
- 1   tsp. grated orange zest
- 1   tsp. vanilla extract
- ¼   tsp. salt
- ¼   tsp. ground cinnamon
- 3   drops red food coloring, optional
- 2   sheets refrigerated pie crust
      Sweetened whipped cream, optional

1. Place the tapioca in a small food processor or spice grinder; process until finely ground.

2. In a large saucepan, combine the strawberries, rhubarb, sugar, orange zest, vanilla, salt, cinnamon, tapioca and, if desired, red food coloring; bring to a boil. Reduce the heat; simmer, covered, for 15-20 minutes or until strawberries are tender, stirring occasionally. Transfer the mixture to a large bowl; cover and refrigerate overnight.

3. Preheat oven to 425°. On a lightly floured surface, roll 1 sheet pie crust to an 18-in. circle. Cut 12 circles with a 4-in. biscuit cutter, rerolling scraps as necessary; press the crust onto bottom and up sides of ungreased muffin cups. Cut 6 more circles with remaining crust. Spoon strawberry mixture into muffin cups.

4. Bake until filling is bubbly and crust golden brown, 12-15 minutes. Cool in pan 5 minutes; remove to wire racks to cool. If desired, serve with whipped cream.

1 mini pie: 207 cal., 10g fat (6g sat. fat), 27mg chol., 171mg sod., 27g carb. (11g sugars, 1g fiber), 2g pro.

COCONUT EGG NESTS

Looking for an Easter activity that kids will enjoy assembling and eating? Try these sweet birds' nest cookies. They're a snap to make and call for just a few ingredients.
—Tonya Hamrick, Wallace, WV

- -

Takes: 20 min. • **Makes:** 1 dozen

- 6   oz. white candy coating, coarsely chopped
- 6   drops green food coloring
- 1   drop yellow food coloring
- 1   cup sweetened shredded coconut
- 36 jelly beans

In a microwave-safe bowl, melt the candy coating; stir in food coloring until blended. Stir in coconut. Drop by tablespoonfuls onto waxed paper into 12 mounds. Make an indentation in the center of each with the end of a wooden spoon handle. Fill each with three jelly beans. Let nests stand until set.

1 nest: 127 cal., 7g fat (6g sat. fat), 0 chol., 22mg sod., 17g carb. (15g sugars, 0 fiber), 0 pro.

COCONUT EGG NESTS

OLD-TIME CAKE DOUGHNUTS

OLD-TIME CAKE DOUGHNUTS

This tender cake doughnut is a little piece of heaven at breakfast. For a variation, add a little rum extract or 1 tablespoon dark rum for a richer flavor.

—Alissa Stehr,
Gau-Odernheim, Germany

- -

Prep: 30 min. + chilling
Cook: 5 min./batch
Makes: about 2 dozen

2	Tbsp. unsalted butter, softened
1½	cups sugar, divided
3	large eggs, room temperature
4	cups all-purpose flour
1	Tbsp. baking powder
3	tsp. ground cinnamon, divided
½	tsp. salt
⅛	tsp. ground nutmeg
¾	cup 2% milk
	Oil for deep-fat frying

1. In a large bowl, beat butter and 1 cup sugar until crumbly, about 2 minutes. Add eggs, 1 at a time, beating well after each addition.
2. Combine the flour, baking powder, 1 tsp. cinnamon, salt and nutmeg; add to butter mixture alternately with milk, beating well after each addition. Cover and refrigerate for 2 hours.
3. Turn onto a heavily floured surface; pat the dough to ¼-in. thickness. Cut with a floured 2½-in. doughnut cutter. In an electric skillet or deep fryer, heat oil to 375°.

4. Fry doughnuts, a few at a time, until golden brown on both sides. Drain doughnuts on paper towels. Combine remaining sugar and cinnamon; roll warm doughnuts in mixture.

Freeze option: Wrap doughnuts in foil and transfer to a resealable freezer container. May be frozen for up to 3 months. To use, remove foil. Thaw at room temperature. Warm if desired. Combine ½ cup sugar and 2 tsp. cinnamon; roll the warm doughnuts in mixture.

1 doughnut: 198 cal., 8g fat (1g sat. fat), 30mg chol., 112mg sod., 29g carb. (13g sugars, 1g fiber), 3g pro.

5i

CHOCOLATE-DIPPED STRAWBERRY MERINGUE ROSES

Eat these kid-friendly treats as is, or crush them into a bowl of strawberries and whipped cream. Readers of my blog went nuts when I posted that idea!
—Amy Tong, Anaheim, CA

- -

Prep: 25 min. + standing
Bake: 40 min. + cooling
Makes: 2 dozen

- 3 large egg whites
- ¼ cup sugar
- ¼ cup freeze-dried strawberries
- 1 pkg. (3 oz.) strawberry gelatin
- ½ tsp. vanilla extract, optional
- 1 cup 60% cacao bittersweet chocolate baking chips, melted

1. Place egg whites in a large bowl; let stand at room temperature 30 minutes. Preheat oven to 225°.
2. Place sugar and strawberries in a food processor; process until powdery. Add gelatin; pulse to blend.
3. Beat egg whites on medium speed until foamy, adding vanilla if desired. Gradually add the gelatin mixture, 1 Tbsp. at a time, beating on high after each addition until sugar is dissolved. Continue beating until stiff glossy peaks form.
4. Cut a small hole in the tip of a pastry bag; insert a #1M star tip. Transfer meringue to bag. Pipe 2-in. roses 1½ in. apart onto parchment-lined baking sheets.

5. Bake 40-45 minutes or until set and dry. Turn off oven (do not open oven door); leave meringues in oven 1½ hours. Remove from oven; cool completely on baking sheets.
6. Remove meringues from paper. Dip bottoms in melted chocolate; allow excess to drip off. Place on waxed paper; let stand until set, about 45 minutes. Store in an airtight container at room temperature.
1 cookie: 33 cal., 1g fat (1g sat. fat), 0 chol., 9mg sod., 6g carb. (5g sugars, 0 fiber), 1g pro.
Diabetic exchanges: ½ starch.

CHOCOLATE-DIPPED STRAWBERRY MERINGUE ROSES

LEMON LAYER CAKE

LEMON LAYER CAKE

This citrusy cake with a luscious cream cheese frosting will garner plenty of applause. The flavor, a duet of sweet and tangy notes, really sings.

—Summer Goddard, Springfield, VA

- -

Prep: 35 min.
Bake: 25 min. + cooling
Makes: 12 servings

- 1 **cup butter, softened**
- 1½ **cups sugar**
- 2 **large eggs, room temperature**
- 3 **large egg yolks, room temperature**
- 1 **Tbsp. grated lemon zest**
- 2 **Tbsp. lemon juice**
- ¾ **cup sour cream**
- ¼ **cup 2% milk**
- 2½ **cups all-purpose flour**
- 1 **tsp. salt**
- 1 **tsp. baking powder**
- ½ **tsp. baking soda**

SYRUP

- ½ **cup sugar**
- ½ **cup lemon juice**

FROSTING

- 2 **pkg. (8 oz. each) cream cheese, softened**
- 1 **cup butter, softened**
- 4 **cups confectioners' sugar**
- 1½ **tsp. lemon juice**
- ⅛ **tsp. salt**
  Optional: Lemon slices or edible flowers

1. Preheat oven to 350°. Line bottoms of 2 greased 9-in. round baking pans with parchment; grease the parchment.

2. Cream butter and sugar until light and fluffy, 5-7 minutes. Add eggs and egg yolks, 1 at a time, beating well after each addition. Beat in lemon zest and juice. In a small bowl, mix sour cream and milk. In another bowl, whisk together flour, salt, baking powder and baking soda; add to creamed mixture alternately with sour cream mixture.

3. Transfer to prepared pans. Bake until a toothpick inserted in center comes out clean, 24-28 minutes. Cool in pans 10 minutes before removing to wire racks; remove parchment. Cool slightly.

4. For syrup, in a small saucepan, combine sugar and lemon juice. Bring to a boil; cook until liquid is reduced by half. Cool completely.

5. For frosting, beat cream cheese and butter until smooth; beat in confectioners' sugar, lemon juice and salt until blended.

6. Using a long serrated knife, cut each cake horizontally in half. Brush the cake layers with warm syrup; cool completely.

7. Place 1 cake layer on a serving plate; spread with 1 cup frosting. Repeat layers twice. Top with the remaining cake layer. Frost top and sides with remaining frosting. If desired, top with lemon slices or edible flowers. Refrigerate leftovers.

1 slice: 841 cal., 48g fat (30g sat. fat), 219mg chol., 656mg sod., 96g carb. (72g sugars, 1g fiber), 8g pro.

CONFETTI BIRTHDAY CAKE

This is a moist and fluffy vanilla cake with lots of sprinkles and a whipped vanilla buttercream. It's almost impossible not to feel happy when you see the fun pop of rainbow confetti!

—Courtney Rich, Highland, UT

- -

Prep: 30 min.
Bake: 35 min. + cooling
Makes: 16 servings

- 1 **cup unsalted butter, room temperature**
- ⅓ **cup vegetable oil**
- 1¾ **cups sugar**
- 3 **large eggs, room temperature**
- 3 **large egg whites, room temperature**
- 1 **Tbsp. vanilla extract**
- 3 **cups cake flour**
- 2 **tsp. baking powder**
- 1 **tsp. salt**
- 1 **cup buttermilk, room temperature**
- ¼ **cup rainbow sprinkles**

BUTTERCREAM

- 1½ **cups unsalted butter, softened**
- 4½ **cups confectioners' sugar, sifted**
- 3 **Tbsp. heavy whipping cream**
- 2 **tsp. clear vanilla extract**
   Soft pink paste food coloring

1. Preheat oven to 325°. Grease a 13x9-in. baking dish. In a large bowl, cream butter, oil and sugar until light and fluffy, 5-7 minutes. Add eggs, then egg whites, 1 at a time, beating well after each addition. Beat in vanilla. In another bowl, whisk flour, baking powder and salt; add to creamed mixture alternately with buttermilk, beating well after each addition. Fold in sprinkles.

2. Transfer to prepared pan. Bake until a toothpick inserted in center comes out clean, 35-40 minutes. Cool completely on a wire rack.

3. For buttercream, in a large bowl, beat butter until creamy. Gradually beat in confectioners' sugar until smooth. Add cream, vanilla and food coloring. Beat until light and fluffy, 5-7 minutes. Frost top of cake with frosting, and top with additional sprinkles if desired.

1 piece: 823 cal., 47g fat (26g sat. fat), 138mg chol., 279mg sod., 97g carb. (75g sugars, 0 fiber), 6g pro.

**CONFETTI
BIRTHDAY CAKE**

LEMONY WALNUT-RAISIN GALETTE

LEMONY WALNUT-RAISIN GALETTE

This flaky, buttery pastry has a filling of fruit, walnuts, coconut and cinnamon. There's a lot to love! For even more appeal, dollop sweetened whipped cream on top of each serving.
—Ellen Kozak, Milwaukee, WI

- -

Prep: 30 min.
Bake: 30 min.
Makes: 10 servings

- 1 **medium lemon**
- 1 **cup finely chopped walnuts**
- 1 **cup raisins**
- 1 **cup apricot spreadable fruit**
- ⅔ **cup unsweetened finely shredded coconut**
- 2 **tsp. ground cinnamon**
- 8 **sheets phyllo dough (14x9-in. size)**
- ⅓ **cup butter, melted**
  Sweetened whipped cream, optional

1. Preheat oven to 350°. Cut unpeeled lemon into 8 wedges; remove seeds. Place wedges in a food processor; process until finely chopped. Transfer to a large bowl; stir in walnuts, raisins, spreadable fruit, coconut and cinnamon.

2. Place 1 sheet of phyllo dough on a parchment-lined baking sheet; brush with butter. Layer with remaining phyllo sheets, brushing each layer. (Keep remaining phyllo covered with a damp towel to prevent it from drying out.)

3. Spoon filling onto center of phyllo, leaving a 2-in. border on all sides. Fold edges of phyllo over filling, leaving center uncovered. Brush folded edges with butter. Bake until golden brown, 30-35 minutes. Using parchment, carefully slide galette onto a wire rack to cool slightly. If desired, serve with whipped cream.

1 piece: 324 cal., 18g fat (8g sat. fat), 16mg chol., 125mg sod., 41g carb. (23g sugars, 3g fiber), 4g pro.

STRAWBERRY MUFFIN CONES

STRAWBERRY MUFFIN CONES

This is a delightful, fun way to serve a cupcake. I share these with the neighborhood kids and they love the ice cream cone look and the ease of eating. The adults say that snacking on them makes them feel like kids again.

—Barb Kietzer, Niles, MI

- -

Prep: 20 min.
Bake: 20 min. + cooling
Makes: 20 servings

- 2 **cups all-purpose flour**
- ½ **cup sugar**
- 2 **tsp. baking powder**
- ½ **tsp. baking soda**
- ½ **tsp. salt**
- 2 **large eggs, room temperature**
- ¾ **cup strawberry yogurt**
- ½ **cup canola oil**
- 1 **cup chopped fresh strawberries**
- 20 **ice cream cake cones (about 3 in. tall)**
- 1 **cup semisweet chocolate chips**
- 1 **Tbsp. shortening**
    Colored sprinkles

1. In a large bowl, combine the first 5 ingredients. In another bowl, beat the eggs, strawberry yogurt, oil and strawberries; stir into dry ingredients just until moistened.

2. Place the ice cream cones in muffin cups; spoon 2 heaping Tbsp. batter into each cone. Bake at 375° for 19-21 minutes or until a toothpick inserted in the center comes out clean. Cool completely.

3. In a microwave, melt chocolate chips and shortening; stir until smooth. Dip the muffin tops in chocolate; allow excess to drip off. Decorate with sprinkles.

1 cone: 253 cal., 13g fat (3g sat. fat), 29mg chol., 196mg sod., 33g carb. (16g sugars, 1g fiber), 4g pro.

CREAMY LEMON ALMOND PASTRIES

I love lemon-filled doughnuts when I can find them. This recipe brings the concept to a new level by placing the filling into a baked beignet and enhancing it with a bit of almond flavoring and toasted almonds. The result? Sunshine in a bite.

—Arlene Erlbach, Morton Grove, IL

- -

Prep: 30 min. + chilling
Bake: 15 min. • **Makes:** 9 servings

- ½ cup plus 1 Tbsp. cream cheese, softened (4½ oz.)
- ⅔ cup confectioners' sugar, divided
- 2 Tbsp. lemon curd
- 2 tsp. grated lemon zest
- ¼ tsp. almond extract
- 1 sheet frozen puff pastry, thawed
- 1 large egg, beaten
- 2 Tbsp. water
- 2 tsp. lemon juice
- 2 tsp. 2% milk
- 3 Tbsp. sliced almonds, toasted

1. Beat cream cheese, 3 Tbsp. confectioners' sugar, lemon curd, lemon zest and almond extract on medium until combined. Refrigerate, covered, for 30 minutes.

2. Preheat oven to 400°. On a lightly floured surface, unfold puff pastry. Roll into a 12x9-in. rectangle. Using a pastry cutter or sharp knife, cut into 9 rectangles. Spoon rounded Tbsp. of cream cheese mixture in center of each rectangle. In a small bowl, whisk egg with water. Brush edges with the egg mixture.

3. Wrap puff pastry around filling to cover completely. Pinch the edges together to form a ball. Place balls seam side down, 2 in. apart, on a parchment-lined baking sheet. Brush pastries with remaining egg mixture. Pierce each once with a fork. Bake until golden brown, 15-18 minutes. Cool on wire rack for 5 minutes. Loosen pastries from parchment.

Meanwhile, combine lemon juice, milk and remaining confectioners' sugar. Brush each pastry with lemon glaze. Top with almonds. When glaze is set, in 1-2 minutes, peel off the parchment. Serve warm.

1 pastry: 255 cal., 14g fat (5g sat. fat), 39mg chol., 148mg sod., 29g carb. (12g sugars, 2g fiber), 4g pro.

CREAMY LEMON ALMOND PASTRIES

Special Menus

We've done the planning for you with 10 magnificent menus. Just add your hospitality and finishing touches.

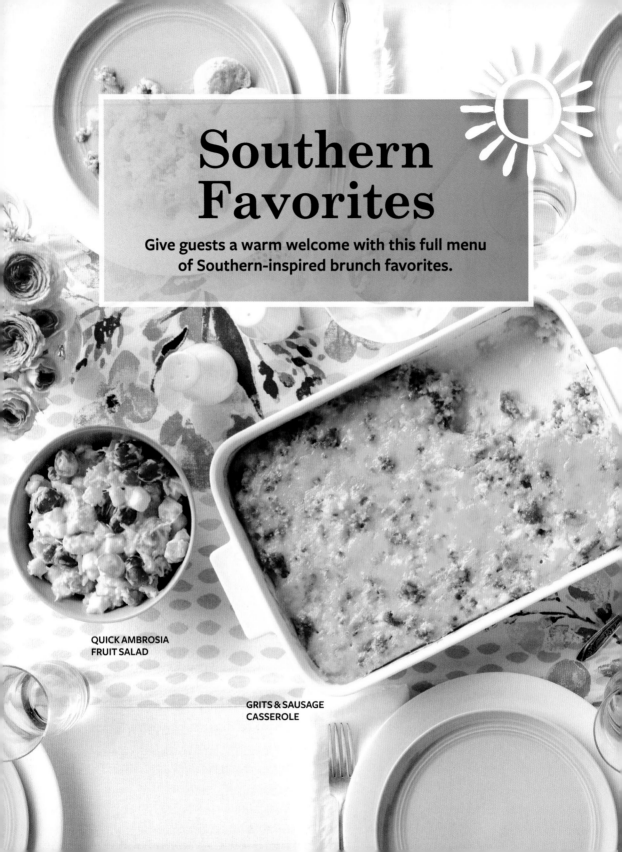

Southern Favorites

Give guests a warm welcome with this full menu of Southern-inspired brunch favorites.

QUICK AMBROSIA
FRUIT SALAD

GRITS & SAUSAGE
CASSEROLE

HOMEMADE BISCUITS & MAPLE SAUSAGE GRAVY

SWEET TEA CONCENTRATE

HAM & COLLARDS QUICHE

HOMEMADE BISCUITS & MAPLE SAUSAGE GRAVY

I remember digging into flaky, gravy-smothered biscuits on Christmas morning and other special occasions when I was a child. What a satisfying way to start the day!

—Jenn Tidwell, Fair Oaks, CA

- -

Prep: 30 min. • **Bake:** 15 min.
Makes: 8 servings

- 2 cups all-purpose flour
- 3 tsp. baking powder
- 1 Tbsp. sugar
- 1 tsp. salt
- ¼ tsp. pepper, optional
- 3 Tbsp. cold butter, cubed
- 1 Tbsp. shortening
- ¾ cup 2% milk

SAUSAGE GRAVY
- 1 lb. bulk maple pork sausage
- ¼ cup all-purpose flour
- 3 cups 2% milk
- 2 Tbsp. maple syrup
- ½ tsp. salt
- ¼ tsp. ground sage
- ¼ tsp. coarsely ground pepper

1. Preheat oven to 400°. In a large bowl, whisk flour, baking powder, sugar, salt and, if desired, pepper. Cut in cubed butter and shortening until mixture resembles coarse crumbs. Add milk; stir just until moistened. Turn onto a lightly floured surface; knead gently 8-10 times.

2. Pat or roll dough to 1-in. thickness; cut with a floured 2-in. biscuit cutter. Place 1 in. apart on an ungreased baking sheet. Bake until golden brown, 15-17 minutes.

3. Meanwhile, in a large skillet, cook sausage over medium heat until no longer pink, 6-8 minutes, breaking into crumbles. Stir in flour until blended; gradually stir in milk. Bring to a boil, stirring constantly; cook and stir until sauce is thickened, 4-6 minutes. Stir in the remaining ingredients. Serve the gravy with warm biscuits.

1 biscuit with ½ cup gravy: 371 cal., 19g fat (8g sat. fat), 41mg chol., 915mg sod., 38g carb. (11g sugars, 1g fiber), 11g pro.

HAM & COLLARDS QUICHE

I love quiche and wanted to make something that celebrates my Southern roots, so I came up with this recipe. With eggs, cheese, ham and collard greens in a flaky crust, it's a complete meal.
—Billie Williams-Henderson, Bowie, MD

- -

Prep: 20 min.
Bake: 35 min. + standing
Makes: 6 servings

- 1 **sheet refrigerated pie crust**
- 2 **Tbsp. olive oil**
- 1 **cup frozen chopped collard greens, thawed and drained**
- 1 **small onion, chopped**
- 1 **garlic clove, minced**
- ¼ **tsp. salt**
- ¼ **tsp. pepper**
- 2 **cups shredded Colby-Monterey Jack cheese**
- ¾ **cup cubed fully cooked ham**
- 6 **large eggs**
- 1 **cup 2% milk**

1. Preheat oven to 375°. Unroll crust into a 9-in. pie plate; flute edge. Chill while preparing filling.
2. In a large skillet, heat oil over medium-high heat. Add collard greens and onion; cook and stir until onion is tender, 5-7 minutes. Add garlic; cook 1 minute longer. Stir in salt and pepper. Cool slightly; stir in cheese and ham. Spoon into crust.
3. In a large bowl, whisk eggs and milk until blended. Pour over top. Bake on lower oven rack until a knife inserted in the center comes out clean, 35-40 minutes. Cover edge loosely with foil during the last 15 minutes if needed to prevent overbrowning. Remove foil. Let stand 10 minutes before cutting.
Freeze option: Cover and freeze unbaked quiche. To use, remove from freezer 30 minutes before baking (do not thaw). Preheat oven to 375°. Place quiche on a baking sheet. Bake as directed, increasing time to 50-60 minutes.
1 piece: 457 cal., 31g fat (15g sat. fat), 240mg chol., 766mg sod., 23g carb. (4g sugars, 1g fiber), 21g pro.

QUICK AMBROSIA FRUIT SALAD

I mix in a little coconut and just enough marshmallows so it tastes like the creamy ambrosia I grew up with. Now everyone in my house loves it, too.
—Trisha Kruse, Eagle, ID

- -

Takes: 10 min. • **Makes:** 6 servings

- 1 **can (8¼ oz.) fruit cocktail, drained**
- 1 **can (8 oz.) unsweetened pineapple chunks, drained**
- 1 **cup green grapes**
- 1 **cup seedless red grapes**
- 1 **cup miniature marshmallows**
- 1 **medium banana, sliced**
- ¾ **cup vanilla yogurt**
- ½ **cup sweetened shredded coconut**

In a large bowl, combine all of the ingredients. Chill until serving.
¾ cup: 191 cal., 4g fat (3g sat. fat), 2mg chol., 48mg sod., 40g carb. (34g sugars, 2g fiber), 3g pro.

HAM & COLLARDS QUICHE

GRITS & SAUSAGE CASSEROLE

GRITS & SAUSAGE CASSEROLE

You could call this the "so good casserole," because that's what people say when they try it. It's a Southern specialty. To make your morning easier, just assemble it and refrigerate overnight.

—Marie Poppenhager, Old Town, FL

- -

Prep: 30 min. • **Bake:** 1¼ hours
Makes: 12 servings

- 3 **cups water**
- 1 **cup quick-cooking grits**
- ¾ **tsp. salt, divided**
- 2 **lbs. bulk pork sausage, cooked and drained**
- 2 **cups shredded cheddar cheese, divided**
- 3 **large eggs**
- 1½ **cups whole milk**
- 2 **Tbsp. butter, melted**
  Pepper to taste

1. In a saucepan, bring water to a boil. Slowly whisk in the grits and ½ tsp. salt. Reduce heat; cover and simmer for 5 minutes, stirring occasionally.

2. In a large bowl, combine grits, sausage and 1½ cups cheese. Beat the eggs and milk; stir into grits mixture. Add the butter, pepper and remaining salt.

3. Transfer to a greased 13x9-in. baking dish. Bake, uncovered, at 350° until a knife inserted in the center comes out clean, about 1 hour. Sprinkle with remaining cheese; bake 15 minutes longer or until cheese is melted. Let stand for 5 minutes before cutting.

To make ahead: This casserole can be covered and refrigerated overnight. Remove from the refrigerator 30 minutes before baking. Bake as directed.

1 cup: 316 cal., 24g fat (11g sat. fat), 110mg chol., 621mg sod., 13g carb. (3g sugars, 1g fiber), 13g pro.

SWEET TEA CONCENTRATE

Sweet iced tea is a Southern classic, and this is a fabulous recipe for sweet-tea lovers or for a party. The concentrate makes 20 servings.

—Natalie Bremson, Plantation, FL

- -

Prep: 30 min. + cooling
Makes: 20 servings
(5 cups concentrate)

- 2 **medium lemons**
- 4 **cups sugar**
- 4 **cups water**
- 1½ **cups English breakfast tea leaves or 20 black tea bags**
- ⅓ **cup lemon juice**

EACH SERVING
- 1 **cup cold water**
  Ice cubes

1. Remove peels from lemons; save fruit for another use.

2. In a large saucepan, combine the sugar and water. Bring to a boil over medium heat. Reduce heat; simmer, uncovered, until sugar is dissolved, 3-5 minutes, stirring occasionally. Remove from the heat; add tea leaves and lemon peels. Cover and steep for 15 minutes. Strain tea, discarding tea leaves and lemon peels; stir in lemon juice. Cool to room temperature.

3. Transfer to a container with a tight-fitting lid. Store in the refrigerator for up to 2 weeks.

To prepare tea: In a tall glass, combine water with ¼ cup of tea concentrate; add ice.

¼ cup concentrate: 165 cal., 0 fat (0 sat. fat), 0 chol., 27mg sod., 43g carb. (40g sugars, 0 fiber), 0 pro.

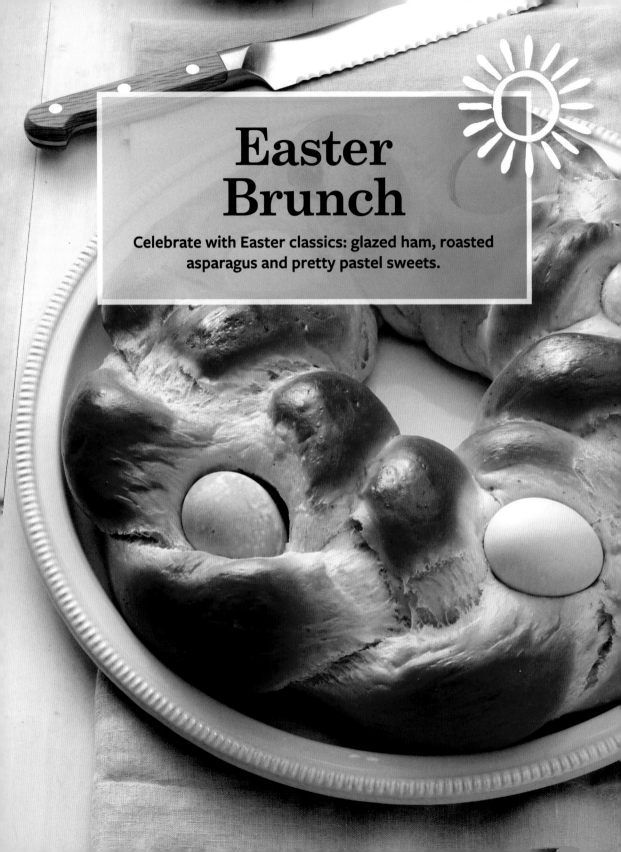

Easter Brunch

Celebrate with Easter classics: glazed ham, roasted asparagus and pretty pastel sweets.

EASTER EGG BREAD

EASTER EGG BREAD

I've made this Easter treat for 20 years! Colored hard-cooked eggs baked in the dough give the sweet bread such a festive look. Leave them out and the recipe can be enjoyed any time of year. My husband especially enjoys this bread with baked ham.
—Heather Durante, Wellsburg, WV

Prep: 55 min. + rising
Bake: 25 min. + cooling
Makes: 1 loaf (16 slices)

½	**cup sugar**
2	**pkg. (¼ oz. each) active dry yeast**
1	**to 2 tsp. ground cardamom**
1	**tsp. salt**
6	**to 6½ cups all-purpose flour**
1½	**cups whole milk**
6	**Tbsp. butter, cubed**
4	**large eggs, room temperature, divided use**
3	**to 6 hard-boiled large eggs, unpeeled**
	Assorted food coloring
	Canola oil
2	**Tbsp. water**

1. In a large bowl, mix sugar, yeast, cardamom, salt and 2 cups flour. In a small saucepan, heat milk and butter to 120°-130°. Add to dry ingredients; beat on medium speed 2 minutes. Add 3 eggs; beat on high 2 minutes. Stir in enough remaining flour to form a soft dough (dough will be sticky).

2. Turn dough onto a floured surface; knead until smooth and elastic, 6-8 minutes. Place in a greased bowl, turning once to grease the top. Cover and let rise in a warm place until doubled, about 45 minutes.

3. Meanwhile, dye hard-boiled eggs with food coloring following package directions. Let stand until completely dry.

4. Punch down dough. Turn onto a lightly floured surface; divide into thirds. Roll each portion into a 24-in. rope. Place ropes on a greased baking sheet and braid. Bring ends together to form a ring. Pinch ends to seal. Lightly coat dyed eggs with oil; arrange on braid, tucking them gently among the ropes.

5. Cover with a kitchen towel; let rise in a warm place until doubled, about 20 minutes. Preheat the oven to 375°.

6. In a bowl, whisk the remaining egg and water; gently brush over dough, avoiding eggs. Bake until golden brown, 25-30 minutes. Remove from pan to a wire rack to cool. Refrigerate leftovers.

1 slice: 281 cal., 8g fat (4g sat. fat), 107mg chol., 231mg sod., 44g carb. (8g sugars, 1g fiber), 9g pro.

READER REVIEW

"Absolutely gorgeous. Rave reviews—everyone loved it. I highly recommend this recipe. We did have some left over, and I cannot wait to make French toast casserole with the leftovers."
—DANIELLEYLEE, TASTEOFHOME.COM

APRICOT GINGER MUSTARD-GLAZED HAM

APRICOT GINGER MUSTARD-GLAZED HAM

One year I decided to bake my holiday ham with a sweet and spicy gingery glaze. This is how you do special-occasion dining.
—Ally Phillips, Murrells Inlet, SC

- -

Prep: 15 min. • **Bake:** 2 hours
Makes: 16 servings

1	**fully cooked bone-in ham (7 to 9 lbs.)**
½	**cup drained canned apricot halves**
½	**cup stone-ground mustard**
⅓	**cup packed brown sugar**
2	**Tbsp. grated fresh gingerroot**
1	**Tbsp. whole peppercorns**
½	**tsp. sea salt**
½	**tsp. coarsely ground pepper**

1. Preheat oven to 325°. Place ham on a rack in a shallow roasting pan. Using a sharp knife, score surface of ham with ¼-in.-deep cuts in a diamond pattern. Cover and bake until a thermometer reads 130°, 1¾-2¼ hours.

2. Meanwhile, place remaining ingredients in a food processor; process until blended.

3. Remove ham from oven. Increase oven setting to 425°. Spread apricot mixture over the ham. Bake ham, uncovered, until a thermometer reads 140°, 15-20 minutes longer. If desired, increase oven setting to broil; broil until golden brown, 2-4 minutes.

4 oz. cooked ham: 201 cal., 6g fat (2g sat. fat), 87mg chol., 1258mg sod., 8g carb. (7g sugars, 0 fiber), 30g pro.

ROASTED
ASPARAGUS WITH
THYME

ROASTED ASPARAGUS WITH THYME

This good-for-you side dish is so easy to prepare, yet it's elegant and special. What a classic way to welcome spring to your table.
—Sharon Leno, Keansburg, NJ

- -

Takes: 20 min. • **Makes:** 12 servings

- 3 **lbs. fresh asparagus, trimmed**
- 3 **Tbsp. olive oil**
- 2 **tsp. minced fresh thyme or ¾ tsp. dried thyme**
- ½ **tsp. salt**
- ¼ **tsp. pepper**

1. Place asparagus in a baking pan lined with heavy-duty foil. Drizzle with oil and toss to coat. Sprinkle with the thyme, salt and pepper.
2. Bake, uncovered, at 425° for 10-15 minutes or until crisp-tender.

7 spears: 55 cal., 4g fat (1g sat. fat), 0 chol., 101mg sod., 4g carb. (0 sugars, 1g fiber), 3g pro.
Diabetic exchanges: 1 vegetable, ½ fat.

ONION-GARLIC HASH BROWNS

Quick to assemble, these slow-cooked hash browns are one of my go-to sides. Stir in hot sauce if you like a bit of heat. I top my finished dish with a little shredded cheddar cheese.
—Cindi Boger, Ardmore, AL

- -

Prep: 20 min. • **Cook:** 3 hours
Makes: 12 servings

- ¼ **cup butter, cubed**
- 1 **Tbsp. olive oil**
- 1 **large red onion, chopped**
- 1 **small sweet red pepper, chopped**
- 1 **small green pepper, chopped**
- 4 **garlic cloves, minced**

- 1 **pkg. (30 oz.) frozen shredded hash brown potatoes**
- ½ **tsp. salt**
- ½ **tsp. pepper**
- 3 **drops hot pepper sauce, optional**
- 2 **tsp. minced fresh parsley**

1. In a large skillet, heat butter and oil over medium heat. Add onion and peppers. Cook and stir until crisp-tender. Add garlic; cook 1 minute longer. Stir in hash browns, salt, pepper and, if desired, hot pepper sauce.
2. Transfer to a 5-qt. slow cooker coated with cooking spray. Cook, covered, 3-4 hours or until heated through. Sprinkle with parsley just before serving.
½ cup: 110 cal., 5g fat (3g sat. fat), 10mg chol., 136mg sod., 15g carb. (1g sugars, 1g fiber), 2g pro.
Diabetic exchanges: 1 starch, 1 fat.

LEMON PUDDING DESSERT

BIRD NESTS

Here's a fun, kid-friendly recipe I started making a few years ago. My kids always love helping me make these.

—Jessica Boivin, Nekoosa, WI

Prep: 40 min. • **Makes:** 2 dozen

- 2 pkg. (10 to 12 oz. each) white baking chips
- 1 pkg. (10 oz.) pretzel sticks
- 24 yellow chicks Peeps candy
- 1 pkg. (12 oz.) M&M's eggs or other egg-shaped candy

1. In a large metal bowl set over simmering water, melt baking chips; stir until smooth. Reserve ½ cup melted chips for decorations; keep warm.

2. Add pretzel sticks to remaining chips; stir to coat evenly. Drop mixture into 24 mounds on waxed paper; shape into bird nests using 2 forks.

3. Dip bottoms of Peeps in reserved chips; place in nests. Attach eggs with remaining chips. Let stand until set.

1 nest: 276 cal., 11g fat (7g sat. fat), 7mg chol., 215mg sod., 41g carb. (30g sugars, 1g fiber), 4g pro.

READER REVIEW

"These were sooo good. I made them with my 7-year-old sister, and she loved to make them. These couldn't have been easier or yummier!"

—DOBYLOVER2008, TASTEOFHOME.COM

LEMON PUDDING DESSERT

After a big meal, folks really go for this light lemon treat. The shortbread crust is the perfect base for the fluffy top layers. I've prepared this sunny dessert for church suppers for years and I always get recipe requests.

—Muriel DeWitt, Maynard, MA

Prep: 20 min. + chilling
Bake: 20 min. • **Makes:** 16 servings

- 1 cup cold butter, cubed
- 2 cups all-purpose flour
- 1 pkg. (8 oz.) cream cheese, softened
- 1 cup confectioners' sugar
- 1 carton (8 oz.) frozen whipped topping, thawed, divided
- 3 cups cold whole milk
- 2 pkg. (3.4 oz. each) instant lemon pudding mix

1. Preheat oven to 350°. Cut butter into flour until crumbly. Press into an ungreased 13x9-in. baking dish. Bake until light brown, 18-22 minutes. Cool on a wire rack.

2. Beat cream cheese and sugar until smooth. Fold in 1 cup whipped topping. Spread over cooled crust.

3. Beat milk and pudding mix on low speed for 2 minutes. Carefully spread over cream cheese layer. Top with the remaining whipped topping. Refrigerate at least 1 hour.

1 piece: 348 cal., 20g fat (13g sat. fat), 49mg chol., 305mg sod., 35g carb. (22g sugars, 0 fiber), 4g pro.

BIRD NESTS

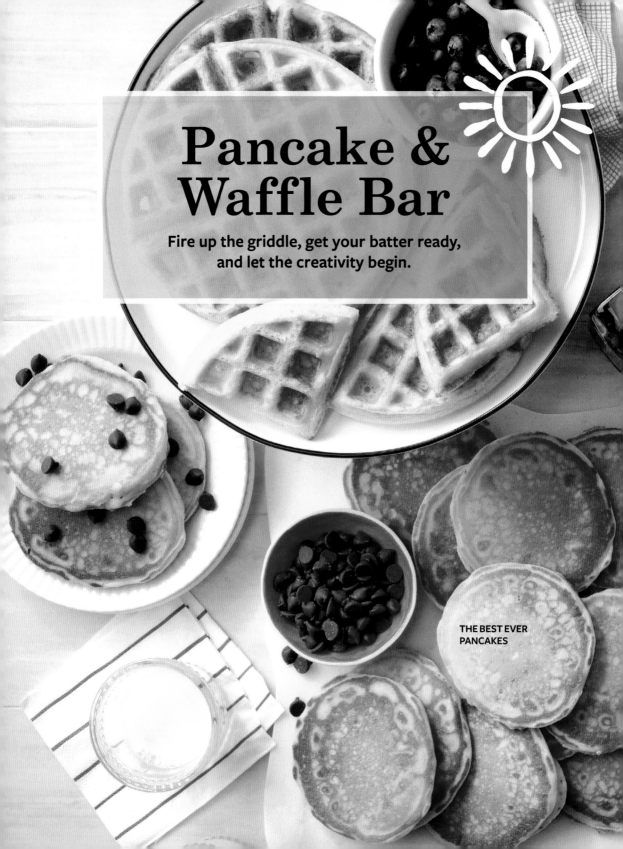

Pancake & Waffle Bar

Fire up the griddle, get your batter ready, and let the creativity begin.

THE BEST EVER
PANCAKES

OVERNIGHT YEAST
WAFFLES

THE BEST EVER PANCAKES

I'm not joking when I say I make pancakes every weekend. I love them in any form and variation, and this is one of my favorite pancake recipes.
—James Schend,
Pleasant Prairie, WI

Prep: 15 min. • **Cook:** 5 min./batch
Makes: 12 pancakes

1½   cups all-purpose flour
2   Tbsp. sugar
1   tsp. baking powder
½   tsp. baking soda
½   tsp. salt
1   cup buttermilk
2   large eggs, room
     temperature
¼   cup butter, melted
1   tsp. vanilla extract
     Optional: Mixed fresh berries,
     whipped cream, maple syrup
     and butter

1. In a large bowl, whisk together the first 5 ingredients. In another bowl, whisk remaining ingredients; stir into dry ingredients just until moistened.
2. Preheat griddle over medium heat. Lightly grease griddle. Pour batter by ¼ cupfuls onto griddle; cook until bubbles on top begin to pop and bottoms are golden brown. Turn; cook until second side is golden brown. Serve with toppings as desired.

3 pancakes: 360 cal., 15g fat (8g sat. fat), 126mg chol., 817mg sod., 45g carb. (10g sugars, 1g fiber), 10g pro.

THE BEST EVER PANCAKES

HOW-TO

Make a Great Pancake Bar

To set up the perfect pancake and waffle bar, provide lots of options! Here are some ideas to get you started.

Spreads
• Butter
• Peanut butter
• Nutella
• Marshmallow fluff
• Jam or preserves
• Pie filling
• Yogurt
• Lemon curd

Toppings
• Fresh fruits: blueberries, strawberries or bananas
• Toasted nuts
• Shredded sweetened coconut
• Sprinkles
• Mini chocolate chips
• Mini marshmallows
• Granola
• Dried fruit: cherries or cranberries
• Crumbled cooked bacon

Finishing Touches
• Honey
• Maple syrup
• Caramel sauce
• Chocolate sauce
• Whipped cream
• Cinnamon sugar

OVERNIGHT YEAST WAFFLES

⑤ᵢ

HOME FRIES

When I was little, my dad and I would get up early on Sundays and make these potatoes for the family. The rest of the gang would be awakened by the tempting aroma.
—Teresa Koide, Manchester, CT

- -

Prep: 25 min. • **Cook:** 15 min./batch.
Makes: 8 servings

1	lb. bacon, chopped
8	medium potatoes (about 3 lbs.), peeled and cut into ½-in. pieces
1	large onion, chopped
1	tsp. salt
½	tsp. pepper

1. In a large skillet, cook chopped bacon over medium-low heat until crisp. Remove bacon from pan with slotted spoon and drain on paper towels. Remove bacon drippings from pan and reserve.
2. Working in batches, add ¼ cup bacon drippings, potatoes, onion, salt and pepper to pan; toss to coat. Cook and stir over medium-low heat until potatoes are golden brown and tender, 15-20 minutes, adding more drippings as needed. Stir in cooked bacon; serve immediately.
1 cup: 349 cal., 21g fat (8g sat. fat), 33mg chol., 681mg sod., 31g carb. (3g sugars, 2g fiber), 10g pro.

MAKE AHEAD

OVERNIGHT YEAST WAFFLES

Starting the day with a hearty breakfast is a step in the right direction when you're trying to follow a healthy eating plan.
—Mary Balcomb, Florence, OR

- -

Prep: 15 min. + chilling
Cook: 5 min./batch
Makes: 10 servings

1	pkg. (¼ oz.) active dry yeast
½	cup warm water (110° to 115°)
1	tsp. sugar
2	cups warm 2% milk (110° to 115°)
½	cup butter, melted
2	large eggs
2¾	cups all-purpose flour
1	tsp. salt
½	tsp. baking soda

1. In a large bowl, dissolve yeast in warm water. Add sugar; let stand for 5 minutes. Add the milk, butter and eggs; mix well. Combine flour and salt; stir into milk mixture. Cover and refrigerate overnight.
2. Stir batter; add baking soda and stir well. Bake waffles in a preheated waffle iron according to manufacturer's directions until golden brown.
2 waffles: 220 cal., 12g fat (7g sat. fat), 74mg chol., 366mg sod., 22g carb. (3g sugars, 1g fiber), 6g pro.

HOW-TO

DIY Waffle Sliders
Cook waffle batter by heaping tablespoonfuls in the waffle iron. Sandwich with whipped cream, berries or other toppers.

CHOCOLATE LOVER'S PANCAKES

These indulgent chocolate pancakes are light and fluffy, with a rich but not-too-sweet flavor from the cocoa. They're delicious with either maple or chocolate syrup—and even better with both swirled together over them!
—Harland Johns, Leesburg, TX

- -

Prep: 15 min. • **Cook:** 5 min./batch
Makes: 4 servings

- 1 **cup all-purpose flour**
- ¼ **cup baking cocoa**
- 2 **Tbsp. sugar**
- 1 **tsp. baking powder**
- ½ **tsp. baking soda**
- ½ **tsp. salt**
- 1 **cup buttermilk**
- 1 **large egg, room temperature**
- 2 **Tbsp. butter, melted**
- 1 **tsp. vanilla extract**
  Maple syrup and chocolate syrup

1. In a large bowl, whisk flour, cocoa, sugar, baking powder, baking soda and salt. In another bowl, whisk buttermilk, egg, melted butter and vanilla until blended. Add to dry ingredients and stir just until moistened.

2. Place a greased large nonstick skillet over medium heat. In batches, pour batter by ¼ cupfuls onto skillet; cook until bubbles on top begin to pop and bottoms are golden brown. Turn; cook until second side is golden brown. Serve with syrups.

2 pancakes: 271 cal., 8g fat (4g sat. fat), 64mg chol., 753mg sod., 42g carb. (16g sugars, 2g fiber), 8g pro.

CHOCOLATE LOVER'S PANCAKES

TROPICAL BERRY
SMOOTHIES

TROPICAL BERRY SMOOTHIES

This fruity, healthy smoothie is a big hit with kids and adults alike because it tastes like a treat while delivering the vitamins. It's easy to increase based on the number of people you'll be serving.
—Hillary Engler,
Cape Girardeau, MO

- -

Takes: 10 min. • **Makes:** 2 servings

1   cup pina colada juice blend
1   container (6 oz.) vanilla yogurt
⅓   cup frozen unsweetened strawberries
¼   cup frozen mango chunks
¼   cup frozen unsweetened blueberries

In a blender, combine all ingredients; cover and process for 30 seconds or until smooth. Pour into chilled glasses; serve immediately.

1¼ cups: 172 cal., 2g fat (1g sat. fat), 4mg chol., 62mg sod., 35g carb. (32g sugars, 2g fiber), 5g pro.

Flavors of Mexico

Choose steak tacos or a Tex-Mex Benedict, add sides and sweets, and wash it down with classic horchata.

GRILLED ONION & SKIRT
STEAK TACOS

SAUTEED SQUASH WITH
TOMATOES & ONIONS

GRILLED ONION & SKIRT STEAK TACOS

I grew up watching my mother and grandmother in the kitchen. My grandparents came from Mexico. This steak marinated in beer and lime juice honors their passion for cooking.
—Adan Franco, Milwaukee, WI

- -

Prep: 15 min. + marinating
Grill: 5 min. • **Makes:** 8 servings

- 2 beef skirt or flank steaks (1 lb. each)
- 1 bottle (12 oz.) beer
- ¼ cup lime juice
- 3 Tbsp. olive oil, divided
- 8 spring onions or green onions
- 1¼ tsp. salt, divided
- ¾ tsp. pepper, divided
  Corn tortillas, minced fresh cilantro and lime wedges

1. Pound beef with a meat mallet to tenderize. In a large bowl, mix beer, lime juice and 2 Tbsp. oil until blended. Add beef to marinade; turn to coat. Refrigerate, covered, at least 30 minutes.
2. Meanwhile, cut partially through onions, leaving tops intact. Drizzle with remaining oil; sprinkle with ¼ tsp. salt and ¼ tsp. pepper.
3. Drain beef, discarding marinade; sprinkle with the remaining salt and pepper. On a greased grill rack, grill steaks and onions, covered, over medium heat or broil 4 in. from the heat until meat reaches desired doneness (for medium-rare, a thermometer should read 135°; medium, 140°; medium-well, 145°) and onions are crisp-tender, 2-4 minutes on each side. Cut steak diagonally across the grain into thin slices. Serve with tortillas, onions, cilantro and lime wedges.

1 serving: 288 cal., 14g fat (5g sat. fat), 67mg chol., 458mg sod., 7g carb. (3g sugars, 1g fiber), 31g pro.

SAUTEED SQUASH WITH TOMATOES & ONIONS

My favorite meals show a love of family and food. This zucchini dish with tomatoes is like a scaled-down ratatouille.
—Adan Franco, Milwaukee, WI

- -

Takes: 20 min. • **Makes:** 8 servings

- 2 Tbsp. olive oil
- 1 medium onion, finely chopped
- 4 medium zucchini, chopped
- 2 large tomatoes, finely chopped
- 1 tsp. salt
- ¼ tsp. pepper

1. In a large skillet, heat olive oil over medium-high heat. Add chopped onion; cook and stir until tender, 2-4 minutes. Add zucchini; cook and stir 3 minutes.
2. Stir in tomatoes, salt and pepper; cook and stir until squash is tender, 4-6 minutes longer. Serve with a slotted spoon.

¾ cup: 60 cal., 4g fat (1g sat. fat), 0 chol., 306mg sod., 6g carb. (4g sugars, 2g fiber), 2g pro.
Diabetic exchanges: 1 vegetable, ½ fat.

LIME-MARINATED SHRIMP SALAD

Ceviche is a seafood dish of raw fish marinated in citrus juice, which cooks the fish without heat. This version starts with cooked shrimp and adds tomatoes, cucumbers and serrano peppers.
—Adan Franco, Milwaukee, WI

- -

Prep: 25 min. + chilling
Makes: 10 cups

1	**large onion, quartered**
2	**to 4 serrano peppers, seeded and coarsely chopped**
2	**medium cucumbers, peeled, quartered and seeds removed**
2	**large tomatoes, cut into chunks**
6	**green onions, coarsely chopped (about ¾ cup)**
2	**lbs. peeled and deveined cooked shrimp (26-30 per lb.)**
¾	**cup lime juice**
½	**tsp. salt**
¼	**tsp. pepper**
	Tortilla chips or tostada shells

1. Place onion and peppers in a food processor; pulse until very finely chopped. Transfer to a large bowl. Place cucumbers, tomatoes and green onions in food processor; pulse until finely chopped. Add to bowl.

2. Pulse shrimp in processor until chopped. Add shrimp, lime juice, salt and pepper to vegetable mixture; toss to coat. Chill. Serve with tortilla chips or tostada shells.

½ cup: 61 cal., 1g fat (0 sat. fat), 69mg chol., 128mg sod., 4g carb. (1g sugars, 1g fiber), 10g pro. **Diabetic exchanges:** 1 lean meat.

MAKE AHEAD

TRES LECHES CUPCAKES

A sweet trio of milks makes these little cakes so good. They soak overnight, making them a great make-ahead dessert.
—*Taste of Home* Test Kitchen

- -

Prep: 45 min. + chilling
Bake: 15 min. + cooling
Makes: 4 dozen

1	**pkg. yellow cake mix (regular size)**
1¼	**cups water**
4	**large eggs, room temperature**
1	**can (14 oz.) sweetened condensed milk**
1	**cup coconut milk**
1	**can (5 oz.) evaporated milk**
	Dash salt

WHIPPED CREAM

3	**cups heavy whipping cream**
⅓	**cup confectioners' sugar**
	Assorted fresh berries

1. Preheat oven to 350°. Line 48 muffin cups with paper liners.

2. In a large bowl, combine cake mix, water and eggs; beat on low speed 30 seconds. Beat on medium for 2 minutes.

3. Fill prepared cups halfway, allowing room in liners for milk mixture. Bake 11-13 minutes or until a toothpick inserted in center comes out clean. Cool 5 minutes before removing from pans to wire racks; cool slightly.

4. Place cupcakes in 15x10x1-in. pans. Poke holes in cupcakes with a skewer. In a small bowl, mix milks and salt; spoon scant 1 Tbsp. mixture over each cupcake. Refrigerate, covered, overnight.

5. In a large bowl, beat cream until it begins to thicken. Add confectioners' sugar; beat until soft peaks form. Spread over cupcakes; top with berries. Store in the refrigerator.

1 cupcake: 143 cal., 9g fat (5g sat. fat), 40mg chol., 99mg sod., 15g carb. (11g sugars, 0 fiber), 2g pro.

TRES LECHES CUPCAKES

SOUTHWESTERN EGGS
BENEDICT WITH
AVOCADO SAUCE

SOUTHWESTERN EGGS BENEDICT WITH AVOCADO SAUCE

I frequently make this spicy spinoff of classic eggs Benedict for my husband, who loves breakfast. I like the heat from the jalapenos and that the avocado sauce is a healthier substitute for the typical hollandaise.
—Kara Scow, McKinney, TX

- -

Takes: 30 min. • **Makes:** 6 servings

- 1   medium ripe avocado, peeled and cubed
- ½   cup water
- ½   cup reduced-fat sour cream
- ¼   cup fresh cilantro leaves
- 2   Tbsp. ranch salad dressing mix
- 2   Tbsp. lime juice
- 2   Tbsp. pickled jalapeno slices
- 1   garlic clove, chopped
- ¼   tsp. salt
- ⅛   tsp. pepper
- 6   slices whole wheat bread, toasted
- 12   slices deli ham
- 6   slices Monterey Jack cheese
- 2   tsp. white vinegar
- 6   large eggs

1. Preheat oven to 425°. Place first 10 ingredients in a blender; cover and process until smooth.
2. Place toast on a baking sheet. Top each piece with 2 slices of ham and 1 slice cheese. Bake until cheese is melted, 6-8 minutes.
3. Meanwhile, place 2-3 in. of water in a large saucepan or skillet with high sides; add vinegar. Bring to a boil; adjust heat to maintain a gentle simmer. Break cold eggs, 1 at a time, into a small bowl; holding bowl close to surface of water, slip egg into pan.
4. Cook, uncovered, until whites are completely set and yolks begin to thicken but are not hard, 3-5 minutes. Using a slotted spoon, lift eggs out of water. Serve immediately with ham and cheese toasts and avocado mixture.

1 serving: 345 cal., 19g fat (8g sat. fat), 232mg chol., 1069mg sod., 19g carb. (4g sugars, 3g fiber), 25g pro.

HORCHATA

HORCHATA

The mixture of ground rice and almonds is accented with a hint of lime in this popular drink. Depending on your preference, you can use more or less of the water to create a thinner or creamier beverage.
—James Schend,
Pleasant Prairie, WI

Prep: 5 min. + standing
Process: 10 min. • **Makes:** 6 servings

¾	cup uncooked long grain rice
2	cups blanched almonds
1	cinnamon stick (3 in.)
1½	tsp. grated lime zest
4	cups hot water
1	cup sugar
1	cup cold water
	Ground cinnamon, optional
	Lime slices, optional

1. Place rice in a blender; cover and process 2-3 minutes or until very fine. Transfer to a large bowl; add almonds, cinnamon stick, lime zest and hot water. Let stand, covered, at room temperature 8 hours.
2. Discard cinnamon stick. Transfer rice mixture to a blender; cover and process 3-4 minutes or until smooth. Add sugar; process until the sugar is dissolved.
3. Place a strainer over a pitcher; line with double-layered cheesecloth. Pour rice mixture over cheesecloth; using a ladle, press mixture through strainer. Stir in cold water.
4. Serve over ice. If desired, sprinkle with cinnamon and serve with lime.
¾ cup: 134 cal., 3g fat (2g sat. fat), 12mg chol., 82mg sod., 25g carb. (21g sugars, 0 fiber), 3g pro.

FRUIT SALAD SALSA WITH CINNAMON TORTILLA CHIPS

Salsa with apples, berries and nectarines makes a refreshing side dish. We scoop it up using tortilla chips sprinkled with cinnamon and sugar.
—Adan Franco, Milwaukee, WI

- -

Prep: 15 min. • **Cook:** 5 min./batch
Makes: 6 cups salsa (80 chips)

MEXICAN CINNAMON COOKIES

- 2 medium apples, finely chopped
- 2 medium nectarines or peaches, finely chopped
- 2 cups chopped fresh strawberries
- 1 cup fresh blueberries
- 2 Tbsp. lemon juice
  Dash salt

CHIPS
- ½ cup sugar
- 2 Tbsp. ground cinnamon
- 10 flour tortillas (8 in.)
  Oil for frying

1. In a large bowl, combine the first 6 ingredients. Refrigerate until serving.
2. In a small bowl, mix the sugar and cinnamon. Cut each tortilla into 8 wedges. In an electric skillet, heat 1 in. of oil to 375°. Fry chips, several at a time, 2-3 minutes on each side or until golden brown. Drain on paper towels.
3. Transfer chips to a large bowl; sprinkle with sugar mixture and gently toss to coat. Serve with salsa.
¼ cup salsa with 3 chips: 122 cal., 4g fat (1g sat. fat), 0 chol., 104mg sod., 21g carb. (8g sugars, 2g fiber), 2g pro.

MEXICAN CINNAMON COOKIES

My extended family shares a meal every Sunday. All the aunts and uncles take turns bringing everything from main dishes to desserts like these traditional Mexican cinnamon cookie called reganadas.
—Adan Franco, Milwaukee, WI

- -

Prep: 25 min. **Bake:** 10 min./batch
Makes: 12 dozen

- 1 large egg, separated
- 2 cups lard
- 4 cups all-purpose flour
- 3 tsp. baking powder
- 1½ tsp. ground cinnamon
  Dash salt
- ¾ cup sugar

COATING
- ⅔ cup sugar
- 4 tsp. ground cinnamon
  Confectioners' sugar, optional

1. Place egg white in a small bowl; let stand at room temperature 30 minutes.
2. Preheat oven to 375°. In a large bowl, beat lard until creamy. In another bowl, whisk flour, baking powder, cinnamon and salt; gradually beat into lard.
3. Beat egg white on high speed until stiff peaks form. Gently whisk in sugar and egg yolk. Gradually beat into lard mixture. Turn onto a floured surface; knead gently 8-10 times.
4. Divide dough into 6 portions. On a lightly floured surface, roll each portion into a 24-in.-long rope; cut diagonally into 1-in. pieces. Place 1 in. apart on ungreased baking sheets. Bake 8-10 minutes or until edges are light brown. Cool on pans 2 minutes.
5. Mix sugar and cinnamon; roll warm cookies in cinnamon-sugar mixture or in confectioners' sugar. Cool on wire racks.
1 cookie: 47 cal., 3g fat (1g sat. fat), 4mg chol., 10mg sod., 5g carb. (2g sugars, 0 fiber), 0 pro.

Celebrate Mom

Treat your mother to a spread that's almost as wonderful as she is.

MIXED BERRY
FRENCH TOAST BAKE

PINK
RHUBARB
PUNCH

MIXED BERRY FRENCH TOAST BAKE

I love this recipe! It's perfect for fuss-free holiday breakfasts or company, utterly delicious and so easy to put together the night before.

—Amy Berry, Poland, ME

- -

Prep: 20 min. + chilling
Bake: 45 min. • **Makes:** 8 servings

6	large eggs
1¾	cups fat-free milk
1	tsp. sugar
1	tsp. ground cinnamon
1	tsp. vanilla extract
¼	tsp. salt
1	loaf (1 lb.) French bread, cubed
1	pkg. (12 oz.) frozen unsweetened mixed berries
2	Tbsp. cold butter
⅓	cup packed brown sugar
	Optional: Confectioners' sugar and maple syrup

1. Whisk together first 6 ingredients. Place bread cubes in a 13x9-in. or 3-qt. baking dish coated with cooking spray. Pour egg mixture over top. Refrigerate, covered, for 8 hours or overnight.

2. Preheat oven to 350°. Remove berries from freezer and French toast from refrigerator and let stand while oven heats. Bake, covered, for 30 minutes.

3. In a small bowl, cut butter into brown sugar until crumbly. Top French toast with berries; sprinkle with brown sugar mixture. Bake, uncovered, until a knife inserted in the center comes out clean, 15-20 minutes. If desired, dust with confectioners' sugar and serve with syrup.

1 serving: 310 cal., 8g fat (3g sat. fat), 148mg chol., 517mg sod., 46g carb. (17g sugars, 3g fiber), 13g pro.

READER REVIEW

"I requested this for Mother's Day breakfast. My hubby isn't a cook, but he easily put this together. It was fantastic. I put a tiny bit of powdered sugar on top. We used a loaf of thick-sliced French toast-type bread. The whole family loved it. Hubby said he would make this again."
—JLDURON, TASTEOFHOME.COM

ASPARAGUS
BACON QUICHE

SAGE TURKEY SAUSAGE PATTIES

Turkey sausage is a good option when you want to cut salt and saturated fat. You'll love the aroma of this recipe when it's sizzling in the pan.

—Sharman Schubert, Seattle, WA

- -

Takes: 30 min. • **Makes:** 12 servings

- ¼   cup grated Parmesan cheese
- 3   Tbsp. minced fresh parsley or 1 Tbsp. dried parsley flakes
- 2   Tbsp. fresh sage or 2 tsp. dried sage leaves
- 2   garlic cloves, minced
- 1   tsp. fennel seed, crushed
- ¾   tsp. salt
- ½   tsp. pepper
- 1½ lbs. lean ground turkey
- 1   Tbsp. olive oil

1. In a large bowl, combine the first 7 ingredients. Crumble turkey over mixture and mix well. Shape into twelve 3-in. patties.

2. In a large skillet, cook patties in oil in batches over medium heat for 3-5 minutes on each side or until meat is no longer pink. Drain on paper towels if necessary.

Freeze option: Place patties on a waxed paper-lined baking sheet; cover and freeze until firm. Remove and transfer to a freezer container. To use, place patties on a baking sheet coated with cooking spray. Bake in a preheated 350° oven 15 minutes on each side or until heated through.

1 patty: 104 cal., 6g fat (2g sat. fat), 46mg chol., 227mg sod., 0 carb. (0 sugars, 0 fiber), 11g pro.

Diabetic exchanges: 1 lean meat, 1 fat.

ASPARAGUS BACON QUICHE

Lovely asparagus peeks out of every slice of this hearty quiche, which is delicious and a little different. I like to make it for special occasions—it's a welcome addition to any brunch buffet.

—Suzanne McKinley, Lyons, GA

- -

Prep: 20 min. • **Bake:** 35 min.

Makes: 8 servings

- 1   pastry shell (9 in.), unbaked
- 1   lb. fresh asparagus, trimmed and cut into 1-in. pieces
- 6   bacon strips, cooked and crumbled
- 3   large eggs
- 1½ cups half-and-half cream
- 1   cup grated Parmesan cheese, divided
- 1   Tbsp. sliced green onions
- 1   tsp. sugar
- ½   tsp. salt
- ¼   tsp. pepper
-     Pinch ground nutmeg

1. Line the unpricked crust with a double thickness of heavy-duty foil. Bake at 450° for 5 minutes; remove foil. Bake 5 minutes longer; remove from the oven and set aside.

2. Cook asparagus in a small amount of water until crisp-tender, about 3-4 minutes; drain well. Arrange the bacon and asparagus in the crust.

3. In a bowl, beat eggs; add cream, ½ cup cheese, onions, sugar, salt, pepper and nutmeg. Pour over asparagus. Sprinkle with remaining Parmesan cheese.

4. Bake at 400° for 10 minutes. Reduce heat to 350°; bake until a knife inserted in the center comes out clean, 23-25 minutes longer.

1 piece: 296 cal., 19g fat (9g sat. fat), 119mg chol., 557mg sod., 18g carb. (5g sugars, 1g fiber), 12g pro.

SAGE TURKEY
SAUSAGE PATTIES

CONTEST-WINNING RASPBERRY CHOCOLATE TORTE

Dazzle your guests with this striking cake that looks fancy but is actually easy to decorate.
—Amy Helbig, Mesa, AZ

- -

Prep: 40 min.
Bake: 20 min. + cooling
Makes: 12 servings

- 1 **cup butter, softened**
- 2 **cups sugar**
- 4 **large eggs, room temperature**
- 1 **tsp. vanilla extract**
- 1½ **cups all-purpose flour**
- ⅓ **cup baking cocoa**

GLAZE

- ¼ **cup boiling water**
- 4 **tsp. raspberry gelatin**
- 2 **Tbsp. seedless raspberry jam**

TOPPING

- 2 **cups semisweet chocolate chips**
- 2 **cartons (8 oz. each) frozen whipped topping, thawed**
- 2 **cups fresh raspberries**
Optional: Confectioners' sugar and chocolate curls

1. Line a greased 15x10x1-in. baking pan with waxed paper; grease the paper. In a large bowl, cream butter and sugar until light and fluffy, 5-7 minutes. Add the eggs, 1 at a time, beating well after each addition. Beat in vanilla. Combine flour and cocoa; gradually beat into creamed mixture.

2. Transfer to prepared pan. Bake at 350° for 20-25 minutes or until a toothpick inserted in center comes out clean. Cool 5 minutes before inverting onto a wire rack to cool completely. Carefully remove paper.

3. For glaze, stir water and gelatin until gelatin is dissolved. Stir in raspberry jam. Brush evenly over bottom of cake. Trim edges; cut cake widthwise into thirds.

4. For topping, in a microwave, melt chips; stir until smooth. Fold in half the whipped topping until blended; fold in remaining whipped topping (mixture will be thick).

5. Place 1 cake layer on a serving platter; spread with ¾ cup topping. Repeat layers; top with raspberries. If desired, decorate top of cake with confectioners' sugar and chocolate curls.

1 slice: 614 cal., 32g fat (21g sat. fat), 111mg chol., 138mg sod., 79g carb. (58g sugars, 4g fiber), 6g pro.

PINK RHUBARB PUNCH

This pretty punch has a crisp, refreshing taste that everyone will love.
—Rebecca Mininger, Jeromesville, OH

Prep: 30 min. + chilling
Makes: 20 servings (about 5 qt.)

- 8 cups chopped fresh or frozen rhubarb
- 8 cups water
- 2½ cups sugar
- 2 Tbsp. strawberry gelatin powder
- 2 cups boiling water
- 2 cups pineapple juice
- ¼ cup lemon juice
- 6 cups ginger ale, chilled
  Optional: Fresh pineapple wedges, sliced strawberries and sliced lemons

1. In a Dutch oven, bring rhubarb and water to a boil. Reduce heat; simmer, uncovered, for 10 minutes. Drain, reserving liquid (save rhubarb for another use).
2. In a large bowl, dissolve sugar and gelatin powder in boiling water. Stir in pineapple and lemon juices. Stir in the rhubarb liquid; refrigerate until chilled.
3. Just before serving, pour into a punch bowl and stir in ginger ale. If desired, garnish with fruit.

1 cup: 152 cal., 0 fat (0 sat. fat), 0 chol., 11mg sod., 38g carb. (37g sugars, 1g fiber), 1g pro.

PECAN
COFFEE CAKE

Country-Style Breakfast

These hearty choices will have everyone
feeling home sweet home on the range.

COLD-BREW
COFFEE

CAMPFIRE
SCRAMBLED EGGS

SOUR CREAM
SWISS STEAK

SAUSAGE
HASH

COWBOY
CORNBREAD

SOUR CREAM
SWISS STEAK

SOUR CREAM SWISS STEAK

I spent a year searching for new beef recipes. This is the dish that my family raves about, and they agree that it's a wonderful change from regular Swiss steak.
—Barb Benting, Grand Rapids, MI

- -

Prep: 50 min. • **Bake:** 1½ hours
Makes: 8 servings

⅓ cup plus 3 Tbsp. all-purpose flour, divided
1½ tsp. each salt, pepper, paprika and ground mustard

3 lbs. beef top round steak, cut into serving-size pieces
3 Tbsp. canola oil
3 Tbsp. butter
1½ cups water
1½ cups sour cream
1 cup finely chopped onion
2 garlic cloves, minced
⅓ cup soy sauce
¼ to ⅓ cup packed brown sugar
Additional paprika, optional

1. In a shallow bowl, combine ⅓ cup of flour, salt, pepper, paprika and ground mustard; dredge the steak.
2. In a large skillet, heat oil and butter. Cook steak on both sides until browned. Carefully add water; cover and simmer for 30 minutes.
3. In a bowl, combine the sour cream, onion, garlic, soy sauce, brown sugar and remaining flour; stir until smooth. Transfer steaks to a greased 2½-qt. baking dish; add sour cream mixture.
4. Cover and bake at 325° for 1½ hours or until tender. Sprinkle with paprika if desired.

1 serving: 460 cal., 23g fat (10g sat. fat), 137mg chol., 1173mg sod., 17g carb. (10g sugars, 1g fiber), 43g pro.

SAUGAGE HASH

5i

Since we always have plenty of pork sausage around, I use this handy recipe when we need a quick meal. The colorful vegetables give the hash a bold look to match its flavor.
—Virginia Krites, Cridersville, OH

Prep: 10 min. • **Cook:** 30 min.
Makes: 6 servings

- 1 lb. bulk pork sausage
- 1 medium onion, chopped
- 2 medium carrots, grated
- 1 medium green pepper, chopped
- 3 cups diced cooked potatoes
- ½ tsp. salt
- ¼ tsp. pepper

In a large cast-iron or other heavy skillet, cook the sausage over medium heat until no longer pink; drain. Add the onion, carrots and green pepper; cook until tender. Stir in the potatoes, salt and pepper. Reduce heat; cook and stir until lightly browned and heated through, about 20 minutes.

1 cup: 245 cal., 14g fat (5g sat. fat), 27mg chol., 519mg sod., 22g carb. (5g sugars, 3g fiber), 8g pro.

COWBOY CORNBREAD

This cornbread is rich and sweet. It's luscious with ham.
—Karen Ann Bland, Gove, KS

Prep: 15 min. • **Bake:** 25 min.
Makes: 12 servings

- 2 cups biscuit/baking mix
- 1 cup yellow cornmeal
- ¾ cup sugar
- ½ tsp. baking soda
- ½ tsp. salt
- 2 large eggs, room temperature
- 1 cup butter, melted
- 1 cup half-and-half cream

1. In a large bowl, combine the first 5 ingredients. In another bowl, combine the eggs, butter and cream; stir into the dry ingredients just until moistened. Spread into a greased 13x9-in. baking pan.
2. Bake at 350° until a toothpick inserted in the center comes out clean, 25-30 minutes. Serve warm.

1 piece: 345 cal., 21g fat (12g sat. fat), 85mg chol., 532mg sod., 34g carb. (14g sugars, 1g fiber), 4g pro.

READER REVIEW
"*Fabulous! I was having 14 dinner guests and needed a good cornbread. I doubled this recipe and baked it in an 11x15-in. pan at 325° for 40 minutes. It turned out wonderfully! The best cornbread I've tasted in a long, long time. Served with honey and butter, it complemented a vegetarian chili.*"
—DEBBIE309, TASTEOFHOME.COM

SAUSAGE HASH

MAKE AHEAD 5i

COLD-BREW COFFEE

Cold-brewing reduces the acidity of coffee, which enhances its natural sweetness and complex flavors. Even those who take hot coffee with sugar and cream might find themselves sipping cold-brew coffee plain.
—*Taste of Home* Test Kitchen

Prep: 10 min. + chilling
Makes: 8 servings

- 1 **cup coarsely ground medium-roast coffee**
- 1 **cup hot water (205°)**
- 6 **to 7 cups cold water**
- 2% **milk or half-and-half cream, optional**

1. Place the coffee grounds in a clean glass container. Pour hot water over the grounds; let stand 10 minutes. Stir in cold water. Cover and refrigerate for 12-24 hours. (The longer the coffee sits, the stronger the flavor.)
2. Strain the coffee through a fine mesh sieve; discard grounds. Strain the coffee again through a coffee filter; discard grounds. Serve over ice, with milk or cream if desired. Store in the refrigerator for up to 2 weeks.
1 cup: 2 cal., 0 fat (0 sat. fat), 0 chol., 4mg sod., 0 carb. (0 sugars, 0 fiber), 0 pro.

BRIGHT IDEA

Freeze some coffee in ice cube trays. The frozen coffee cubes will chill your beverage without watering it down.

CAMPFIRE SCRAMBLED EGGS

Every bit as quick as scrambled eggs are meant to be, my dish is also hearty, colorful and just a bit different.

—Fern Raleigh, Windom, KS

- -

Takes: 20 min. • **Makes:** 6 servings

- 12 **large eggs**
- 1½ **cups 2% milk, divided**
- ½ **to 1 tsp. salt**
- ¼ **tsp. pepper**
- 2 **Tbsp. diced pimientos**
- 2 **Tbsp. minced fresh parsley or chives**
- 2 **Tbsp. all-purpose flour**
- ¼ **cup butter, cubed**

In a large bowl, beat eggs and 1 cup milk. Add the salt, pepper, pimientos and parsley. In a small bowl, combine the flour and remaining milk until smooth; stir into egg mixture. In a large skillet, melt butter over medium heat. Add egg mixture. Cook and stir over medium heat until eggs are completely set.

1 serving: 185 cal., 11g fat (4g sat. fat), 377mg chol., 369mg sod., 6g carb. (3g sugars, 0 fiber), 15g pro.

PECAN COFFEE CAKE

My mom serves this nutty coffee cake for Christmas breakfast each year. The simple recipe is a big timesaver on such an event-filled morning. Everyone loves the crunchy topping.

—Becky Wax, Tuscola, IL

- -

Prep: 15 min. • **Bake:** 30 min.
Makes: 15 servings

PECAN
COFFEE CAKE

- 1 **pkg. yellow cake mix (regular size)**
- 1 **pkg. (3.4 oz.) instant vanilla pudding mix**
- 1 **cup sour cream**
- 4 **large eggs, room temperature**
- ⅓ **cup canola oil**
- 2 **tsp. vanilla extract**
- ⅔ **cup chopped pecans**
- ⅓ **cup sugar**
- 2 **tsp. ground cinnamon**
- ½ **cup confectioners' sugar**
- 2 **Tbsp. orange juice**

1. In a large bowl, beat the first 6 ingredients on low speed for 30 seconds. Beat on medium for 2 minutes. Pour into a greased 13x9-in. baking pan. Combine pecans, sugar and cinnamon; sprinkle over batter. Cut through batter with a knife to swirl.

2. Bake at 350° for 30-35 minutes or until a toothpick inserted in the center comes out clean.

3. Meanwhile, in a small bowl, combine confectioners' sugar and orange juice until smooth; drizzle over warm coffee cake. Cool on a wire rack.

1 piece: 335 cal., 16g fat (4g sat. fat), 67mg chol., 332mg sod., 44g carb. (29g sugars, 1g fiber), 4g pro.

Ladies' Luncheon

Gather friends for some quality girl time and this elegant array.

CUCUMBER PARTY SANDWICHES

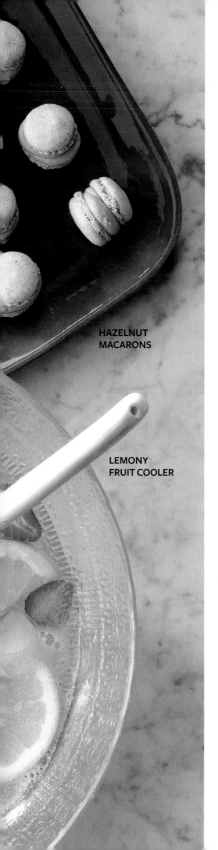

HAZELNUT MACARONS

LEMONY FRUIT COOLER

CUCUMBER PARTY SANDWICHES

This is one of my favorite appetizers. We have lots of pig roasts here in Kentucky, and these small sandwiches are perfect to serve while the pig is cooking.
—Rebecca Rose,
Mount Washington, KY

- -

Prep: 20 min. + standing
Makes: 2½ dozen

- 1 pkg. (8 oz.) cream cheese, softened
- 2 Tbsp. mayonnaise
- 2 tsp. Italian salad dressing mix
- 30 slices cocktail rye or pumpernickel bread
- 60 thin cucumber slices
  Optional: Fresh dill sprigs and slivered red pearl onions

1. Beat cream cheese, mayonnaise and dressing mix until blended; let stand 30 minutes.
2. Spread cream cheese mixture on bread. Top each with 2 cucumber slices and, if desired, dill and red onion slivers. Refrigerate, covered, until serving.

1 open-faced sandwich: 53 cal., 4g fat (2g sat. fat), 8mg chol., 92mg sod., 4g carb. (1g sugars, 1g fiber), 1g pro.

LEMONY FRUIT COOLER

This punch looks so pretty with all the colorful fruit floating in the bowl. It has a refreshing taste and is easy to put together.
—Dawn Shackelford,
Fort Worth, TX

- -

Takes: 10 min. • **Makes:** 2½ qt.

- ½ cup sugar
- ½ cup lemon juice
- 4 cups cold white grape juice
- 1 liter club soda, chilled
- 1 orange, halved and sliced
- ½ cup sliced strawberries
- ½ cup sliced fresh peaches
  Ice cubes, optional

1. In a punch bowl or pitcher, mix sugar and lemon juice until sugar is dissolved. Stir in grape juice.
2. To serve, stir in club soda and fruit. If desired, serve with ice.

1 cup: 107 cal., 0 fat (0 sat. fat), 0 chol., 29mg sod., 28g carb. (25g sugars, 0 fiber), 0 pro.

BRIGHT IDEA

Keep the fruit cooler cold and flavorful on a buffet with special-made ice cubes. Freeze your favorite lemonade in an ice cube tray or mini muffin tins, with or without sliced berries or lemons inside.

CAYENNE PECANS

These toasted nuts are crunchy and mildly seasoned. The cayenne pepper adds a little zing.
—Phyllis Stanley, Avery, TX

Takes: 20 min. • **Makes:** 4 cups

- ¼ cup butter, cubed
- 3 Tbsp. Worcestershire sauce
- ¾ tsp. salt
- ¾ tsp. cayenne pepper
- 4 cups pecan halves (about 15 oz.)

1. Preheat oven to 350°. In a microwave, melt butter; stir in Worcestershire sauce, salt and cayenne. Toss pecans with butter mixture; spread evenly in an ungreased 15x10x1-in. pan.
2. Bake until lightly toasted, about 15 minutes, stirring occasionally. Cool in pan on a wire rack. Store cooled nuts in an airtight container.
⅓ cup: 266 cal., 28g fat (4g sat. fat), 10mg chol., 220mg sod., 5g carb. (2g sugars, 3g fiber), 3g pro.

HAM SALAD

I first made this for a shower, and everyone raved about it. Now when I go to a potluck, I take it, along with copies of the recipe.
—Patricia Reed, Pine Bluff, AR

Takes: 15 min. • **Makes:** 10 servings

- ¾ cup mayonnaise
- ½ cup finely chopped celery
- ¼ cup sliced green onions
- 2 Tbsp. minced fresh chives
- 1 Tbsp. honey
- 2 tsp. spicy brown mustard
- ½ tsp. Worcestershire sauce
- ½ tsp. seasoned salt
- 5 cups diced fully cooked ham or turkey
- ⅓ cup chopped pecans and almonds, toasted
  Slider buns, split, optional

1. Mix first 8 ingredients. Stir in ham. Refrigerate, covered, until serving.
2. Stir in pecans before serving. If desired, serve on buns.
½ cup ham salad: 254 cal., 20g fat (3g sat. fat), 43mg chol., 1023mg sod., 4g carb. (2g sugars, 1g fiber), 16g pro.

HAM SALAD

STRAWBERRY CHEESECAKE BITES

These treats are a perfect mouthful of strawberry, sweet cream cheese filling and just a drizzle of chocolate. Easy to fill and prepare ahead, they add tempting variety to brunch or party offerings—and make a delicious homemade gift.

—Linda Baldt, Croydon, PA

- -

Takes: 30 min. • **Makes:** 20 servings

- 1 **pkg. (8 oz.) cream cheese, softened**
- ⅓ **cup confectioners' sugar**
- ¼ **tsp. vanilla extract**
- 20 **large fresh strawberries (about 1½ lbs.)**
- ¼ **cup semisweet chocolate chips**
- 1 **tsp. shortening**
  Graham cracker crumbs, optional

1. For filling, beat cream cheese, confectioners' sugar and extract until smooth.

2. Remove stems from strawberries. Using a paring knife or small melon baller, cut a 1-in.-deep opening in the stem end of strawberries. Pipe or spoon the cream cheese mixture into openings. Place on a waxed paper-lined baking sheet.

3. In a microwave, melt chocolate and shortening; stir until smooth. Drizzle over strawberries; if desired, sprinkle with the graham cracker crumbs. Refrigerate until set.

1 filled strawberry: 70 cal., 5g fat (3g sat. fat), 11mg chol., 36mg sod., 7g carb. (5g sugars, 1g fiber), 1g pro.

STRAWBERRY
CHEESECAKE BITES

⑤i

ROASTED GARLIC DEVILED EGGS

I love incorporating new flavors into old classics, and these garlic deviled eggs were a big hit with everyone! You can roast the garlic and hard-boil the eggs up to three days in advance.

—Ellen Weaver, Denver, CO

- -

Prep: 15 min.
Bake: 50 min. + cooling
Makes: 2 dozen

1	whole garlic bulb
1	Tbsp. olive oil
12	hard-boiled large eggs
½	cup mayonnaise
2	Tbsp. grated Parmesan cheese
1	tsp. paprika
	Chopped fresh chives, optional

1. Preheat oven to 350°. Remove papery outer skin from garlic bulb, but do not peel or separate the cloves. Cut off top of garlic bulb, exposing individual cloves. Drizzle cut cloves with olive oil. Wrap in foil. Bake until cloves are soft and light golden, 50-60 minutes. Unwrap; cool completely.

2. Meanwhile, cut eggs lengthwise in half. Remove yolks to a bowl; reserve whites. Squeeze garlic from skins and add to yolks; mash yolks and garlic with a fork. Stir in the mayonnaise, cheese and paprika.

3. Spoon or pipe filling into egg whites. If desired, sprinkle with chives. Refrigerate until serving.

1 stuffed egg half: 78 cal., 7g fat (1g sat. fat), 94mg chol., 62mg sod., 1g carb. (0 sugars, 0 fiber), 3g pro.

⑤i

GINGER MINT JULEP

Mint juleps aren't just for serving on Kentucky Derby day! Enjoy one while gathering with friends for a baby shower or luncheon.

—Ellen Riley, Murfreesboro, TN

- -

Prep: 15 min. + chilling
Cook: 5 min. + cooling
Makes: 10 servings

2	cups sugar
2	cups water
2	cups loosely packed chopped fresh spearmint

EACH SERVING

½	to ¾ cup crushed ice
1	oz. bourbon
2	tsp. lime juice
1½	oz. ginger beer

1. For mint syrup, place the sugar, water and chopped mint in a large saucepan; bring to a boil over medium heat. Cook until sugar is dissolved, stirring occasionally. Remove from heat; cool completely.

2. Strain syrup through a fine mesh strainer; discard mint. Refrigerate, covered, until cold, at least 2 hours.

3. For each serving, place ice in a mint julep cup or rocks glass. Add bourbon, lime juice and ¼ cup mint syrup; stir until mixture is cold. Top with ginger beer.

1 serving: 238 cal., 0 fat (0 sat. fat), 0 chol., 4mg sod., 45g carb. (44g sugars, 0 fiber), 0 pro.

GINGER MINT JULEP

HAZELNUT MACARONS

HAZELNUT MACARONS

You don't have to be an expert in French cooking to whip up these sandwich cookies. Crisp, chewy macarons require attention to detail, but they're not hard to make—and they're simply a delight to serve and eat!
—*Taste of Home* Test Kitchen

- -

Prep: 50 min.
Bake: 10 min./batch + cooling
Makes: about 5 dozen

- 6 **large egg whites**
- 1½ **cups hazelnuts, toasted**
- 2½ **cups confectioners' sugar**
    Dash salt
- ½ **cup superfine sugar**
  COFFEE BUTTERCREAM
- 1 **cup sugar**
- 6 **Tbsp. water**
- 6 **large egg yolks**
- 4 **tsp. instant espresso powder**
- 1 **tsp. vanilla extract**
- 1½ **cups butter, softened**
- 6 **Tbsp. confectioners' sugar**

1. Place egg whites in a small bowl; let stand at room temperature for 30 minutes.

2. Preheat oven to 350°. Place hazelnuts and confectioners' sugar in a food processor; pulse until nuts are finely ground.

3. Add salt to egg whites; beat on medium speed until soft peaks form. Gradually add the superfine sugar, 1 Tbsp. at a time, beating on high until stiff peaks form. Fold in the hazelnut mixture.

4. With a pastry bag, pipe 1-in.-diameter cookies 2 in. apart onto parchment-lined baking sheets. Bake until lightly browned and firm to the touch, 9-12 minutes. Transfer cookies on parchment to wire racks; cool completely.

5. For buttercream, in a heavy saucepan, bring sugar and water to a boil; cook over medium-high heat until sugar is dissolved. Remove from heat. In a small bowl, whisk a small amount of hot syrup into egg yolks; return all to pan, whisking constantly. Cook until thickened, 2-3 minutes, stirring constantly; remove from heat. Stir in espresso powder and vanilla; cool completely.

6. In a stand mixer with the whisk attachment, beat butter until creamy. Gradually beat in cooled syrup. Beat in confectioners' sugar until fluffy. Chill until mixture firms to a spreading consistency, about 10 minutes.

7. Spread about 1½ tsp. buttercream onto the bottom of each of half the cookies; top with remaining cookies. Store macarons in airtight containers in the refrigerator.

1 macaron: 117 cal., 8g fat (3g sat. fat), 31mg chol., 67mg sod., 12g carb. (11g sugars, 0 fiber), 1g pro.

Oatmeal & Smoothie Bar

Bowl guests over with wholesome, healthy smoothie bowls and hearty oats with customizable toppings.

FRUIT SMOOTHIE
BOWLS

RAISIN NUT
OATMEAL

**LIME COCONUT
SMOOTHIE BOWL**

LIME COCONUT SMOOTHIE BOWL

This bowl is the most refreshing thing on the planet!
—Madeline Butler, Denver, CO

- -

Takes: 15 min. • **Makes:** 2 servings

1	medium banana, peeled and frozen
1	cup fresh baby spinach
½	cup ice cubes
½	cup cubed fresh pineapple
½	cup chopped peeled mango or frozen mango chunks
½	cup plain Greek yogurt
¼	cup sweetened shredded coconut
3	Tbsp. honey
2	tsp. grated lime zest
1	tsp. lime juice
½	tsp. vanilla extract
1	Tbsp. spreadable cream cheese, optional
	Optional: Lime wedges, sliced banana, sliced almonds, granola, dark chocolate chips and additional shredded coconut

Place the first 11 ingredients in a blender; if desired, add cream cheese. Cover and process until smooth. Pour into chilled bowls. Serve immediately, with optional toppings if desired.

1 cup: 325 cal., 10g fat (7g sat. fat), 15mg chol., 80mg sod., 60g carb. (51g sugars, 4g fiber), 4g pro.

SLOW-COOKER COCONUT GRANOLA

Here's a versatile treat with a taste of the tropics. Mix it up by subbing dried pineapple or tropical fruits for the cherries.
—*Taste of Home* Test Kitchen

- -

Prep: 15 min. • **Cook:** 3½ hours
Makes: 6 cups

- 4   cups old-fashioned oats
- 1   cup sliced almonds
- 1   cup unsweetened coconut flakes
- 1   tsp. ground cinnamon
- 1   tsp. ground ginger
- ¼   tsp. salt
- ½   cup coconut oil, melted
- ½   cup maple syrup
- 1   cup dried cherries

1. Combine oats, almonds, coconut, cinnamon, ginger and salt in a 3-qt. slow cooker. In small bowl, whisk together oil and maple syrup. Pour into slow cooker; stir to combine. Cook, covered, on low, stirring occasionally, 3½-4 hours. Stir in cherries.

2. Transfer mixture to a baking sheet; let stand until cool.

½ cup: 343 cal., 19g fat (12g sat. fat), 0 chol., 55mg sod., 41g carb. (18g sugars, 5g fiber), 6g pro.

SLOW-COOKER
COCONUT
GRANOLA

RAISIN NUT OATMEAL

There's no better feeling than waking up to a hot ready-to-eat breakfast. This homey meal simmers away while you sleep!
—Valerie Sauber, Adelanto, CA

- -

Prep: 10 min. • **Cook:** 7 hours
Makes: 6 servings

- 3½ cups fat-free milk
- 1   large apple, peeled and chopped
- ¾   cup steel-cut oats
- ¾   cup raisins
- 3   Tbsp. brown sugar
- 4½ tsp. butter, melted
- ¾   tsp. ground cinnamon
- ½   tsp. salt
- ¼   cup chopped pecans

In a 3-qt. slow cooker coated with cooking spray, combine the first 8 ingredients. Cover and cook on low for 7-8 hours or until liquid is absorbed. Spoon oatmeal into bowls; sprinkle with pecans.

¾ cup: 289 cal., 9g fat (3g sat. fat), 10mg chol., 282mg sod., 47g carb. (28g sugars, 4g fiber), 9g pro.

READER REVIEW
"Love overnight oatmeal! This is a great recipe and the nicest thing is that you can change the add-ins if you want. "
—333MELLO333, TASTEOFHOME.COM

FRUIT SMOOTHIE BOWLS

What's not to love about smoothie bowls? They're easy, gorgeous, totally customizable and healthy. Blend up a big batch and have your friends over for a feel-good brunch.
—*Taste of Home* Test Kitchen

Takes: 15 min. • **Makes:** 6 servings

- 2½ cups 2% milk
- 2 cups frozen unsweetened sliced peaches
- 2 cups frozen unsweetened strawberries
- ½ cup orange juice
- ¼ cup honey
  Optional toppings: Fresh berries, chia seeds, pumpkin seeds, flax seeds and toasted chopped nuts

In a blender, combine half of the milk, peaches, strawberries, orange juice and honey; cover and process until smooth. Transfer to a large pitcher. Repeat, adding second batch to the same pitcher; stir to combine. Serve immediately. Add toppings as desired.

1 cup: 140 cal., 2g fat (1g sat. fat), 8mg chol., 49mg sod., 27g carb. (24g sugars, 2g fiber), 4g pro.

OVERNIGHT FLAX OATMEAL

Fans of the healthy benefits of flaxseed will enjoy this hearty oatmeal. It's full of yummy raisins and dried cranberries, too. Many variations will work, so get creative!
—Susan Smith, Ocean View, NJ

Prep: 10 min. • **Cook:** 7 hours
Makes: 4 servings

- 3 cups water
- 1 cup old-fashioned oats
- 1 cup raisins
- ½ cup dried cranberries
- ½ cup ground flaxseed
- ½ cup 2% milk
- 1 tsp. vanilla extract
- 1 tsp. molasses
  Optional: Sliced almonds, whole milk and additional molasses

In a 3-qt. slow cooker, combine all ingredients. Cover and cook on low for 7-8 hours or until the liquid is absorbed and oatmeal is tender. If desired, top with sliced almonds, whole milk and additional molasses.

1 cup: 322 cal., 9g fat (1g sat. fat), 2mg chol., 28mg sod., 63g carb. (34g sugars, 8g fiber), 9g pro.

OVERNIGHT FLAX OATMEAL

SWEET KAHLUA COFFEE

Want to perk up your java? With Kahlua, creme de cacao and a dollop of whipped cream, this chocolaty coffee makes a perfect indulgent treat.
—Ruth Gruchow, Yorba Linda, CA

- -

Prep: 10 min. • **Cook:** 3 hours
Makes: 8 servings (about 2 qt.)

- 2 **qt. hot water**
- ½ **cup Kahlua (coffee liqueur)**
- ¼ **cup creme de cacao**
- 3 **Tbsp. instant coffee granules**
- 2 **cups heavy whipping cream**
- ¼ **cup sugar**
- 1 **tsp. vanilla extract**
- 2 **Tbsp. grated semisweet chocolate**

1. In a 4-qt. slow cooker, mix water, Kahlua, creme de cacao and coffee granules. Cook, covered, on low 3-4 hours or until heated through.
2. In a large bowl, beat cream until it begins to thicken. Add sugar and vanilla; beat until soft peaks form. Serve warm coffee with whipped cream and chocolate.

1 cup: 337 cal., 23g fat (15g sat. fat), 68mg chol., 19mg sod., 21g carb. (18g sugars, 0 fiber), 2g pro.

SWEET KAHLUA COFFEE

Christmas Morning Feast

A leisurely brunch makes a fabulous present. Check it off your list with this great make-ahead menu.

THREE-CHEESE QUICHE

CHRISTMAS MORNING
SWEET ROLLS

FESTIVE
CRANBERRY
FRUIT SALAD

MONTE CRISTO CASSEROLE WITH RASPBERRY SAUCE

My husband likes the ham and cheese sandwich known as the Monte Cristo, so I came up with a baked casserole based on the classic recipe. It makes a terrific brunch dish.

—Mary Steiner, Parkville, MD

- -

Prep: 20 min. + chilling
Bake: 30 min. + standing
Makes: 10 servings (1¾ cups sauce)

- 1 loaf (1 lb.) French bread, cut into 20 slices
- 2 Tbsp. Dijon mustard
- ½ lb. sliced deli ham
- ½ lb. sliced Swiss cheese
- ½ lb. sliced deli turkey
- 6 large eggs
- 1½ cups whole milk
- 2 tsp. sugar
- 2 tsp. vanilla extract

TOPPING

- ½ cup packed brown sugar
- ¼ cup butter, softened
- ½ tsp. ground cinnamon

RASPBERRY SAUCE

- ⅓ cup sugar
- 1 Tbsp. cornstarch
- ¼ cup cold water
- ¼ cup lemon juice
- ¼ cup maple syrup
- 2 cups fresh or frozen raspberries

1. Line a greased 13x9-in. baking dish with half the bread. Spread mustard over bread. Layer with ham, cheese, turkey and remaining bread (dish will be full).

2. In a large bowl, whisk eggs, milk, sugar and vanilla; pour over top. Refrigerate, covered, overnight.

3. Preheat oven to 375°. Remove casserole from refrigerator while oven heats. In a small bowl, mix topping ingredients; sprinkle over casserole. Bake, uncovered, until golden brown, 30-40 minutes.

4. Meanwhile, in a small saucepan, combine sugar and cornstarch. Stir in the water, lemon juice and maple syrup until smooth. Add raspberries. Bring to a boil; cook and stir until thickened, about 2 minutes. Cool sauce slightly.

5. Let casserole stand 10 minutes before cutting. Serve with sauce.

1 piece with about 3 Tbsp. sauce: 476 cal., 17g fat (8g sat. fat), 167mg chol., 906mg sod., 55g carb. (29g sugars, 3g fiber), 25g pro.

MONTE CRISTO CASSEROLE WITH RASPBERRY SAUCE

**MAKE-AHEAD
EGGS BENEDICT
TOAST CUPS**

MAKE AHEAD

MAKE-AHEAD EGGS BENEDICT TOAST CUPS

When I was growing up, we had a family tradition of eggs Benedict with champagne and orange juice for Christmas breakfast. Now that I'm cooking, a fussy meal isn't my style. So I made this creation!
—Lyndsay Wells, Ladysmith, BC

- -

Prep: 30 min. • **Bake:** 10 min.
Makes: 1 dozen

6	**English muffins, split**
1	**envelope hollandaise sauce mix**
12	**slices Canadian bacon, quartered**
1	**tsp. pepper**
1	**Tbsp. olive oil**
6	**large eggs**
1	**Tbsp. butter**

1. Preheat oven to 375°. Flatten muffin halves with a rolling pin; press into greased muffin cups. Bake until lightly browned, about 10 minutes.
2. Meanwhile, prepare hollandaise sauce according to the package directions; cool slightly. Sprinkle bacon with pepper. In a large skillet, cook bacon in oil over medium heat until partially cooked but not crisp. Remove to paper towels to drain. Divide bacon among muffin cups. Wipe skillet clean.
3. Whisk eggs and ½ cup cooled hollandaise sauce until blended. In the same skillet, heat butter over medium heat. Pour in egg mixture; cook and stir until eggs are thickened and no liquid egg remains. Divide egg mixture among muffin cups; top with remaining hollandaise sauce. Bake until heated through, 8-10 minutes.

Overnight option: Refrigerate unbaked cups, covered, overnight. Bake until cups are golden brown, 10-12 minutes.

Freeze option: Cover and freeze unbaked cups in muffin cups until firm. Transfer to an airtight container; return to freezer. To use, bake cups in muffin tin as directed, increasing time to 25-30 minutes. Cover the cups loosely with foil if needed to prevent overbrowning.

1 toast cup: 199 cal., 11g fat (5g sat. fat), 114mg chol., 495mg sod., 15g carb. (2g sugars, 1g fiber), 9g pro.

CHRISTMAS MORNING SWEET ROLLS

CHRISTMAS MORNING SWEET ROLLS

These rolls have been a holiday tradition for years. The eggnog in the frosting makes them extra special on Christmas morning.
—Kimberly Williams, Brownsburg, IN

- -

Prep: 45 min. + chilling
Bake: 20 min. • **Makes:** 1 dozen

- 1   pkg. (¼ oz.) active dry yeast
- 1   cup warm water (110° to 115°)
- ½   cup sugar
- 1   tsp. salt
- 4   to 4½ cups all-purpose flour
- ¼   cup canola oil
- 1   large egg, room temperature

FILLING

- ⅓   cup sugar
- 1½   tsp. ground cinnamon
- ¼   tsp. ground nutmeg
- 3   Tbsp. butter, softened

FROSTING

- 2½   cups confectioners' sugar
- 5   Tbsp. butter, softened
- ½   tsp. ground cinnamon
- ½   tsp. vanilla extract
- 2   to 3 Tbsp. eggnog

1. In a small bowl, dissolve yeast in warm water. In a large bowl, combine sugar, salt, 1 cup flour, oil, egg and the yeast mixture; beat on medium speed until smooth. Stir in enough remaining flour to form a soft dough (dough will be sticky).

2. Do not knead. Place in a greased bowl, turning once to grease the top. Cover and refrigerate overnight.

3. For filling, in a small bowl, mix sugar, cinnamon and nutmeg. Punch down dough; turn onto a lightly floured surface. Roll into a 18x8-in. rectangle. Spread with butter to within ½ in. of edges; sprinkle with sugar mixture. Roll up jelly-roll style, starting with a long side; pinch seam to seal. Cut into 12 slices.

4. Place in a greased 13x9-in. baking pan, cut side down. Cover with a kitchen towel; let rise in a warm place until doubled, about 45 minutes.

5. Preheat oven to 350°. Bake rolls until golden brown, 20-25 minutes. Place pan on a wire rack. Beat the confectioners' sugar, butter, ground cinnamon, vanilla extract and enough eggnog to reach desired consistency; spread over warm rolls.

1 roll: 424 cal., 13g fat (5g sat. fat), 37mg chol., 267mg sod., 72g carb. (39g sugars, 2g fiber), 5g pro.

FESTIVE CRANBERRY FRUIT SALAD

This fruit salad is a tradition on my Christmas table. It goes together quickly, which is a plus on such a busy day.

—Rousheen Arel Wolf, Delta Junction, AK

Takes: 25 min. • **Makes:** 14 servings

1 pkg. (12 oz.) fresh or frozen cranberries
¾ cup water
½ cup sugar
5 medium apples, diced
2 medium firm bananas, sliced
1½ cups fresh or frozen blueberries, thawed
1 can (11 oz.) mandarin oranges, undrained
1 cup fresh or frozen raspberries, thawed
¾ cup fresh strawberries, halved

1. In a large saucepan, combine the cranberries, water and sugar. Cook and stir over medium heat until berries pop, about 15 minutes. Remove from the heat; cool slightly.
2. In a large bowl, combine the remaining ingredients. Add the cranberry mixture; stir gently. Refrigerate until serving.
¾ cup: 105 cal., 0 fat (0 sat. fat), 0 chol., 2mg sod., 27g carb. (21g sugars, 4g fiber), 1g pro.

MAKE AHEAD
THREE-CHEESE QUICHE

Try eggs and cheese at their best. Guests often mention how tall, light and fluffy my crustless quiche is. You'll love it!

—Judy Reagan, Hannibal, MO

Prep: 15 min.
Bake: 45 min. + standing
Makes: 6 servings

7 large eggs
5 large egg yolks
1 cup heavy whipping cream
1 cup half-and-half cream
1 cup shredded part-skim mozzarella cheese
¾ cup shredded sharp cheddar cheese, divided
½ cup shredded Swiss cheese
2 Tbsp. finely chopped oil-packed sun-dried tomatoes
1½ tsp. salt-free seasoning blend
¼ tsp. dried basil

1. Preheat oven to 350°. In a large bowl, combine eggs, egg yolks, whipping cream, half-and-half, mozzarella cheese, ½ cup cheddar cheese, Swiss cheese, tomatoes, seasoning blend and basil; pour into a greased 9-in. deep-dish pie plate. Sprinkle with remaining cheddar cheese.
2. Bake 45-50 minutes or until a knife inserted in the center comes out clean. Let stand 10 minutes before cutting.
Freeze option: Securely wrap individual portions of cooled quiche in plastic and foil; freeze. To use, partially thaw in the refrigerator overnight. Remove from refrigerator 30 minutes before baking. Preheat oven to 350°. Unwrap quiche; reheat in oven until heated through and a thermometer inserted in center reads 165°.
1 piece: 449 cal., 37g fat (21g sat. fat), 524mg chol., 316mg sod., 5g carb. (3g sugars, 0 fiber), 22g pro.

FESTIVE CRANBERRY FRUIT SALAD

Breakfast at Midnight

Keep New Year's Eve guests full and happy with breakfast foods special enough for after dark.

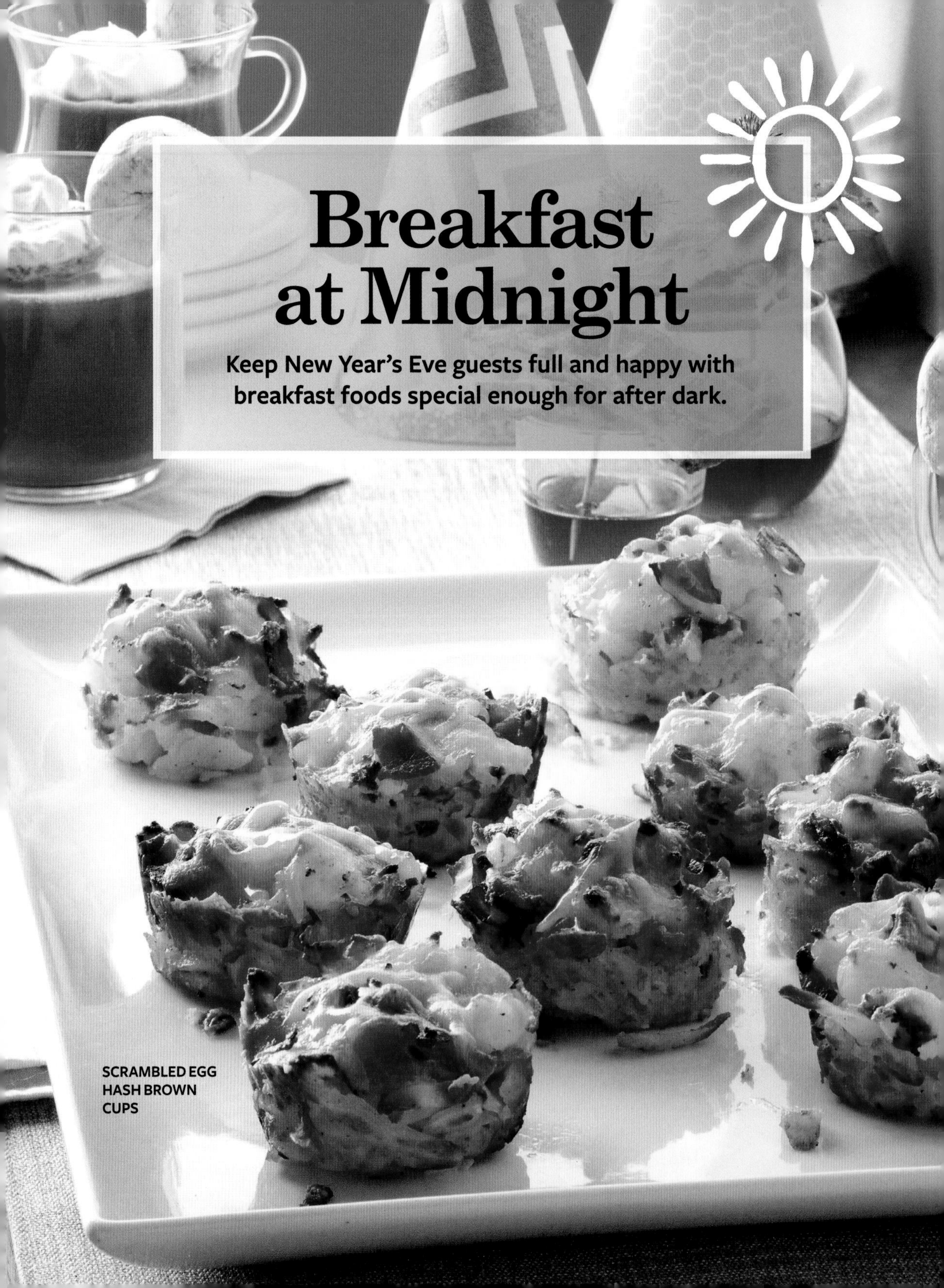

SCRAMBLED EGG
HASH BROWN
CUPS

SCRAMBLED EGG HASH BROWN CUPS

These cuties combine all of your favorite breakfast foods—eggs, hash browns and bacon—in one single serving-sized cup. Grab one and get mingling.
—Talon DiMare, Bullhead City, AZ

- -

Prep: 10 min. • **Bake:** 25 min.
Makes: 1 dozen

- 1 pkg. (20 oz.) refrigerated Southwest-style shredded hash brown potatoes
- 6 large eggs
- ½ cup 2% milk
- ⅛ tsp. salt
- 1 Tbsp. butter
- 10 thick-sliced bacon strips, cooked and crumbled
- 1¼ cups shredded cheddar-Monterey Jack cheese, divided

1. Preheat oven to 400°. Divide potatoes among 12 greased muffin cups; press onto bottoms and up sides to form cups. Bake until light golden brown, 18-20 minutes.
2. Meanwhile, in a small bowl, whisk eggs, milk and salt. In a large nonstick skillet, heat the butter over medium heat. Pour in egg mixture; cook and stir until eggs are thickened and no liquid egg remains. Stir in bacon and ¾ cup cheese. Spoon into cups; sprinkle with the remaining ½ cup of cheese.
3. Bake until the cheese is melted, 3-5 minutes. Cool 5 minutes before removing from pan.
1 hash brown cup: 180 cal., 10g fat (5g sat. fat), 113mg chol., 487mg sod., 11g carb. (1g sugars, 1g fiber), 10g pro.

HOLIDAY PEPPERMINT MOCHA

It's so easy to make this for a group on a snowy night. The mocha is also good with a coffee liqueur instead of peppermint. Trust me, I've tried it both ways several times!
—Lauren Brien-Wooster, South Lake Tahoe, CA

- -

Takes: 10 min. • **Makes:** 8 servings

- 4 cups 2% milk
- 8 packets instant hot cocoa mix
- 1½ cups brewed espresso or double-strength dark roast coffee
- ¾ cup peppermint schnapps liqueur or 1 tsp. peppermint extract plus ¾ cup additional brewed espresso
    Whipped cream, optional

1. In a large saucepan, heat the milk over medium heat until bubbles form around sides of pan. Add cocoa mix; whisk until blended. Add espresso and heat through.
2. Remove from heat; stir in liqueur. If desired, serve mocha cups with whipped cream.
¾ cup: 197 cal., 6g fat (4g sat. fat), 10mg chol., 234mg sod., 22g carb. (18g sugars, 1g fiber), 5g pro.

APPLE & PEAR KABOBS

Instead of scooping chunks of fruit on a platter, be adventurous and go kabob-style. Drizzled with a rich butter pecan sauce, these are irresistible.

—Robin Boynton, Harbor Beach, MI

- -

Takes: 30 min. • **Makes:** 12 servings

- 5 **medium apples, cut into 1-in. chunks**
- 4 **medium pears, cut into 1-in. chunks**
- 1 **Tbsp. lemon juice**

BUTTER PECAN SAUCE

- ⅓ **cup packed brown sugar**
- 2 **Tbsp. sugar**
- 4 **tsp. cornstarch**
- ¾ **cup heavy whipping cream**
- 1 **Tbsp. butter**
- ½ **cup chopped pecans**

1. Toss apples and pears with lemon juice. Thread fruit alternately onto 12 metal or soaked wooden skewers; place on an ungreased baking sheet. Bake at 350° for 15-20 minutes or until tender.

2. Meanwhile, in a small saucepan, combine sugars and cornstarch. Gradually stir in cream until smooth. Bring to a boil, stirring constantly; cook and stir for 2-3 minutes or until slightly thickened.

3. Remove from the heat; stir in butter until smooth. Add pecans. Serve warm with kabobs.

1 serving: 195 cal., 10g fat (4g sat. fat), 23mg chol., 18mg sod., 27g carb. (21g sugars, 3g fiber), 1g pro.

BANANA BEIGNET BITES

When I was a little girl, my grandmother took me aside one day and taught me how to make her famous banana beignets. Although we made them during the holidays, they're pretty fantastic any time of the year.

—Amy Downing, South Riding, VA

- -

Takes: 30 min.
Makes: about 3 dozen

- ¾ **cup sugar**
- ¼ **cup packed brown sugar**
- 1½ **tsp. ground cinnamon**

BEIGNETS

- 2 **cups cake flour**
- ¾ **cup sugar**
- 2½ **tsp. baking powder**
- ½ **tsp. ground cinnamon**
- 1 **tsp. salt**
- 1 **large egg, room temperature**
- 1 **cup mashed ripe bananas (about 2 medium)**
- ½ **cup 2% milk**
- 2 **Tbsp. canola oil**
  Oil for deep-fat frying

1. In a small bowl, mix sugars and cinnamon until blended. In a large bowl, whisk the first 5 beignet ingredients. In another bowl, whisk egg, bananas, milk and 2 Tbsp. oil until blended. Add to flour mixture; stir just until moistened.

2. In an electric skillet or deep fryer, heat oil to 375°. Drop tablespoonfuls of batter, a few at a time, into hot oil. Fry about 45-60 seconds on each side or until golden brown. Drain on paper towels. Roll warm beignets in sugar mixture.

1 beignet: 72 cal., 4g fat (0 sat. fat), 6mg chol., 88mg sod., 9g carb. (3g sugars, 0 fiber), 1g pro.

BANANA
BEIGNET BITES

FRENCH TOAST WAFFLES

MAKE AHEAD

FRENCH TOAST WAFFLES

I'm a from-scratch cook but also like shortcuts. Since we all love French toast and waffles, I use a waffle iron to make a hybrid French toast!
—Linda Martindale, Elkhorn, WI

- -

Prep: 15 min. • **Cook:** 5 min./batch
Makes: 16 waffles

- 8 large eggs
- 2 cups 2% milk
- ½ cup sugar
- 1 tsp. vanilla extract
- ½ tsp. ground cinnamon
- ½ tsp. ground nutmeg
- 16 slices Texas toast
- Maple syrup

In a large bowl, whisk the first 6 ingredients until blended. Dip both sides of bread in egg mixture. Place in a preheated waffle iron; bake until golden brown, 4-5 minutes. If desired, cut waffles into thirds. Serve with maple syrup.

Freeze option: Cool waffles on wire racks. Freeze between layers of waxed paper in freezer containers. Reheat frozen waffles in a toaster on medium setting.

2 waffles: 340 cal., 9g fat (3g sat. fat), 192mg chol., 476mg sod., 51g carb. (19g sugars, 2g fiber), 14g pro.

BREADED BRUNCH BACON

Make bacon even more delicious with this recipe. It earned a permanent spot in my tried-and-true recipe collection after just one bite! Guests can't resist it.
—Rebecca Novakovich, Dallas, TX

- -

Prep: 15 min. • **Bake:** 30 min.
Makes: 10 servings

- 2 large eggs
- 2 Tbsp. white vinegar
- 1 tsp. prepared mustard
- ½ tsp. cayenne pepper
- 1½ cups finely crushed reduced-sodium saltines (about 45 crackers)
- 10 thick-sliced bacon strips, halved widthwise

1. In a shallow dish, whisk the eggs, vinegar, mustard and cayenne. Place cracker crumbs in another shallow dish. Dip bacon in egg mixture, then roll in crumbs.

2. Arrange in a single layer on 2 foil-lined 15x10x1-in. baking pans. Bake at 350° for 15 minutes; turn. Bake 15-20 minutes longer or until golden brown. Remove to paper towels to drain. Serve warm.

2 pieces: 111 cal., 6g fat (2g sat. fat), 44mg chol., 296mg sod., 8g carb. (0 sugars, 0 fiber), 5g pro.

SPARKLING CRANBERRY KISS

Cranberry and orange juices are a terrific pairing with ginger ale in this party punch. We always use cranberry juice cocktail, but other blends like cranberry-apple also sparkle.
—Shannon Copley,
Upper Arlington, OH

Takes: 5 min. • **Makes:** 14 servings

  6   **cups cranberry juice**
1½ **cups orange juice**
  3   **cups ginger ale**
      Ice cubes
      Orange slices, optional

In a pitcher, combine the cranberry juice and orange juice. Just before serving, stir in the ginger ale; serve over ice. If desired, serve with orange slices.
¾ cup: 81 cal., 0 fat (0 sat. fat), 0 chol., 9mg sod., 21g carb. (20g sugars, 0 fiber), 1g pro.
Mock Champagne Punch: Substitute 3 cups white grape juice for cranberry and orange juices. Garnish with fresh raspberries.
Orange Juice Spritzer: Omit cranberry juice; increase orange juice to 3 cups and add 3 Tbsp. maraschino cherry juice. Garnish servings with maraschino cherries and orange slices.

PIGS IN A POOL

My kids love sausage and pancakes, but making them for breakfast on a busy weekday was out of the question. My homemade version of pigs in a blanket is a thrifty alternative to the packaged kind, and they freeze like a dream.

—Lisa Dodd, Greenville, SC

- -

Prep: 45 min. • **Bake:** 20 min.
Makes: 4 dozen

- 1 **lb. reduced-fat bulk pork sausage**
- 2 **cups all-purpose flour**
- ¼ **cup sugar**
- 1 **Tbsp. baking powder**
- 1 **tsp. salt**
- ½ **tsp. ground cinnamon**
- ¼ **tsp. ground nutmeg**
- 1 **large egg, room temperature, lightly beaten**
- 2 **cups fat-free milk**
- 2 **Tbsp. canola oil**
- 2 **Tbsp. honey**
  Maple syrup, optional

1. Preheat oven to 350°. Coat 48 mini muffin cups with cooking spray.
2. Shape sausage into forty-eight ¾-in. balls. Place meatballs on a rack coated with cooking spray in a shallow baking pan. Bake until cooked through, 15-20 minutes. Drain on paper towels.
3. In a large bowl, whisk the flour, sugar, baking powder, salt and spices. In another bowl, whisk egg, milk, canola oil and honey until blended. Add to the flour mixture; stir just until moistened.
4. Place a sausage ball in each mini muffin cup; cover with batter. Bake until lightly browned, 20-25 minutes. Cool 5 minutes before removing from pans to wire racks. Serve warm, with syrup if desired.
Freeze option: Freeze cooled muffins in airtight freezer containers.

To use, microwave each muffin on high until heated through, 20-30 seconds.
4 mini muffins: 234 cal., 10g fat (3g sat. fat), 45mg chol., 560mg sod., 26g carb. (9g sugars, 1g fiber), 10g pro.
Diabetic exchanges: 1½ starch, 1 medium-fat meat, ½ fat.

HAM & CHEDDAR SCONES

Flecks of cheese, ham and green onions add great color to these tasty scones. I first got the recipe from a friend, and I now prepare it often.

—Felicity La Rue, Palmdale, CA

- -

Prep: 25 min. • **Bake:** 20 min.
Makes: 1 dozen

- 3 **cups all-purpose flour**
- ½ **cup sugar**
- 2 **Tbsp. baking powder**
- ½ **tsp. salt**
- 2 **cups heavy whipping cream**
- 1 **cup diced fully cooked ham**
- ½ **cup diced cheddar cheese**
- 4 **green onions, thinly sliced**

1. Preheat oven to 400°. In a large bowl, combine flour, sugar, baking powder and salt. Stir in cream just until moistened. Stir in ham, cheese and onions. Turn onto a floured surface; knead 10 times.
2. Transfer dough to a greased baking sheet. Pat into a 9-in. circle. Cut into 12 wedges, but do not separate. Bake 20-25 minutes or until golden brown. Serve warm.
1 scone: 321 cal., 17g fat (10g sat. fat), 58mg chol., 527mg sod., 34g carb. (10g sugars, 1g fiber), 8g pro.

PIGS IN A POOL

CATEGORY INDEX

ALPHABETICAL INDEX